THE STRUGGLE FOR PALESTINE

The struggle
for Palestine

Edited by Lance Selfa

HAYMARKET BOOKS
CHICAGO

Map on p. vii copyright Jan de Jong, used with permission from PASSIA (the Palestinian Academic Society for the Study of International Affairs).

Front cover photo by David Silverman, Getty Images. Palestinians flash V-for-victory sign during a rally May 15, 2001, commemorating al-Nakbah (the "Great Catastrophe" of 1948, when Zionists drove 750,000 Palestinians from their homes upon the foundation of Israel).

Back cover photo by Josh On. Pro-Palestinian demonstrators in San Francisco on April 20, 2002.

Book design by David Whitehouse. Copyediting by Mikki Smith.

Entered into digital printing January 2019.

Library of Congress Control Number: 2002106485

ISBN: 978-1-93185-900-4

HAYMARKET BOOKS is a project of the Center for Economic Research and Social Change, a nonprofit 501(c)3 organization.

We take inspiration—and our name—from the Haymarket Martyrs, who gave their lives fighting for a better world. Their struggle for the eight-hour day in 1886 gave us May Day, the international workers' holiday, a symbol for workers around the world that ordinary people can organize and struggle for their own liberation.

Write us at P.O. Box 258082, Chicago, IL 60625, or visit www.haymarketbooks.org on the Web.

Contents

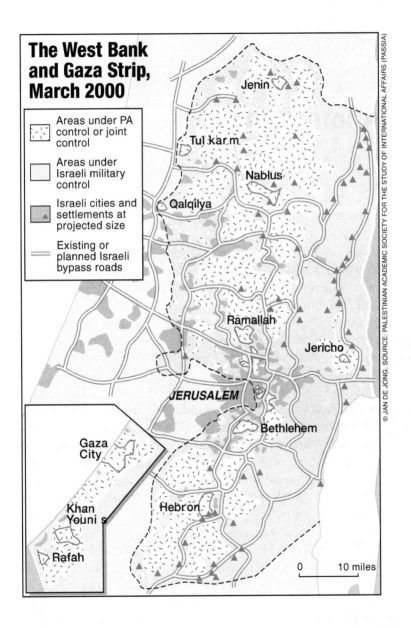

The West Bank and Gaza Strip, March 2000

Legend:

- Areas under PA control or joint control
- Areas under Israeli military control
- Israeli cities and settlements at projected size
- Existing or planned Israeli bypass roads

Jenin

Tul karm

Nablus

Qalqilya

Ramallah

Jericho

JERUSALEM

Bethlehem

Gaza City

Khan Younis

Rafah

Hebron

0   10 miles

LANCE SELFA

About this book

THE PUBLICATION of this book takes on a greater urgency than it did when we first began to compile its chapters. When we began this project in August 2001, the situation in Palestine was already grave. Israel and the Palestinians stood on the verge of all-out war. Israeli troops and police occupied Orient House, the anticipated home of a future Palestinian parliament, in East Jerusalem. Leaks to the press from Israeli military sources suggested that Israeli preparations were underway to smash the Palestinian Authority and to fight a region-wide war.[1]

As this book went to press in May 2002, Israel was engaged in a war to break all Palestinian resistance. Its armed forces had already killed hundreds of Palestinians and arrested thousands. It held the Palestinian Authority's president, Yasser Arafat, as a prisoner in the ruins of his Ramallah headquarters. Meanwhile, it laid siege to millions of Palestinians in the West Bank and Gaza. As Anthony Arnove and Ahmed Shawki point out in the foreword to this volume, Israeli politicians and military officials now openly speak of "transfer," the euphemism for the mass, forcible expulsion of Palestinians from their land.

The September 11, 2001, attacks on the World Trade Center and the Pentagon, and President George W. Bush's declared "war on terrorism," gave Israel's prime minister, Ariel Sharon, the ideological cover for his assault on the Palestinians. Within hours of the attacks, the level of Israeli repression against the Palestinians took a quantum leap in intensity.

Images of handfuls of Palestinians celebrating the attacks appeared on television screens around the world. For the war hawks in Israel and the U.S., these images helped to link the Palestinian struggle to the terrorists who organized the September 11 hijackings. It made no difference to them that every major Palestinian political and social organization denounced the attacks. Normally "liberal" and "tolerant" opinion contemplated the murder of Palestinian children.[2]

In the days following September 11, right-wingers smeared almost any mainstream commentator who dared to suggest that U.S. policy in the Middle East might help to explain the widespread resentment toward the U.S. around the world. Writer Susan Sontag asked, "Where is the acknowledgment that this was not a 'cowardly' attack on 'civilization' or 'liberty' or 'humanity' or 'the free world' but an attack on the world's self-proclaimed superpower, undertaken as a consequence of specific American alliances and actions?"[3]

A chorus of abuse branded her a near-traitor. But Sontag's question was sound. Even if U.S. policy can't explain the hijackers' motivations, it can certainly help to explain why the U.S. had a hard time selling its "war on terrorism" to millions of people in the Arab and Muslim worlds. No U.S. policy is more widely despised in the Middle East than U.S. support for Israel's dispossession of the Palestinian people.

The U.S. (and Western) political, military, and media establishments would have us believe that history began again on September 11, 2001. It was as if nothing that happened before the September 11 attacks—from CIA support for Osama bin Laden to U.S. sanctions against Iraq—mattered. It mattered only whether you were "with us, or with the terrorists," as Bush put it.

This simpleminded dichotomy may make for good sound bites, but it provides neither context nor understanding of the real issues at stake. Similarly, the U.S. media's presentation of the Palestinian conflict exclusively through Israel's "war on terrorism" lens deliberately distorts reality.

The articles collected here attempt to fill in some of the historical void that commonly exists in discussions around the struggle for Palestine. This collection—which contains previously published articles from the *International Socialist Review* (ISR),[4] original material, and reprints from the socialist tradition—aims to provide a framework for understanding present-day developments in the Middle East. In assembling this collection, we want to give readers more than simply historical facts and data.[5] We also want to put forward a point of view that can help readers to make sense of the facts and data.

The ISR's analysis of the struggle for Palestine is distinctive. In broad outlines, it follows (and seeks to update) the revolutionary socialist analysis that is associated largely with the Trotskyist tradition. This analysis of the "Jewish question," Zionism, and the struggle for Palestinian liberation dates from the pioneering works of socialists such as Abram Leon, Tony Cliff, and Nathan Weinstock. It was given concrete expression in the formation of the revolutionary Israeli Socialist Organization (ISO), made up of Jews and Arabs who were active in the 1960s.

The ISO, known by its newspaper *Matzpen*, collapsed in the mid-1970s. Former members who remain active are involved in a number of projects that bring together Israeli and Palestinian activists. Present-day organizations such as the Jerusalem-based Alternative Information Center and Kav La'Oved (the "Workers' Hotline"), which organizes immigrant workers in Israel, embody some of these efforts. Unfortunately, no explicitly political organization unites activists committed to a socialist solution on both sides of the Green Line.

Three features of the revolutionary socialist perspective on Palestine separate it from other views on the political left of the conflict. First, it is unequivocally anti-Zionist. It argues that Zionism is a "colonial-settler" movement that has linked its fortunes to imperial powers. Those powers used the Zionist movement to establish a foothold in the Middle East. Therefore, the revolutionary socialist perspective opposes the state of Israel and the Zionist project. It rejects any notion that one religious or national group should hold special privileges over another. It asserts that only a secular, democratic, socialist Palestine, where Jews and Arabs live together, can solve the "question of Palestine."

On its face, it may seem like common sense for a journal of the socialist left, such as the ISR, to hold this anti-Zionist position. Unfortunately, that is not the case. For years, Zionism and the state of Israel received their most fervent ideological backing from self-proclaimed socialists.

Despite the presence of Israeli Labor Party members in the right-wing government of Ariel Sharon that took office in 2001—as defense minister and foreign minister—the Socialist International of social-democratic and labor parties continues to claim the Israeli Labor Party as one of its affiliates. Liberals in the U.S., including Democratic Party leaders and the editors of *Dissent*, specialize in producing apologies for Israeli repression.

Second, the revolutionary socialist view insists that the conflict between Israel and the Palestinians can only be understood in the context of imperialist domination of the Middle East. The Zionist project only became viable when the British Empire's 1917 "Balfour Declaration" promised a Jewish state in Palestine. The anti-Semites who ran the British Empire had no more interest in helping the Jewish people than the U.S. government, which turned away thousands of Jewish refugees who were fleeing Nazi Germany in the 1930s. Yet both the British and their imperial successors in the Middle East, the U.S., found an imperialist-backed Jewish state useful to their designs on the oil-rich region.

Israel is one part of an imperialist protected system of Middle Eastern states designed to divide the region in order to enable Western exploitation of its oil riches. U.S. backing of Israel goes hand in hand with U.S. backing of Egypt, Jordan, and the Gulf monarchies.

Third, the revolutionary socialist position asserts that Palestinian liberation depends on a region-wide challenge by Arab workers and peasants to these corrupt, Western-backed regimes. This strategy identifies a force with both the power and an interest in fighting the imperialist setup that leaves millions in poverty. It also addresses the structural weakness of the Palestinian population, which faces one of the world's most powerful and ruthless militaries.

As a result of Israel's 1948 expulsion of almost a million Palestinians from Palestine, more Palestinians live outside historic Palestine than live within its borders. Palestinians also remain marginalized in the Israeli economy. To win a free Palestine, the revolutionary socialist position argues, Palestinians must connect their struggle to those who have the social power to shake the region and their own regimes. It follows that workers' power offers the only road to liberation and socialism in the Middle East.

Chapters 1 and 2, Lance Selfa's "Zionism: False messiah" and Phil Gasper's "Israel: Colonial-settler state," lay to rest many Zionist myths about the founding of the state of Israel. Selfa's "Israel: The U.S. watchdog" (chapter 3) and Paul D'Amato's "Blood for oil" (chapter 4) situate U.S. support for Israel within imperialist plans for Middle Eastern oil.

Chapters 5–9 provide a more contemporary perspective on the failure of the Oslo peace process and on the Al-Aqsa Intifada, which began in September 2000. Selfa's "Standing up to Goliath" (chapter 5) took the ISR's first look at the Al-Aqsa Intifada. Rania Masri's "The Al-Aqsa Intifada" (chapter 6) and the interview with Naseer Aruri, "Oslo: Cover for territorial conquest" (chapter 7), document why most Palestinians consider Oslo a sham.

Hadas Thier's "Ariel Sharon: War criminal" (chapter 8) exposes the career of the Israeli prime minister and the "security establishment" that encouraged his war crimes. Tanya Reinhart's "Evil unleashed" (chapter 9) lays out this security establishment's explicit plans to overthrow the Palestinian Authority, implemented as part of Sharon's self-described "war on terrorism."

The final four chapters include original material produced for this collection and a reprint from the socialist tradition. These chapters respond to many of the issues that the Palestinian movement has had to face since the September 11, 2001, attacks.

Excerpts from two of David Barsamian's interviews with Palestinian intellectual and activist Edward Said, conducted prior to September 11, appear in chapter 10. Said, one of the most eloquent defenders of Palestinian rights and a fierce critic of the undemocratic Palestinian Authority, answers the standard U.S.-

Israeli rhetoric that equates Palestinian resistance to "terrorism."

Jerusalem-based activists Toufic Haddad and Tikva Honig-Parnass assess the impact of the attacks on politics in the region and the Palestinian struggle in an interview conducted by Anthony Arnove in November 2001, which was then updated in February 2002 (chapter 11).

Despite the terrible conditions faced by the Palestinian movement today, Palestinians have continued their resistance to Israeli repression. What kind of Palestine should the movement fight for? The last two chapters give expression to a vision of a free, democratic, and socialist Palestine.

Chapter 12, the reprinted "Joint declaration" from the Israeli Socialist Organization and the Palestinian Popular Democratic Front, first produced in response to the 1967 war, offers a revolutionary socialist perspective on the Middle East crisis.

Mostafa Omar's "The Palestinian national liberation movement: A socialist analysis" (chapter 13) provides a Marxist analysis of the dominant nationalist and Islamist tendencies in the Palestinian opposition to Israel.

As the ISR has attempted to develop the revolutionary socialist analysis of the Palestinian question, it has always maintained a dialogue with activists and organizations—several of whom contributed to this volume—that do not share all of our assumptions. These activists share with the ISR an opposition to Zionism and imperialism and a commitment to Palestinian liberation. We hope that this collection will contribute to the ongoing dialogue among different tendencies committed to building a left in the movement for Palestinian liberation.

We have arranged the chapters in this book in a rough chronological order so that they can be read as a short and selective history of Israel, Zionism, and the struggle for Palestine. Since each contribution was originally written as a stand-alone essay, some repetition exists between chapters. Moreover, as the materials collected here were written over a period of five years in response to developments in the Middle East, they refer to events and political developments that do not necessarily hold today.[6] We think that these are minor drawbacks, as readers also gain an advantage in their ability to read and discuss each chapter without reference to the others.

To encourage further investigation of the issues presented in this reader, we have included an appendix that contains a full bibliography and a list of other resources.

Chicago, April 2002

---

1   See Agence France Press, "Israeli generals' plans to 'smash' Palestinians: Report," *Middle East Times*, July 12, 2001.

2   Richard Roeper's repugnant column, "You want to wring their little necks, right?" *Chicago Sun-Times*, September 13, 2001, is a good example. The column accompanied a picture of Palestinian children in Jerusalem reportedly celebrating the September 11 attacks. Yuppie film critic/columnist Roeper wrote: "You want to kill those kids in the picture, don't you?... If you think I'm going to dissuade you of those emotions, you're wrong. I'm with you. I'd like to knock their teeth out."

3   Susan Sontag, "Talk of the town," *New Yorker*, September 24, 2001.

4   Articles from the ISR have been slightly modified in this volume to minimize repetition between adjacent chapters and to correct errors that appeared in the original published versions; however, no attempt has been made to rewrite articles to reflect present circumstances, which will be most noticeable in those first published several years ago.

5   Many excellent book-length studies can be found in this volume's bibliography.

6   For instance, my November 2000 assessment of the Al-Aqsa Intifada as an "advance" on the 1987–93 Intifada proved premature. While involving a higher level of military confrontation with Israel and the settlers than the 1987–93 Intifada, the Al-Aqsa Intifada didn't subsequently approach the level of popular mobilization or leadership of the earlier uprising. See Nancy Murray, "Rebuilding our activism: What we can learn from the example of South Africa and the civil rights movement," in *The New Intifada: Resisting Israel's Apartheid*, Roane Carey, ed. (New York: Verso, 2001), pp. 333–42, for a similar assessment.

Foreword

LIFE FOR Palestinians today is immeasurably worse than it was when the Clinton administration, the Palestine Liberation Organization (PLO), and Israel began the much-heralded Oslo "peace process." Since the famous signing on the White House lawn in September 1993—said to signal a new era for the Middle East—illegal Israeli settlements have doubled, some 170,000 Palestinians who used to work in Israel have been barred from the country, Palestinians have lived under a state of siege, the Palestinian economy has been shattered, and Israeli state terrorism has continued—reaching, in the spring of 2002, levels not seen in more than 20 years.

As we write this foreword, the Al-Aqsa Intifada continues—and faces intense military repression. In late February and early March 2002, Israel sent soldiers and tanks into the largest Palestinian refugee camp in the West Bank, the Balata camp in Nablus—only one square mile with a population of 20,000 people—and a camp in Jenin. Britain's *Guardian* newspaper described in detail how Israel quickly "killed around 30 Palestinians, and sowed fear and panic as soldiers went from house to house by smashing their way through the walls.... Palestinian witnesses...described how Apache helicopters peppered homes with machine-gun fire."[1] One refugee explained why he wouldn't leave, even though his life was in danger: "'We were refugees already twice,' said Mahmoud Diyab, 80, who said he was pushed out of homes in 1967 as well as 1948. 'Where to go now?'"[2]

After invading the refugee camps, Israeli F-16 warplanes fired rockets into Bethlehem and Ramallah.[3] The following week, Israeli troops entered refugee camps in Jabalia, Dheisheh, Bureij, and Tulkarm. More than 1,500 Palestinians were arrested, many of them blindfolded and brutalized, and dozens were killed.[4]

After briefly withdrawing from parts of the Palestinian territory it seized in early March, Israel escalated its violent invasions in late March and early April. Saying that Israel is "in an uncompromising war to uproot these savages," and that Palestinian Authority president Yasser Arafat is "the enemy of the entire free world," Israel's prime minister, Ariel Sharon, launched a major offensive into Ramallah and ordered the army to target Arafat's headquarters, "smashing through walls and battling room to room," cutting off electricity to the building, and firing on his office, leaving Arafat sitting at his desk by candlelight.[5]

As the army went house to house and rounded up all men in Ramallah aged 15 to 45, Israel ordered out foreign reporters and solidarity activists, who were trying to disrupt the army's operation. Reporters were shot at and teargassed as they tried to report on Israel's operations in the West Bank. "[J]ournalists are banned, and [Israeli] government officials have warned that those caught [in Ramallah] could have their press cards revoked. A new list today of closed military zones includes every city and town the army has entered."[6]

Conditions were so grim that even the World Bank protested that "the [Israeli] army had destroyed water and electricity facilities, homes, schools and public buildings" in the towns it had occupied.[7] The Red Cross protested Israel's attacks on its ambulances and facilities, which limited its ability to "feed and provide medical care to Palestinian civilians," while the Israeli human rights group B'Tselem petitioned Israel's High Court "after receiving reports of torture at the Ofer detention center near Ramallah."[8]

Israeli troops moved into Bethlehem, Hebron, Jenin, Salfit, Beit Jala, Nablus, and Tulkarm, and also conducted house-to-house searches in Qalqilya. "In each city," the *New York Times* reported, "the [Israeli] army was proving more intense, ruthless and thorough than in any prior incursion, including the raids last month."[9] Major General Yitzhak Eitan of the Israeli army announced, "This operation will last as long as necessary, without a time limit," as Israel called up 20,000 reservists for duty.[10]

What was the response of the Bush administration to these atrocities? "U.S. puts onus on Palestinians to stop terror," a *New York Times* headline neatly summed up on March 30. "Arafat should be doing more to stop the violence," President Bush said from his ranch in Texas.[11] "We understand the Israeli government's need to respond to these acts of terror and the right of the Israeli government to decide what actions best serve the interest of the Israeli people," added Secretary of State Colin Powell, noting that he asked "the Israelis to show the necessary restraint."[12]

Even when Powell and Bush were finally pressured into calling for an end to Sharon's brutal assault, "Israel's West Bank offensive continued unabated...as the government of Ariel Sharon sought to beat what was seen as a warning," the *Financial Times* reported. "I'm not sure that we have to be concerned," one Israeli official said of the Bush call for Israel to pull back.[13]

In light of such intense repression, and the blank check given to Israel by its masters in Washington, it is not surprising that the desperate tactic of suicide bombing has sharply escalated in the second Intifada. The suicide bombings are a product of hopelessness and despair in the face of Israel's military offensive and years of occupation and humiliation, with little or no prospect for change. The young Palestinian men and women who blow themselves up do so in the belief that all hope for justice has failed and that this is the only way to lash back at their oppressors. It is clear that the suicide bombings haven't advanced the Palestinian resistance. Each time, they have provided the Israeli military—and its allies in Washington—with an excuse to crack down more viciously.

Israel's escalation of its war on Palestinians will only create more desperation. Yet Israel and the United States both insist that the symptom, not the disease, is the root of the problem, directing their outrage selectively against suicide bombings—while creating conditions that ensure only more suicide bombings. Israeli antiwar activist Ran HaCohen gets to the heart of the matter: "Reducing the struggle to the issue of suicide bombing is just another way of dehumanizing and legitimizing the killing of Palestinians, instead of removing the reasons for their horrible desperation.... Dehumanizing an entire people in the name of the 'sacredness of every human life'...is an especially repulsive example of demagoguery."[14]

On a recent trip to the West Bank, we witnessed the appalling humiliation and repression that Israel deals the Palestinians. Even the small amount of historic Palestine that is now controlled by the PA is broken into more than 220 bantustans, with numerous checkpoints controlled by heavily armed Israeli security guards. At these checkpoints, Israeli soldiers practice a form of racial profiling that regularly leaves Palestinians dead. Israeli soldiers murder Palestinians, secure in the universal knowledge that they can claim they fired their weapons in self-defense. On numerous occasions, guards have held ambulances at checkpoints for hours—deliberately endangering the lives of those seeking treatment for medical emergencies.

Palestinians face brutal attacks not only from Israeli soldiers, but also from fanatical settlers determined to drive Palestinians out of their homes and off their land. As we sat in his living room in the village of Medar, Ahmed Hofash told us how he lost his son Amin in the fall of 1999 to a settler who drove his car off an Israeli-only bypass road and headed deliberately toward seven-year-old Amin and his 15-year-old brother. No Israeli officials came to investigate the murder. "Nobody cared," Ahmed explained.

"The economic losses to Palestinians during the post-Oslo period have been devastating," observes Harvard University researcher Sara Roy. As Roy notes, the Oslo accords "were designed not to alter the structures of occupation but to maintain them, albeit in new, somewhat less direct forms."[15] In a classic colonial model, the Israeli government sought to shift the primary burden for repressing the Palestinian population onto the Palestinians themselves, a task that Arafat and the PLO leadership were quite willing to take up.

By April 2001, as a result of the persistent closure imposed by Israel, 2 million Palestinians—64.2 percent of the population—lived below the poverty line. "During the 123 days between October 1, 2000, and January 31, 2001," Roy adds, "economic borders were closed 93 days, or 75.6 percent of the time. Internal closures were in effect 100 percent of the time in the West Bank and 89 percent of the time in the Gaza Strip."[16] According to the United Nations (UN), "nearly half of the [Palestinian] population [is] living on $2 a day or less."[17]

While Palestinians live in horrendous poverty, their economic lifelines almost entirely closed off because of Israel, Israeli settlers live in heavily subsidized and armed outposts. We drove by one settlement, Ariel, that has a university with 6,500 students, a modern sports complex, and high-speed Internet access. "The faculty says it is holding fast to...a master plan that calls for 20,000 students [at Ariel] by the year 2020," the *Jerusalem Post* reports.[18] Ariel's lush lawns are kept green with water taken from Palestinian lands.

Israel routinely uses methods of collective punishment to destroy Palestinian infrastructure, agriculture, and homes. On one day during our visit, the Israeli army destroyed 14 homes in the Shufat refugee camp in East Jerusalem. Residents were given only a day's notice that their homes would be torn down because of "permit violations." Although it is almost impossible for a Palestinian to obtain a building permit from Israeli authorities, Israelis are able to expand their homes with government encouragement and subsidies.

"They came with bulldozers and just tore them down," Hassan, whose home was destroyed, told us. When neighbors and anti-demolition activists tried to stop the army, soldiers beat them. Journalists trying to cover the demolition and lawyers trying to stop it were brutally pushed aside. Hassan, who walks on crutches because of a childhood case of polio, now has difficulty making his way through the rubble that remains of his home. Because of the demolition, Hassan and his brothers, one with scars on his back from an Israeli soldier's rifle, are forced to share a small room with their mother and her grandchildren. One brother was planning to get married, but now, Hassan's mother fears, "we think she will not come."

The same week, Israelis tore town 22 Palestinian homes in Rafah, a southern town in the Gaza Strip near the Egyptian border. "The only thing I have left is the red shirt I am wearing," said Mohammed Abu Lideh, whose home was destroyed. "I spent all my savings to build this house."[19] In an even larger demolition during our visit, Israel destroyed the homes of hundreds of Palestinian shepherds in the South Hebron hills. "The destroyers blocked up the wells—the source of life for these families that have neither running water nor electricity," *Ha'aretz Magazine* reported. "Now hundreds of children have no roof over their heads in the midsummer sun, and nowhere to go."[20]

During our visit, Sharon appeared at a settlement in the Golan Heights to proclaim, "Only through developing the Golan, expanding the Jewish population, expanding the settlements, and bringing in new residents...will we be able to turn the settlement of the Golan to a reality that cannot be reversed."[21] Not long after that, Sharon traveled to Russia, where he openly worried that improved conditions for Russian Jews would make it harder to bring them to Israel as underpaid laborers or pawns in his aggressive settlement policy. "[President] Putin has energized Jewish communal life here, with Hebrew schools in 400 communities. It's like a golden era with freedom of worship. Matter of fact, it worries me because we want a million more Russian Jews. So I tell them, 'don't get used to it—move to Israel,'" Sharon told William Safire of the *New York Times*.[22]

Sharon's statements fall firmly within the logic and historical experience of Zionism, an ideology that asserts an exclusive Jewish right to a state in historic Palestine. Zionism has always been less concerned with promoting the well-being of the Jewish people than with colonizing Palestine. Like the colonizers of white-ruled South Africa or French-ruled Algeria, the Zionists have fought to dispossess and repress the indigenous people of the region. The most powerful and aggressive military machine in the Middle East imposes an apartheid existence on millions of Palestinians.

Unfortunately, the power imbalance between the Palestinian movement and the Israel-U.S. alliance means that PA officials grasp at virtually any "peace" plan offered. When Saudi Arabia floated a proposal in February 2002 that the Arab League countries would collectively recognize Israel in exchange for its withdrawal to 1967 borders, supporters of the peace process deemed it a breakthrough. However, it restated long-established positions.

What's more, the Saudi proposal made no mention of the right of return for the more than 4 million Palestinian refugees living in the Palestinian diaspora—families forcibly evicted from their homes in

1948 and 1967, and their children and grandchildren, who have lived their whole lives in miserable refugee camps. The Arab League declaration of late March 2002 spoke only of a "return of refugees," language favored by those who would severely limit the number of exiled Palestinians allowed to return or receive compensation.[23]

As pathetic as this plan was, Israeli officials immediately raised objections and sought to water down the offer ever further. A desperate Arafat, rather than point out the glaring problems with the Saudi initiative or criticize the blank check given to Israel by the U.S. government, reacted by arguing that "its chances for success depended on immediate American support." In an interview with the *New York Times*, Arafat begged for more U.S. intervention: "[T]he peace process started through the initiative which had been declared by Bush the father at the Madrid conference, and we hope that President Bush his son will complete this very international, historical initiative. For this there must be a very important and very strong and very quick push from outside."[24]

The history of various peace proposals, whether made by Arab politicians or the great powers seeking to extend their influence in the oil-rich region, teaches a numbingly familiar lesson: Negotiations dominated by Israel and the U.S. only lead to the further entrenchment of Israel's power and to further disenfranchisement and suffering for Palestinians. In every case, the massive power imbalance between Israel and the Palestinians has determined the outcome, as we see again in the case of the latest Saudi proposal.

Although Prince Abdullah spoke of "full withdrawal from all the Occupied Territories, in accordance with UN resolutions, including in Jerusalem," the terms of debate have quickly shifted. In the words of Israel's American mouthpiece, the *New York Times*, the Saudi initiative called merely for "withdrawal to a modified version of [Israel's] pre-1967 borders," to be determined in negotiations with Israel.[25] Soon after the Saudi proposal was floated, Sharon said, "Israel cannot return to the '67 borders," which he referred to as "Auschwitz borders."[26]

One reason for the interest in the Saudi proposal is that even Israel's allies found it a bit hard to defend the level of open brutality against the Palestinians reached in 2001 and 2002. Consider

the Gaza Strip diary entry of *New York Times* reporter Chris
Hedges on June 17, 2001, later published in *Harper's*: "Yesterday
at this spot the Israelis shot eight young men, six of whom were
under the age of eighteen. One was twelve. This afternoon they
kill an eleven-year-old boy, Ali Murad, and seriously wound four
more, three of whom are under eighteen. Children have been shot
in other conflicts I have covered—death squads gunned them
down in El Salvador and Guatemala, mothers with infants were
lined up and massacred in Algeria, and Serb snipers put children
in their sights and watched them crumple onto the pavement in
Sarajevo—but I have never before watched soldiers entice children
like mice into a trap and murder them for sport."[27]

Hedge's honesty in this report remains a rare exception. Many
newspapers now follow Israel's practice of referring to Palestinian
land as "disputed," rather than "occupied," even though the occupation is the central fact of life for Palestinians—and is essential
for understanding the conflict. Even in Israel, one can find more
open criticism of Israel and its policies than in the United States. In
fact, the Al-Aqsa Intifada and Israel's brutality have sharply polar-
ized Israeli society.

The leader of the Moledet party, Israel's tourism minister, Benny
Elon, is one of the many Israelis now openly calling for the "transfer" of Palestinians, a euphemism for mass ethnic cleansing. "We
must not fear bringing up again the idea of a transfer and of open
discussion of the various possibilities that it offers," Elon said on Israeli public radio.[28] Moledet has purchased billboard space in Tel
Aviv to promote its message: "Only transfer will bring peace."
Sharon did not object to Elon's proposals, spokesperson Ra'anan
Gissin, explained, only its practicality: "If the Palestinians would
have a change of heart and move elsewhere, OK, but Sharon realizes
transfer cannot be done because of the stance of the Israeli public.
What Elon is saying is not something that today seems possible."[29]

However, Elon may be behind the curve of Israeli opinion. A
March 2002 poll showed that almost half of Israelis (46 percent)
would support forcibly expelling Palestinians from their homeland.[30] This Israeli support for ethnic cleansing may shock those in
the West conditioned to think of Israel as "the only democracy in

the Middle East," but it is the logical conclusion of Zionism. If Jews have an exclusive right to historic Palestine, as Zionism argues, then Palestinians have no right to live there.

Indeed, Israeli activist Tikva Honig-Parnass, co-editor of *Between the Lines*, suggests that Sharon has been seeking to create the preconditions for transfer: "Israel wants a freer hand to smash the Palestinian resistance and ultimately to commit mass expulsion of the Palestinians. A 'full-scale war' for conquering control over all of historic Palestine—instead of the current 'low-intensity war'—is a necessary condition for the implementation of Sharon's 'big plan' to scrap Oslo and get rid of Arafat."[31]

In the words of Robert Fisk, an outstanding observer and one of the few honest journalists reporting on the Middle East, "Israel, in Mr. Sharon's own words, is fighting a colonial war. Not the 'war against terror,' which he tries to mimic in miniature with the United States, but a war to colonize Arab land with colonies for Jews and Jews only, as the colonized (the 'terrorists,' of course) rise up against them."[32]

The level of violence against Palestinians during the second Intifada reached such a level in 2001 and early 2002 that more than 250 Israeli reservists have signed a letter that reads, in part: "We will no longer fight beyond the Green Line for the purpose of occupying, deporting, destroying, blockading, killing, starving and humiliating an entire people," referring to the border between Israel and the West Bank.[33] Lt. David Zonshein, who helped to draft the petition, told *Yediot Aharonot*, "[Y]ou are asked to do things that should not be asked of you—to shoot people, to stop ambulances, to destroy houses in which you don't know if there are people living."[34]

Peretz Kidron, a member of the Yesh Gvul, a campaign to support soldiers and reservists who refuse to fight in the Occupied Territories, told the *Jerusalem Post* that more than 400 soldiers have refused to serve in the territories since October 2000.[35] According to Honig-Parnass, this development "indicates cracks in the public consensus around the occupation. And it has the potential to become a mass refusal to serve in the Occupied Territories— a development which could challenge blind obedience among soldiers to the most criminal orders they're given by their superiors."[36]

The protest of the reservists stands in contrast to the timidity of much of the so-called Israeli peace camp, which has only recently shown signs of revival in response to Sharon's deliberate escalation of violence. Most of the Israeli left, which supported the Oslo process despite its fundamental flaws, largely collapsed when Arafat rejected the supposedly generous offer granted to the Palestinians at Camp David in July 2000. With the start of the current Intifada only a few months later, in response to deliberate provocation by Sharon, the "peace camp" felt "betrayed" and bought into the Israeli government's argument that Arafat had deliberately chosen the path of violence. The peace camp drew these conclusions even though the Intifada was, in large part, a grassroots protest against Arafat and his strategy of collaboration.

Some have said that the only solution to this conflict is for the U.S. government to be more engaged in the peace process. The problem, however, is that the United States is already far too engaged in the Middle East. Though the U.S. government claims to be an "honest broker" between Israel and the Palestinians, it is anything but. Once Bush launched his "war on terrorism," he gave Sharon a green light to suppress the Palestinians. The U.S. supplied the Apache helicopters and F-16s that Israel uses in attacks on refugee camps. The U.S. has even defended Israel's right to assassinate Palestinians accused of terrorism and to use "pre-emptive" attacks on Palestinians. "I think there's some justification in their trying to protect themselves by pre-empting," Vice President Dick Cheney said in early August 2001.[37]

Without massive public protest, as Robert Fisk points out, "The United States will do nothing to stop [Israel]." Fisk adds: "The American press made much of U.S. Secretary of State Colin Powell's criticism of Mr. Sharon. But read what Mr. Powell actually said: he asked whether Sharon's military policy—of killing more Palestinians—would work. One of his spokesmen, speaking two days ago, announced that 'we had to make clear to him [Sharon] there is simply no evidence that approach will succeed.' Mr. Powell and his minions were not attacking Mr. Sharon be-

cause the Israeli policy was immoral. It was the military ineffec-
tiveness of killing Palestinians, not the abuse of human rights that
this embodies, to which the Americans took objection."[38]

The United States has long committed itself to Israel as a
strategic asset in the oil-rich and geostrategically crucial Middle
East. It gives more than $3 billion a year to Israel, and provides it
with invaluable military, economic, and political backing. In its
fiscal year 2001 budget, the State Department explained: "The
United States has a significant interest in a stable, democratic, and
economically and militarily strong Israel" and is committed to
"maintaining the qualitative edge of the Israel Defense Forces in
the regional balance of power."[39]

As Noam Chomsky has rightly pointed out, "It is highly misleading to use the phrase 'Israel-Palestine conflict'.... [I]t should be
termed the 'U.S./Israel–Palestine' conflict."[40] Viewed in that light,
the key to resolving the historic and ongoing crimes committed
against the Palestinian people is not the self-activity of Palestinians
alone, but broader Arab working-class solidarity and activism, as
well as anti-imperialist struggle in the United States, the guarantor
of Israel's repression. Palestine must be a central part of a global
struggle for a future based on democratic control of the world's resources and production for human needs. Otherwise, a world run
on profit will continue to produce the horrors of F-16s, Apache
helicopters, and refugee camps.

The socialist vision of a secular, democratic state in all of Palestine, in which Jews, Muslims, Christians, and others can live side by
side in peace, remains the only vision for the future of Palestine that
offers any hope. It is the only vision that presents any meaningful
alternative to Israel's vision of crushing, or "transferring," the
Palestinians, or to Arafat's vision of winning a bantustan state for a
small percentage of the Palestinian people alongside Israel. Given
the clear failure of the Oslo process and the glaring power imbalance between Israel and Palestine, it is not surprising that many activists are once again discussing the need for a one-state solution.

Such discussions should be a vital part of the new Palestine solidarity movement. The United States has seen a welcome resurgence
of protest against Israeli apartheid, with many people seeking to

draw on lessons from protests against apartheid South Africa. Students for Justice in Palestine brought a network of activists from dozens of schools together at a February 2002 conference at the University of California at Berkeley. The conference called on the national student movement for solidarity with Palestine to work for divestment of schools and corporations from Israel and for the end of U.S. aid to Israel. It also called on the movement to support Palestinians' right of return and for "public demonstrations and rallies...[and] civil disobedience or direct action."[41] Checkpoints like the one UC-Berkeley students set up on their campus to dramatize what life is like under Israeli occupation should be set up on every campus—and in every city and town—around the country. The conference represented a significant step forward for the movement.

In March 2002, 100,000 demonstrated in Italy against Israel's war, and in early April, protesters faced tear gas, water cannons, and police repression as they demonstrated in Amman, Cairo, Khartoum, Alexandria, and elsewhere in the Middle East.[42] And on April 20, 2002, more than 75,000 in Washington, D.C., and 25,000 in San Francisco turned out for the largest pro-Palestinian demonstrations ever in the United States. But much remains to be done.

A new movement in solidarity with the people of Palestine must deliver a clear message: Without justice in Palestine, there will be no peace.

Anthony Arnove and Ahmed Shawki
April 2002

---

1   Phil Reeves, "Israel isolated after refugee camp attacks," *Guardian* (London), March 3, 2002.

2   James Bennet, "Israeli troops raid Arab camps, killing 11 in West Bank fighting," *New York Times*, March 1, 2002.

3   Eric Silver, "Israeli gunships fire on Palestinian police after 21 die in weekend violence," *Independent* (London), March 4, 2002.

4   Charles A. Radin, "Rightists quit Israel's unity government," *Boston Globe*, March 12, 2002.

5   James Bennet, "Israelis besiege a defiant Arafat in his office," *New York Times*, March 30, 2002; John Kifner and James Bennet, "Israelis increase West Bank forces as Arabs protest," *New York Times*, April 2, 2002.

6 Kifner, "Under siege, without power or water," *New York Times*, April 5, 2002; Mark Jurkowitz, "News outlets decry Israel's coverage limit," *Boston Globe*, April 3, 2002.

7 Harvey Morris, "Israeli invasion 'threat to Arab aid scheme,'" *Financial Times*, April 5, 2002.

8 Elizabeth Becker, "Red Cross criticizes attacks on its facilities," *New York Times*, April 6, 2002; Morris, "Israeli push continues as U.S. envoy meets Arafat," *Financial Times*, April 6–7, 2002.

9 Serge Schmemann, "Israeli armor units continue sweeping through West Bank," *New York Times*, April 4, 2002.

10 Kifner, "In Israel, press kits roll out with tanks," *New York Times*, March 30, 2001; Kifner and Bennet, "Israelis increase West Bank forces."

11 Michael R. Gordon, "U.S. puts onus on Palestinians to stop terror," *New York Times*, March 30, 2002.

12 "In Powell's words, a plea to both sides," *New York Times*, March 30, 2002.

13 Morris, "Israeli push continues"; Edward Alden, Carola Hoyos, and Harvey Morris, "Bush urges Israel to halt offensive in West Bank," *Financial Times*, April 5, 2002.

14 Ran HaCohen, "Suicidal truths," April 5, 2002, available online at www.palestinechronicle.com.

15 Sara Roy, "Decline and disfigurement: The Palestinian economy after Oslo," in *The New Intifada: Resisting Israel's Apartheid*, Roane Carey, ed. (New York and London: Verso, 2001), pp. 91, 93.

16 Roy, p. 104.

17 William A. Orme Jr., "Palestinian economy in ruins, UN says," *New York Times*, December 6, 2001.

18 Tovah Lazaroff, "Education under the gun," *Jerusalem Post*, July 13, 2001.

19 Associated Press, "Israelis level Gaza houses in night raid," *International Herald-Tribune*, July 11, 2001.

20 Giddeon Levy, "No water in the pipes," *Ha'aretz Magazine*, July 13, 2001.

21 Reuters, "Sharon calls for expansion in Golan," *Jerusalem Post*, July 11, 2001.

22 William Safire, "Sharon in Moscow," *New York Times*, September 6, 2001.

23 Neil MacFarquhar, "Saudi in strong plea to Israel and Arabs," *New York Times*, March 28, 2002.

24 James Bennet and Serge Schmemann, "Arafat says plan outlined by Saudis needs U.S. backing," *New York Times*, February 28, 2002; Yasser Arafat, "Arafat's words: 'A push from outside,'" *New York Times*, February 28, 2002.

25 Schmemann, "Quickly, a Saudi peace idea gains momentum in Mideast," *New York Times*, March 3, 2002; "Support for the Saudi initiative," *New York Times*, editorial, February 28, 2002.

26 William Safire, "A talk with Sharon," *New York Times*, April 1, 2002.

27 Chris Hedges, "A Gaza diary," *Harper's*, October 2001, pp. 59–71.

28 Agence France-Presse, "Extreme right-wing Israeli minister threatens expulsion of Palestinians," February 1, 2002.

29 Ben Lynfield, "Israeli expulsion idea gains steam," *Christian Science Monitor*, February 6, 2002.

30 Amnon Barzilai, "More Israeli Jews favor transfer of Palestinians, Israeli Arabs—poll finds," *Ha'aretz* (English edition), March 12, 2002.

31 Tikva Honig-Parnass and Toufic Haddad, "'Everything is a struggle,'" interview with Eric Ruder, *Socialist Worker*, March 8, 2002. See also Joseph Algazy, "Transfer is a clear and present danger," *Ha'aretz* (English edition), April 5, 2002.

32 Robert Fisk, "Bush is doing nothing to stop Israel's immoral civil war," *Independent* (London), March 9, 2002.

33 Schmemann, "Saudi peace idea gains momentum."

34 Lee Hockstader, "Israeli reservists refuse Territories duty," *Washington Post*, January 29, 2001.

35 Tovah Lazaroff, "'We will not continue to fight...,'" *Jerusalem Post*, February 1, 2002.

36 Honig-Parnass and Haddad, "'Everything is a struggle.'"

37 Hoyos, "UN admits blame for debacle over kidnap video," *Financial Times*, August 4, 2001.

38 Fisk, "Bush is doing nothing."

39 Assistant Secretary Edward S. Walker Jr., "Congressional Budget Justification for Foreign Operations, Fiscal Year 2001: Near East," statement, Office of the Secretary of State, Bureau of Near Eastern Affairs, March 15, 2000.

40 Noam Chomsky, introduction to *The New Intifada*.

41 "Points of unity adopted by the Student Conference of the Palestine Solidarity Movement," Berkeley, California, February 2002, available online at: www.justiceinpalestine.org.

42 MacFarquhar, "Across the Mideast, an outpouring of anger," *New York Times*, April 2, 2002; MacFarquhar, "Arab protesters focus ire on U.S.," *New York Times*, April 6, 2002.

LANCE SELFA

Zionism: False messiah

IN MAY 1948, Israel's first prime minister, David Ben-Gurion, proclaimed the founding of the state of Israel. Immediately, Jewish commandos in Palestine launched what Israel called its "War of Independence." When Israel concluded an armistice with the armies of Egypt, Transjordan, and Syria in 1949, more than 750,000 Palestinians had been forced to flee their homes. They became refugees, since the Jewish Zionist armies now controlled their country. The founding of Israel marked the culmination of a 50-year campaign, waged by political Zionists, to establish a Jewish state.

The Zionists claimed that they expressed world Jewry's yearning for "national liberation." Yet, if Zionism was a movement for national liberation, it was like no other. Rather than seeking to break free from imperialism, it actively courted patronage from imperialist powers. Rather than promising self-determination to the people of Palestine—the vast majority of whom were Arab—it expelled them. And rather than representing a widely popular expression of the fight against national oppression, Zionism counted as little more than a sect for most of its existence prior to the Second World War.

What is Zionism?

Political Zionism, "a doctrine which, starting from the postulate of the incompatibility of the Jews and the gentiles, advocated massive emigration to an underdeveloped country with the aim of es-

First published in the International Socialist Review, *Spring 1998.*

tablishing a Jewish state,"[1] developed as a response to an upsurge of anti-Jewish racism (anti-Semitism) in Europe at the end of the 19th century. In Western Europe, the formation of openly anti-Semitic political parties challenged the assumption of many middle-class Jews that they could simply blend (or "assimilate") into non-Jewish society.

In the Russian Empire, where the majority of world Jewry lived, Jews fell victim as the feudal order gave way to capitalist economic development. As feudalism collapsed, Jews lost the specific roles that they had played as moneylenders and organizers of commerce in the feudal economy. Forced out of the feudal economy, Jewish artisans and shopkeepers fell into competition with non-Jews (gentiles). Meanwhile, capitalist development destroyed the artisanal economy, turning craftspeople into wageworkers. These two processes—the destruction of the feudal economy and the undermining of the artisanal economy—combined in fewer than 50 years to create a massive Jewish working class in Eastern Europe. These wrenching changes in the position of Jews in society impelled millions to emigrate from Eastern Europe. Those who stayed behind often faced pogroms, or anti-Jewish riots. Taking advantage of rising anti-Semitism among the gentile middle class and seeking to keep the Jewish working class divided from its gentile brothers and sisters, tsarist police stirred up pogroms against the Jews.[2]

This atmosphere of despair and oppression stirred several responses in the Jewish population, among them a growing nationalism. Nathan Weinstock emphasizes that "Jewish nationalism, in particular, its Zionist variant, was an absolutely new conception born of the socio-political context of Eastern Europe in the 19th century."[3] For centuries, the idea of a return to "Zion" (i.e., the "Holy Land" in Palestine) occupied a significant place in Judaism, but this belief had no *political* significance. Passover's ritual toasts to "next year in Jerusalem" didn't imply the desire to found a Jewish state with its "eternal capital" there. Jewish religious pilgrims immigrated to Palestine in the late 1800s to form religious communities, not to establish a state. Yet political Zionism had just that goal in mind.

Political Zionism received its most powerful statement in *The*

Jewish State, an 1896 tract by Jewish Austrian journalist Theodor Herzl, considered the father of political Zionism. Herzl, a widely traveled man, covered the 1894 Paris trial of Captain Alfred Dreyfus, a Jewish military officer framed by French military authorities as a spy. The Dreyfus Affair brought out shocking displays of anti-Semitism from official French society. On the other hand, it spurred an international antiracist campaign led by the gentile journalist and novelist Émile Zola. Mass pressure—which the socialist movement helped to organize—forced the French government to retry Dreyfus. The courts later found "extenuating circumstances" to lessen Dreyfus's sentence. The outcry against the Dreyfus trial dealt severe blows to the French right wing and to institutions—such as the army and the Catholic church—that stoked anti-Semitism.

One could have read the Dreyfus case as an example of the potential for Jews and non-Jews to unite to fight anti-Semitism. Herzl did not. As he later wrote in his diary:

> In Paris…I achieved a freer attitude toward anti-Semitism, which I now began to understand historically and to pardon. Above all, I recognized the emptiness and futility of trying to "combat" anti-Semitism.[4]

Herzl's "pardoning" of anti-Semitism reflected a core assumption of Zionism—that all non-Jews are anti-Semites. Anti-Semitism is "like a psychic affliction, it is hereditary and as a disease has been incurable for 2,000 years," wrote Leo Pinsker, a Zionist contemporary of Herzl.[5] If persecution or death awaited Jews who tried to assimilate into largely gentile societies, then the only solution to the "Jewish problem" would be the physical separation of Jews and non-Jews. It followed that only a Jewish state could provide a haven from persecution. On this point, the Zionists and anti-Semites converged. Both believed Jews to be a "foreign" presence in gentile society. And both believed that gentile society would be better off without Jews.

Herzl convened the first Zionist Congress in Basel, Switzerland, in 1897. Two hundred delegates from 17 countries authorized the creation of the World Zionist Organization to campaign for a "publicly recognized, legally secured homeland in Palestine." Later, Herzl modestly claimed, "If I were to sum up the Basel congress in a single phrase, I would say, 'In Basel, I created the Jewish

State.'"[6]

Yet Herzl found one major problem in building the Jewish state in Palestine: Very few Jews were interested in it. Between 1880 and 1929, almost 4 million Jews emigrated from Russia, Austria-Hungary, Poland, Romania, and other countries. Only 120,000 of them immigrated to Palestine. More than 3 million immigrated to the U.S. and Canada. In 1914, Zionist organizations in the U.S. could claim only about 12,000 members. At the same time, in the Lower East Side neighborhoods of Manhattan, the Socialist Party had as many Jewish members![7]

Socialism and the fight against anti-Semitism

Unlike Herzl, socialists defended Jews who faced persecution. Socialists also combated anti-Jewish racism as a poison to the workers' movement. In this period, August Bebel, a leader of the German Social Democratic Party (SPD), denounced anti-Semitism as "the socialism of fools" for diverting workers' anger from their true enemy, the ruling class, and onto Jewish scapegoats. Karl Kautsky, another German SPD leader, argued that the differentiation of the Jewish population into classes meant that the condition of the Jews would be bound up inextricably with the overall working-class movement. Connecting the fight against anti-Semitism to the fight for workers' power became the Marxist approach to fighting anti-Semitism.[8]

Because socialists stressed the need to fight anti-Semitism in the countries where most Jews lived, the socialist movement recruited Jews in large numbers. Many Jews played active roles as founders, leaders, and activists in the socialist parties in Europe. Count Sergey Witte, the tsar's finance minister, once complained to Herzl that Jews "comprise about 50 percent of the membership of the revolutionary parties," while constituting only 5 percent of the Russian Empire's population.[9] One such party that earned Witte's hatred was the General Jewish Workers League, known as the Jewish Bund. The Bund, launched in 1897—the same year as Herzl's Zionist Congress—became Russia's first mass socialist organization. It bitterly opposed Zionist calls for a Jewish state. Over the course of the next decade, the Bund grew among Jewish workers, swelling to 40,000 members in Russia during the 1905 Russian Revolution. In the revolutionary period, Jewish socialists, both in the Bund and in the other socialist parties, assumed leadership of the working-class and communal organizations in Jewish communities.

The Bund opposed political Zionism, but it accommodated to Jewish nationalism. Because of this, Vladimir Lenin and other Russian revolutionaries engaged in fierce polemics with Bund leaders. At the 1903 founding congress of the Russian Social Democratic Labor Party (RSDLP), Bund leaders argued for the official right to represent and to speak for Jewish workers inside the broader Russian socialist movement. Lenin and prominent Jewish socialists such as Yuli Martov and Leon Trotsky opposed the Bund. Lenin argued that the Bund was wrong to "legitimize Jewish isolation, by propagating the idea of a Jewish 'nation.'" The task of socialists was "not to segregate nations, but to unite the workers of all nations," Lenin later wrote. "Our banner does not carry the slogan 'national culture' but international culture." The Bund lost the vote to represent Jewish workers and subsequently left the RSDLP.[10]

The 1917 October Revolution in Russia showed what the socialist strategy for Jewish emancipation meant in practice. In a country where the tsar and his henchmen used anti-Semitism to divide workers, Russian workers elected Jewish Bolsheviks such as Trotsky, Grigory Zinoviev, Lev Kamenev, and Yakov Sverdlov to leading roles in the revolutionary government. The revolution declared freedom of religion and abolished tsarist restrictions on education and residence for Jews. During the 1918–22 civil war against counterrevolutionary armies that slaughtered Jews by the thousands, the revolutionary Red Army meted out stern punishment—including execution—to any pogromists in its ranks. In the workers' government, Yiddish was given equal status with other languages. A Commissariat of Jewish Affairs and a special Jewish Commission inside the Bolshevik Party simultaneously worked to involve Jews in the affairs of the workers' state and to win the Jewish masses to socialism. The revolution's early years saw an unprecedented flowering of Yiddish and Jewish cultural life. In 1926–27, more than half of the Jewish school population attended Yiddish schools and 10 state theaters performed Yiddish plays. By the late 1920s, nearly 40 percent of the Jewish working population worked for the government.[11]

Thus, by the 1920s, the Zionists had been marginalized on all sides. The majority of the world's Jews clearly desired to immigrate to Western countries, and thousands of Jews who remained in Eastern Europe fought for a better life, winning solidarity from many of their gentile brothers and sisters. By 1927, as many people were leaving Palestine as were migrating to it. The entire Zionist enterprise seemed in doubt.[12]

Appealing to imperialism

When embarking on their campaign for a Jewish homeland, the Zionists didn't let any ideological attachment to Palestine stand in their way. In fact, in the first years after Herzl formed the World Zionist Organization, Zionists debated a number of alternative targets for colonization: Uganda, Angola, North Africa. In 1903, Herzl accepted a British government proposal to colonize Jews in Uganda, a decision that proved controversial in Zionist ranks. Herzl's death in 1904 put an end to schemes involving colonization outside Palestine. Yet the debate on alternative sites for the Jewish state exposed the Zionist enterprise in two respects. First, it showed that political Zionism placed the colonizing project ahead of any 2,000-year longing for the Jewish people to "return" to Palestine. Second, it showed that Zionism depended, from its inception, on the sponsorship by European powers of its colonial-settler aims.

Early Zionists made no secret that they hoped the Jewish state would be what Herzl called "a portion of the rampart of Europe against Asia, an outpost of civilization as opposed to barbarism."[13] Herzl's writings abound with praise for the leading imperialist powers in Europe. He admired the German Kaiser's dictatorship: "To live under the protection of a strong, great, moral, splendidly governed and thoroughly organized Germany is certain to have most salutary effects upon the national character of the Jews."[14] In 1902, he wrote to Lord Rothschild, a British Zionist with connections in the highest reaches of the British state:

> So far, you [the British empire] still have elbow room. Nay, you may claim high credit from your government if you strengthen British influences in the Near East by a substantial colonization of our people at the strategic point where Egyptian and Indo-Persian interests converge.[15]

Zionism's founders exuded pro-imperialist racism against what they considered the "backward peoples" of Asia and Africa.

When it came to seeking imperialist sponsors, the Zionists had no scruples about dealing with any regime, no matter how rotten or anti-Semitic. Herzl himself negotiated for increased Jewish immigration to Palestine with Vyacheslav Von Plehve, the Russian tsar's interior minister and the architect of one of the worst pogroms in history, at Kishinev in the Russian Empire in 1903. During the First World War, leading Zionists ingratiated themselves to British imperialism. They hoped that Britain would reward them after it defeated the Ottoman Empire, which controlled Palestine. They achieved their goal with the 1917 declaration by Tory politician Lord Arthur Balfour proclaiming British support for "the establishment in Palestine of a national home for the Jewish people" under British protection. That Balfour had sponsored legislation in 1905 to bar Jewish immigrants from entering Britain didn't faze the Zionists.

The Balfour Declaration grew out of discussions between France and Britain over how to carve up the Ottoman Empire's lands following the First World War. In 1915, Britain's cabinet minister, Herbert Samuel, proposed that Britain establish a Jewish protectorate in Palestine. The cabinet majority opposed the plan. Samuel wrote:

> Curiously enough, the only other partisan of this proposal is Lloyd George, who, I need not say, does not care a damn for the Jews or their past or their future, but thinks it will be an outrage to let the Holy Places pass into the possession or under the protectorate of "agnostic, atheistic France."[16]

Yet, two years later, Britain issued the Balfour Declaration. What had changed in Britain's calculations? One clue comes from the fact that Britain issued the Balfour Declaration days before the October Revolution in Russia. Both Britain and the Zionists saw a Jewish state as a bulwark of imperialism against the spread of Bolshevism. Winston Churchill, then a Tory cabinet minister, later explained Britain's motivations in meeting Zionist expectations:

> A Jewish state under the protection of the British Crown...would from every point of view be beneficial and would be especially in

harmony with the truest interests of the British Empire.

Chief among those interests was stopping Trotsky's "schemes of a world-wide communistic state under Jewish domination." Thus, Churchill showed himself to be both an ardent Zionist and a rabid anti-Semite![17]

Zionism: Left and right

Under the Balfour Declaration, Britain promised the Zionists both Palestine and Transjordan (modern-day Jordan). Pressure from Arab countries forced Britain to renege on the promise of Transjordan in 1922. The Zionist movement's mainstream, led by David Ben-Gurion and Chaim Weizmann, accepted Britain's decision. Later, they agreed to accept British decisions to limit Jewish immigration into Palestine. This provoked a major split in the Zionist movement, as a minority led by writer Vladimir Jabotinsky protested Ben-Gurion and Weizmann's realpolitik.

Jabotinsky argued that Zionists should insist on capturing "both sides of the Jordan" and refuse to abide by any limitations the British imposed. To placate Arab opinion, the World Zionist Organization called its colony in Palestine "a homeland." But Jabotinsky insisted that Zionists speak openly of their goal to build a Jewish state in Palestine. Jabotinsky's program amounted to a call for revising the World Zionist Organization's strategy, thereby earning his followers the description "Revisionists" in the Zionist movement. Jabotinsky wrote bluntly in his 1923 essay "The Iron Wall":

> We cannot give any compensation for Palestine, neither to the Palestinians nor to other Arabs. Therefore, a voluntary agreement is inconceivable. All colonization, even the most restricted, must continue in defiance of the will of the native population. Therefore, it can continue and develop only under the shield of force which comprises an Iron Wall which the local population can never break through. This is our Arab policy. To formulate it any other way would be hypocrisy.[18]

Jabotinsky posed the first major challenge to the dominance in mainstream Zionism of the ideology of "Labor Zionism." Labor Zionism, which traced its roots to the Eastern European Poale Zion movement in the early 1900s, dominated all of the major institutions of Zionism and of the *Yishuv*, the Jewish settler community in Palestine. If the Bund represented socialists who caved in to nationalism, the Labor Zionists represented nationalists who used socialist rhetoric to win supporters away from genuine socialist parties.

The defining institutions of Labor Zionism in pre-state Palestine were the Histadrut "trade union" and the kibbutzim, a network of communal settlements that some have compared to utopian socialist communities. Both of these institutions carried over into the state of Israel. Many supporters of Israel even point to them as evidence of socialism in the Zionist enterprise. Yet this is another part of the Zionist story where myth collides with reality.

When it was launched, the Histadrut strictly limited its membership to Jewish workers. Only in 1960 did it it officially allow Palestinians with Israeli citizenship to join. One year after its founding, it owned a holding company and a bank. The capital for these ventures came not from the Histadrut's original 5,000 members, but from the international Zionist movement's Jewish Agency. In other words, the Histadrut subsisted (and continues to subsist) on its role as a conduit for investment from world Zionism. The Histadrut formed the backbone of the Jewish "state-in-waiting, controlling the mainstream of Zionist colonization efforts, economic production and marketing, labor employment and defense (the Haganah)."[19] One of its early leaders (and later Israel's defense minister), Pinhas Lavon, described it this way: "Our Histadrut is a general organization to the core. It is not a workers' trade union although it copes perfectly well with the real needs of the worker."[20]

Kibbutzim also restricted membership to Jews. Kibbutz land was defined as the possession of "the nation," which in pre-state and Israeli law was defined as the property of the "Jewish people." Therefore, no Arab can hope to join a kibbutz. What is more, in the pre-state period, kibbutzim served as forward military bases in the strategic plan of Zionist settlement. The "strategic consideration which had underlain the plan of Zionist settlement, decided, in large measure, the fate of many regions of the country" because Haganah militia detachments attacked

Palestinians from kibbutz bases.[21]

Until 1977, when self-described terrorist Menachem Begin became Israel's first Revisionist prime minister, the Labor Zionists effectively represented Zionism in most people's minds. But Labor (the Zionist "left") and the Revisionists (the Zionist "right") differed on means rather than ends. Both supported an exclusively Jewish state. Like apartheid South Africa's rulers, the Revisionists were willing to employ the native Palestinian population. Labor sought to replace Palestinian workers with Jewish workers. Both looked for support from imperialism. Labor Zionists oriented toward British and U.S. imperialism, while the Revisionists made overtures to Italian and German fascism.[22]

Colonizing Palestine

The Zionists tried to convince themselves that Palestine was an unoccupied land. Yet for more than 1,300 years, a Muslim Arab majority—living side by side with Jews and Christians—had resided in the Ottoman province. In 1882, Palestine had a population of 24,000 Jews and 500,000 Arabs. By 1922, after more than two decades of Zionist-sponsored immigration, the country had a population of nearly 760,000 total, 89 percent of it Palestinian Arab.[23]

Zionists purchased land—and a foothold in Palestine—from absentee Arab landowners in the 1920s. Later, in the 1930s, rich Palestinians sold their land to Zionists. Individual Jewish "pioneers" didn't buy the land. Zionist organizations such as the Jewish National Fund bought it to provide a foundation for Jewish settlement in the country. Zionists drove Palestinian peasants off their land, forcing them into destitution. British authorities assured the Zionists privileged access to water and other essential resources in Palestine.

After establishing themselves in Palestine, the Zionists proceeded to set up a separate Jewish economy and government under the noses of British mandate authorities. They called their economic policy "the conquest of Jewish land and labor," a flowery description for the expulsion of Palestinians from the country's economic life. Under the slogan, "Jewish land, Jewish labor, Jewish produce," the Histadrut, the kibbutzim, and the moshavim (agricultural cooperatives) proceeded to drive Palestinians out of their jobs and their livelihoods. Histadrut members acted as goon squads against Palestinians:

> Members of the Histadrut would picket and stand guard at Jewish orchards to prevent Arab workers from getting jobs. Squads of activists stormed through market places, pouring kerosene on tomatoes grown in Arab gardens or smashing eggs that Jewish housewives might buy from Arab merchants.[24]

The Palestinians fought back against their dispossession. In 1936, Palestinian organizations launched a general strike against increased poverty, the Zionists, and the Zionists' British sponsors. The strike and subsequent armed uprisings lasted for three years before collapsing under the weight of Zionist and British repression. The Zionists' role in the Palestinian Revolt clearly showed that Labor Zionism had nothing in common with genuine workers' solidarity. The Histadrut organized scabbing against the strike. It worked with the British to replace Arab strikers with Jewish workers in the Port of Haifa and on Palestine railroads.[25] The British also armed Zionist militias to crush the Palestinian uprising. "With two divisions, squadrons of airplanes, the police force, the Transjordanian frontier forces, and 6,000 Jewish auxiliaries, British troops outnumbered the Palestinians ten to one." Yet it still took three years to crush the revolt.[26]

The revolt's intensity derived from the fact that the Zionist threat to Palestine was becoming clear in the 1930s. Throughout the 1930s, the Jewish population in Palestine exploded. Thousands of Jews fleeing persecution in Central and Eastern Europe—and denied admission to Britain, the U.S., and other Western countries—made their way to Palestine. Between 1931 and 1945, the Jewish population in Palestine swelled from 174,000 to 608,000. While Jews accounted for only one-third of the population of Palestine on the eve of Israel's declaration of statehood in 1948, they were a well-armed and powerful minority. As the Jewish population increased, so did Zionist provocations against the Palestinians.

Zionism and the Holocaust

Today's Israeli and Zionist leaders regularly accuse critics of Israel's policies of being anti-Semites who want to engineer "another Holocaust" against Israel. From these extreme statements, it might be inferred that Zionist leaders fought the Nazi Holocaust. The historical record shows the contrary. A few months after Hitler came to power, the leading German Zionist organization sent Hitler a long memo offering formal collaboration with the Nazis. This stomach-turning memo reads, in part:

> On the foundation of the new state, which has established the principle of race, we wish to fit our community into the total structure so that for us too, in the sphere assigned to us, fruitful activity for the Fatherland is possible....
>
> For its practical aims, Zionism hopes to be able to win the collaboration even of a government fundamentally hostile to Jews, because in dealing with the Jewish question no sentimentalities are involved but a real problem whose solution interests all peoples, and at the present moment especially the German people.[27]

At the time, collaboration meant that leading organizations of Zionism worked to undermine a worldwide anti-German boycott that had been called to protest the Nazis' anti-Semitism. Instead, the World Zionist Organization worked out a "transfer agreement" by which money from German Jews could be sent to Palestine to finance imports into Germany. Meanwhile, inside Germany, the Nazis shut down all socialist and Jewish resistance organizations and arrested their leaders. But the Nazis allowed the Zionists to operate. An American Zionist leader confessed his embarrassment: "It was a painful distinction for Zionism to be singled out for favors and privileges by its Satanic counterpart [Nazi Germany]."[28]

Throughout the 1930s and the Second World War, Zionists always placed the interests of Palestine ahead of the fight against anti-Semitism in Europe. Seeking allies against Britain, the Zionist militia, the Haganah, negotiated for support from the German SS. In one secret meeting in Haifa in 1937, Haganah agent Feivel Polkes told the SS's Adolph Eichmann that "Jewish nationalist circles are very pleased with the radical German policy, since the strength of the Jewish population would be so far increased" that it would overwhelm the Palestinians. For a period in the late 1930s, the Nazis allowed Polkes to set up Haganah recruiting and training camps inside Germany, and for some time, Polkes' sole income was "secret funds from the SS."[29]

The Zionists impressed Eichmann. Years later in exile in Argentina, he recalled:

> I did see enough to be very impressed by the way the Jewish colonists were building up their land. I admired their desperate will to live, the more so since I was myself an idealist. In the years that followed I often said to Jews with whom I had dealings that, had I been a Jew, I would have been a fanatical Zionist. I could not imagine being anything else. In fact, I would have been the most ardent Zionist imaginable.[30]

This is the man who oversaw Hitler's Final Solution!

Thousands of Jews, including the rank and file of Zionist groups, resisted Hitler's attempt to herd them into death camps. Zionists united with Communists and Bundists in the 1943 armed uprising against the Nazis in the Warsaw Ghetto. But even at the Holocaust's height, Jewish Agency and settler leaders in Palestine offered little help. "The disaster facing European Jewry is not directly my business," said Ben-Gurion in 1943.

Zionist leaders believed that the fight in Europe diverted them from their main task: building the Jewish state in Palestine. The chair of the Jewish Agency's committee refused to divert Jewish Agency funds from Palestine into rescuing Europe's Jews. "They will say that I am anti-Semitic, that I don't want to save the Exile, that I don't have a warm Jewish heart," said Yitzhak Gruenbaum at a 1943 Jewish Agency meeting.

> Let them say what they want. I will not demand that the Jewish Agency allocate a sum of 300,000 or 100,000 pounds sterling to help European Jewry. And I think that whoever demands such things is performing an anti-Zionist act.

During the war, the agency spent far more money to acquire land in Palestine than to mount rescues.[31]

Preserving the "remnant" of Jewry for transfer to Palestine, not saving the Jews, guided Zionist leaders. Ben-Gurion opposed a plan to allow German Jewish children to immigrate to Britain in 1938. To justify himself, Ben-Gurion said,

> If I knew that it would be possible to save all the children in Ger-

many by bringing them over to England, and only half of them to [Israel], then I would opt for the second alternative. For we must weigh not only the life of these children but also the history of the people of Israel.[32]

Unfortunately, plans like the British proposal to rescue Jewish children were few. In general, Western governments turned their backs on Jews fleeing Germany. In one celebrated case, the U.S. Coast Guard in 1939 turned away a ship, the SS *St. Louis*, that carried more than 900 refugees who wished to immigrate to the United States. Until several European countries agreed to accept the refugees, they were destined to return to Germany—and to certain death. Still, American Zionist organizations refused to press for the abolition of immigration restrictions that prevented Jews fleeing Germany to move to the United States. Only the left—the Trotskyist Communist League and the Communist Party—called for the lifting of all restrictions on Jewish immigration.

Without the Holocaust, the state of Israel probably wouldn't have been founded. Zionists recruited immigrants to Israel from among the thousands of Holocaust survivors whose communities in Europe had been destroyed. Perhaps more importantly, the Holocaust provided a convincing justification for a Jewish state. The Holocaust proved that gentiles were inherently anti-Semitic, the Zionists argued. Jews living in gentile societies, therefore, faced the constant danger of extermination. What was more, the Nazis' physical elimination of alternative political currents in Jewish society increased support for Zionism. While the Nazis willingly dickered with Zionist leaders throughout the 1930s and 1940s, they made sure to kill every communist, socialist, or Jewish resistance fighter they could get their hands on.[33] By the end of the war, most Jews agreed with the Zionists.

The road to al-Nakbah

The Second World War forced Britain to evacuate much of its empire, including Palestine. Britain left to the United Nations (UN) the task of deciding Palestine's fate. In November 1947, the UN agreed to a partition plan. The plan granted the Zionists control of 55 percent of Palestine (although they still represented only one-third of the country's population). The Palestinian majority was left with 45 percent of their own country. Jerusalem was to be an "international city" with equal access granted to Jews, Christians, and Muslims.

Zionist leaders accepted the UN partition plan in public. In private, they planned a military assault to seize as much Palestinian land as possible. In 1947, Judah L. Magnes, president of Hebrew University of Jerusalem and a supporter of a binational Arab and Jewish state, explained the Zionists' logic:

> A Jewish state can only be obtained, if it ever is, through war.... You can talk to an Arab about anything, but you cannot talk to him about a Jewish state. And that is because, by definition, a Jewish state means that the Jews will govern other people, other people who are living in this Jewish state. Jabotinsky knew that long ago. He was the prophet of the Jewish state. Jabotinsky was ostracized, condemned, excommunicated. But now we see that the entire Zionist movement has adopted his point of view.[34]

As Magnes predicted, the Zionist right and left united to hijack the country. They used terror, psychological warfare, and massacres to instill fear among Palestinians. In the most well-known massacre, two Revisionist militias, the Irgun and Fighters for Freedom of Israel—whose chief leaders were future Israeli prime ministers Menachem Begin and Yitzhak Shamir—murdered the entire Palestinian village of Deir Yassin. The commandos "lined men, women and children up against walls and shot them," according to a Red Cross description of the massacre.[35] After Deir Yassin, Zionists used the threat of massacre to compel Palestinians to flee their homes, including those in cities such as Haifa and Jaffa.

Israeli military commander and future prime minister Yitzhak Rabin oversaw the expulsion of the Palestinian population of Lydda. He described the events:

> Yigal Allon asked Ben-Gurion what was to be done with the civilian population. Ben-Gurion waved his hand in a gesture of "drive them out." "Driving out" is a term with a harsh ring. Psychologically, this was one of the most difficult actions we undertook. The population of Lydda did not leave willingly. There was no way of avoiding the use of force and warning shots in order to make the inhabitants march the ten or fifteen miles to the point where they

met up with the Arab Legion.[36]

For years, Zionist history asserted a number of "facts" about the 1948 war: that little Israel faced overwhelming Arab firepower, that Palestinian leaders encouraged Palestinians to leave the country, that there was no Zionist plan to drive the Palestinians out, that Palestinians rejected partition and started the war. Yet recent historical research, based on formerly top secret Israel Defense Forces documents, proves that all of these assertions are lies.

When the war ended, the Zionists held more than 77 percent of Palestine, including 95 percent of all of the good agricultural land. The state of Israel stole 80 percent of privately owned Palestinian land. More than 750,000 Palestinians were expelled from their homes, which Jews moved into. Palestinian society was destroyed. For this reason, Palestinians refer to 1948 as "al-Nakbah" ("the catastrophe").

In 1949, a kibbutz welcomed members of the "socialist" Hashomer Hatzair from the U.S. and Canada to colonize a Palestinian village seized in 1948. One of the kibbutz's first acts was to raze the village mosque. A Hashomer member's diary noted:

> It had to be done. It would have been useless to preserve this symbol of a population which showed itself to be, when one views the thing factually and unsentimentally, our hardened enemies whom we have no intention of permitting to return. It's now a mass of ruins, and yet most of us agree it's better this way. The hovels, the filth, the medieval atmosphere—it's gone now for the most part. Bring on the bulldozers and let's plant trees.[37]

On a foundation of war and murder, the Israeli state was built. Zionism gained its long-standing aim: a Jewish state. But as the 100-year history of political Zionism and the 50-year history of the state of Israel shows, this is nothing to celebrate. Members of the revolutionary Israeli Socialist Organization said it best in 1972:

> Zionism promised national awakening and fraternal solidarity; it has produced a society of increasing inequality and of racist discrimination and cultural oppression. Zionism promised independence; it has produced a society in which the Prime Minister must periodically affirm to the people that the existence of the nation depends on the delivery of fifty or a hundred Phantom jets from the United States.... Zionism promised physical security to the Jews; Is-

rael is the most dangerous place on earth today for a Jew, and it will remain so as long as Israeli-Jewish society retains its colonial character and its function as an instrument of imperialism.[38]

1   Nathan Weinstock, *Zionism: False Messiah* (London: Ink Links, 1979), p. 32.

2   This description of the roots of anti-Semitism in late 19th-century Eastern Europe can be found in the classical Marxist text, Abram Leon's *The Jewish Question* (New York: Pathfinder Press, 1970). Leon, a Belgian Jewish Trotskyist, wrote most of the book while conducting underground political activity in Nazi-occupied Belgium. Leon died in Auschwitz in 1944.

3   Weinstock, *Zionism*, p. 32.

4   Theodor Herzl, *The Diaries of Theodore Herzl* (New York: Dial Press, 1956), p. 6.

5   This idea is no mere 19th-century relic. Daniel Goldhagen's recent book *Hitler's Willing Executioners* starts from the assumption that all non-Jews were culturally programmed to slaughter Jews if given the chance. See Henry Maitles's December 1997 review of *Hitler's Willing Executioners* in *International Socialism*, pp. 103–10, or Annie Zirin's review in *International Socialist Review*, Fall 1997, pp. 47–48. The Pinsker quote comes from Maitles, p. 109.

6   Herzl's quote can be found in "The Zionist century, 1897–1997," on the Jewish Agency for Israel Web site at www.jajz-ed.org.il.

7   Immigration figures come from Weinstock, *Zionism*, p. 12. Figures comparing the number of Zionists and Jewish socialists are from Arthur Liebman, *Jews and the Left* (New York: John Wiley and Sons, 1979), p. 163.

8   Weinstock, introduction to Abram Leon, *The Jewish Question*, translated by Ernest Mandel (New York: Pathfinder Press, 1970), p. 32.

9   Liebman, p. 111.

10 Quoted in Peter Alexander, *Racism, Resistance, and Revolution* (London: Bookmarks, 1987), pp. 149–50.

11 Weinstock, *Zionism*, pp. 15–18.

12 Phil Marshall, *Intifada: Zionism, Imperialism, and Palestinian Resistance* (London: Bookmarks, 1989), p. 37.

13 Quoted in Maxime Rodinson, *Israel and the Arabs* (Harmondsworth, England: Penguin Books, 1973), p. 14.

14 Quoted in Richard P. Stevens, "Zionism as Western imperialism," in *The Transformation of Palestine,* edited by Ibrahim Abu-Lughod (Evanston, Ill.: Northwestern University Press, 1971), p. 35.

15 Quoted in Stevens, p. 36.

16 Quoted in Stevens, p. 46.

17 Quoted in Weinstock, *Zionism*, p. 96.

18 Quoted in Ralph Schoenman, *The Hidden History of Zionism* (San Francisco: Socialist Action, 1988), p. 13.

19 Uri Davis, *Israel: Apartheid State* (London: Zed Press, 1987), p. 49.

20 Quoted in Jim Higgins, "The Middle East crisis" *International Socialism*, mid-November 1973, p. 16.

21 Erskine B. Childers, "The wordless wish: From citizens to refugees," in Abu-Lughod, p. 165.

22 Lenni Brenner describes the history of Zionism's dealings with fascism in his *Zionism in the Age of the Dictators* (Westport, Conn.: Lawrence Hill and Company, 1983).

23 Samih K. Farsoun and Christine E. Zacharia, *Palestine and the Palestinians* (Boulder, Col.: Westview Press, 1997), p. 75.

24 John Rose, *Israel: The Hijack State* (London: Bookmarks, 1986), p. 33.

25 Zachary Lockman, *Comrades and Enemies* (Berkeley: University of California, 1996), pp. 240–65. This extremely detailed book documents many attempts by the Histadrut to organize Arab workers into "separate but equal" affiliates. The history shows that Zionists viewed Palestinian workers as "enemies" much more than "comrades."

26 Farsoun and Zacharia, p. 107.

27 Brenner, pp. 48–49.

28 Brenner, p. 85.

29 Christopher Simpson, *Blowback* (New York: Collier Books, 1988), p. 253.

30 Quoted in Brenner, p. 98.

31 Quoted in Tom Segev, *The Seventh Million* (New York: Hill and Wang, 1993), p. 98. Gruenbaum quote and comparison of Jewish Agency spending in Segev, p. 102.

32 Quoted in Brenner, p. 149.

33 In saying this, I do not mean to minimize Hitler's determination to kill all Jews regardless of their political beliefs. But it is important to understand the Nazi regime in class terms. Long before they devised plans for the Final Solution, the Nazis crushed working-class and socialist opposition. The first concentration camps were set up for communists and trade unionists. The Nazis understood that only the working class held the power to break their regime. That is why they so ruthlessly crushed all working-class resistance. Only after they crushed opposition to their rule could the Nazis launch the war and carry out genocide.

34 Quoted in Rodinson, *Israel: A Colonial-Settler State?* (New York: Pathfinder Press, 1973), p. 68.

35 Quoted in Simha Flapan, *The Birth of Israel* (New York: Pantheon Books, 1987), p. 94.

36 Quoted in Flapan, p. 81.

37 Joel Beinin, *Was the Red Flag Flying There?* (Berkeley: University of California Press, 1990), p. 81.

38 Arie Bober, ed., *The Other Israel: The Radical Case against Zionism* (Garden City, N.J.: Anchor Books, 1972), pp. 200–01.

PHIL GASPER

Israel: Colonial-settler state

ZIONISM IS a political movement that originally emerged in the
late 19th century as a response to anti-Semitism, particularly in
Eastern Europe. Capitalist development undermined the traditional commercial roles that many Jews had played in the old feudal economy. As the economic system moved into periodic crises,
ruling groups in many countries would deflect mass anger at economic hardship and political repression by scapegoating Jews.

Zionists drew the pessimistic conclusion that anti-Semitism
could not be eliminated, and that to escape persecution, Jews had
to immigrate to a region where they could set up an exclusively
Jewish state. At the time of the Dreyfus Affair in France, in which
a Jewish army officer was falsely accused of espionage, Theodor
Herzl—who is generally regarded as the father of Zionism—set
out the Zionist program in 1896 in a pamphlet called *The Jewish State*. He called for a Jewish state to be set up in an un-
developed country outside Europe. Herzl was explicit that the
program could be carried out only with the backing of one of the
major imperialist powers, which were at that time carving up the
world between them. Once such support had been won, the Zionist movement would conduct itself like other colonizing ventures.

Various sites for the new state were considered, including Argentina and Madagascar, but the influence of religious Jews led

First published in the International Socialist Review, *December 2000–January 2001.*

the Zionists to decide on Palestine, the Biblical "promised land."

Once Palestine was chosen, the Zionist movement attempted to persuade one of the imperialist powers to give it support in colonizing the country. The new state would be part of the system of colonial domination of the rest of the world. Initially, Turkey and Germany were approached. According to one Zionist spokesperson,

> Turkey can be convinced that it will be important for her to have in Palestine and Syria a strong and well-organized group which...will resist any attack on the authority of the Sultan and defend his authority with all its might.[1]

Similar advances were made toward Germany.

The founders of Zionism were even prepared to ally themselves with the most vicious anti-Semites. Herzl approached Count Vyacheslav Von Plehve, the sponsor of the worst anti-Jewish pogroms in Russia: "Help me to reach the land sooner and the revolt [against tsarist rule] will end." Herzl and other Zionist leaders offered to help guarantee tsarist interests in Palestine and to rid Eastern Europe and Russia of those "noxious and subversive Anarcho-Bolshevik Jews"—in other words, to get rid of the people who wanted to fight anti-Semitism rather than capitulate to it. Von Plehve agreed to finance the Zionist movement as a way of countering socialist opposition to the tsar:

> The Jews have been joining the revolutionary parties. We were sympathetic to your Zionist movement as long as it worked toward emigration. You don't have to justify the movement to me. You are preaching to a convert.[2]

When Britain took control of Palestine at the end of the First World War, Zionists turned their attention to lobbying the British government. The Zionist leader Chaim Weizmann argued, "A Jewish Palestine would be a safeguard to England, in particular in respect to the Suez Canal."[3] This argument became increasingly attractive to the British ruling class. The war had underlined the importance of the Middle East, which guarded the sea routes to the Far East and contained the immensely profitable and strategically vital Persian oil fields.

Britain was eager to find ways to consolidate its power in the region, in opposition both to the other imperial powers and to the emerging anticolonial nationalist movements in Egypt and other countries. On November 2, 1917, the British foreign minister, Lord Arthur Balfour, a notorious anti-Semite, issued the following declaration:

> His Majesty's Government views with favor the establishment in Palestine of a national home for the Jewish people, and will use their best endeavors to facilitate the achievement of this object.[4]

One person who played an important role in winning support for the declaration was the South African delegate to the British war cabinet, General Jan Smuts, a close friend of Weizmann and a future South African prime minister. In fact, Zionist leaders Herzl and Weizmann frequently compared their aims with the South African conception of a racially distinct colonizing population, and built close ties with South Africa. In his diaries, Herzl explicitly drew parallels between himself and the most prominent representative of British imperialism in South Africa, Cecil Rhodes:

> Naturally there are big differences between Cecil Rhodes and my humble self, the personal ones very much in my disfavor, but the objective ones greatly in favor of our [Zionist] movement.[5]

The Balfour Declaration did not create a Jewish state, but it did encourage mass immigration to Palestine and the construction of an extensive settler community that was to become the basis of the state of Israel. But there was one problem. Contrary to Zionist propaganda that Palestine was "a land without a people for a people without a land," the area was in fact the most densely populated region of the Eastern Mediterranean, with an Arab population that had lived there for more than 1,000 years and had developed an extensive economy.[6]

Small Jewish settlements had existed in Palestine from the late 19th century, but after 1917, the colonization process accelerated considerably. Jewish organizations bought large areas of land from absentee landlords, displacing large numbers of Palestinian peasants. The Zionists also began to build an exclusively Jewish "enclave" economy, organized around the Histadrut, the general confederation of Hebrew workers in Palestine. The settlers refused to employ Arab labor and boycotted Arab goods.

In the 1930s, the rise of fascism in Europe gave a further boost to Jewish emigration, even though most Jews had no interest in moving to Palestine. Zionism was still very much a fringe movement among Jews, and only 8.5 percent of Jewish migrants went to Palestine during this period. The number would have been even smaller if countries such as the U.S. and Britain had not had racist immigration policies that excluded most Jews. The refugees who did arrive in Palestine, however, strengthened the settler community. As Ralph Schoenman notes in *The Hidden History of Zionism*:

> Throughout the late thirties and forties, Jewish spokespersons in Europe cried out for help, for public campaigns, for organized resistance, for demonstrations to force the hand of allied governments— only to be met not merely by Zionist silence but by active Zionist sabotage of the meager efforts which were proposed or prepared in Great Britain and the United States.
>
> The dirty secret of Zionist history is that Zionism was threatened by the Jews themselves. Defending the Jewish people from persecution meant organizing resistance to the regimes which menaced them. But these regimes embodied the imperial order which comprised the only social force willing or able to impose a settler colony on the Palestinian people. Hence, the Zionists needed the persecution of the Jews to persuade Jews to become colonizers afar, and they needed the persecutors to sponsor the enterprise.

Meanwhile, Jews in Palestine were given privileged status by the British colonial regime. The British helped to establish and train a Zionist militia, granted Jewish capital 90 percent of economic concessions, and paid Jews higher wages than Arabs for equal work. From the 1920s onward, the British government used Jewish settlers to help suppress mass Arab demonstrations against landlessness and unemployment and for independence. The most sustained uprising by the Palestinians took place from 1936 to 1939, and included a general strike of several months, the withholding of taxes, civil disobedience, and armed insurrection. The British responded by declaring martial law and instituting mass repression, relying heavily on Zionist forces. Hundreds of Palestinians were executed or assassinated, thousands were imprisoned, and thousands of homes were demolished.[7]

The foundation of Israel

Britain, greatly weakened by the Second World War, was forced to withdraw from Palestine. In 1947, the leading imperialist powers, including the U.S. and the USSR, decided to partition the country into separate Jewish and Palestinian states. Even though Jews at this time comprised only 31 percent of the population, the Zionists were given 54 percent of the fertile land.

Even this was not satisfactory for the Zionists, however. In 1938, Ben-Gurion had declared:

> The boundaries of Zionist aspiration include southern Lebanon, southern Syria, today's Jordan, all of Cis-Jordan [the West Bank] and the Sinai.... After we become a strong force as the result of the creation of the state, we shall abolish partition and expand to the whole of Palestine. The state will only be a stage in the realization of Zionism and its task is to prepare the ground for our expansion. The state will have to preserve order...with machine guns.[8]

The Zionist project could only be completed if the local Arab population was expelled. As Joseph Weitz, head of the Jewish Agency's Colonization Department, had put it in 1940:

> There is no room for both peoples together in this country.... We shall not achieve our goal of being an independent people with the Arabs in this small country.... And there is no other way than to transfer the Arabs from here to the neighboring countries. To transfer all of them; not one village, not one tribe should be left.[9]

Another Zionist document, the "Koenig Report," was even more blunt:

> We must use terror, assassination, intimidation, land confiscation and the cutting of all social services to rid the Galilee of its Arab population.[10]

In 1948, this policy was put into effect. Zionist forces seized three-quarters of the land and expelled close to 1 million Palestinians. Military groups, whose leaders included future prime ministers Menachem Begin and Yitzhak Shamir, carried out massacres at Deir Yassin and other villages that were designed to terrorize

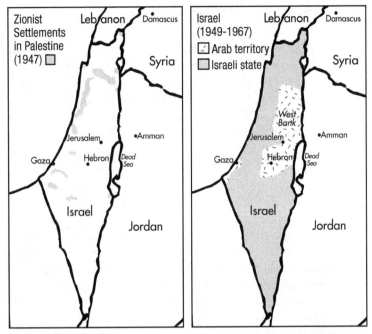

Jewish settlements in Palestine in 1947 (left) were tiny. By means of terrorist violence, the Zionists drove the Palestinians away and, in 1948, seized territory beyond what they had been granted by the 1947 UN partition plan.

the rest of the Palestinian population into fleeing for their lives. At Deir Yassin, 254 men, women, and children were murdered. In Begin's own words:

> All in the Jewish forces proceeded to advance through Haifa like a knife through butter. The Arabs began fleeing in panic, shouting "Deir Yassin."[11]

Other massacres were carried out by the official Israel Defense Forces. At the village of Dueima, according to the eyewitness account of one soldier:

> They killed between eighty to one hundred Arab men, women and children. To kill the children they fractured their heads with sticks. There was not one home without corpses.... Educated and well-mannered commanders who were considered "good guys"...be-

came base murderers, and this not in the storm of battle, but as a method of expulsion and extermination.[12]

Nearly 500 Palestinian villages existed in the territory that came under Israeli occupation after partition in 1947. During 1948 and 1949, nearly 400 of these were razed to the ground. More were destroyed in the 1950s. In 1969, Moshe Dayan, former chief of staff and minister of defense, summarized the nature of the Zionist colonization:

> We came here to a country that was populated by Arabs, and we are building here a Hebrew, Jewish state. Instead of Arab villages, Jewish villages were established…. There is not a single [Jewish] settlement that was not established in the place of a former Arab village.[13]

Zionist apologists have defended Israel's expansion on the grounds that the survival of the Jewish state was threatened by hostile Arab neighbors. On the pretext of defending the Palestinians, Arab countries did launch a military offensive in 1948, but as John Rose notes, "It was a totally unreal exercise. There were military clashes—but key Arab governments were already in negotiations with the Israelis."[14] Israel's forces vastly outmatched their Arab counterparts, and they used the opportunity to seize as much territory as possible.

In his diary, Moshe Sharett, Israel's prime minister in the 1950s, admits that the security argument has always been a fraud. According to Sharett, the Israeli political and military leadership never believed in any Arab danger to Israel. Rather, Israel has "sought to maneuver and force the Arab states into military confrontations which the Zionist leadership were certain of winning so Israel could carry out the destabilization of Arab regimes" and occupy more territory. According to Sharett, Israel's aim has been to "dismember the Arab world, defeat the Arab national movement and create puppet regimes under regional Israeli power" and "to modify the balance of power in the region radically, transforming Israel into the major power in the Middle East."[15]

Before 1947, Jews owned about 6 percent of the land in Palestine. In the process of establishing the state of Israel, the Zionists expropriated 90 percent of the land, the vast majority of which formerly belonged to Arabs. Entire cities were emptied of Palestinians, and Palestinian orchards, industry, rolling stock, factories, houses, and possessions were seized. Close to 1 million Palestinians were ethnically cleansed from their homeland.

The Arabs who remained in Israel became second-class citizens, while Palestinians who were driven out of the country were forced to live in poverty in refugee camps throughout the Middle East. Israel passed the "Law of Return," which allows every person of Jewish descent to immigrate to Israel, but the Palestinians were not allowed to return to their homeland.

Following the Six Day War in 1967, Israel occupied further territory, including the West Bank and the Gaza Strip. In the West Bank, 55 percent of the land and 70 percent of the water were seized for the benefit of Jewish settlers, who constituted only a tiny fraction of the population. In Gaza, 2,200 settlers were given more than 40 percent of the land, while 500,000 Palestinians were confined to crowded camps and slums.

Israel's actions have been repeatedly condemned by the United Nations (UN), but the U.S. government has ensured that nothing has been done to enforce a series of UN resolutions. Since its creation, Israel has been a defender of Washington's interests in the oil-rich region of the Middle East. The U.S. wanted a client state in the region that could help to prevent popular resistance to its control of oil. As a consequence, Israel has received billions of dollars in U.S. aid every year, which has made it one of the most heavily armed states in the world.

---

1   Quoted in Ralph Schoenman, *The Hidden History of Zionism* (San Francisco: Socialist Action, 1988), pp. 19–20.

2   See Andre Chouraqui, *The Life of Theodor Herzl* (Jerusalem: Keter Books, 1970), p. 230, for an account of Herzl's meeting with Von Plehve.

3   Quoted in Nathan Weinstock, *Zionism: False Messiah* (London: Pluto Press, 1989), p. 96.

4   Quoted in Weinstock, p. 97.

5   Quoted in Uri Davis, *Israel: An Apartheid State* (London: Zed Books, 1987), pp. 3–4.

6   See, for example, Rashid Khalidi, "Palestinian peasant resistance to
    Zionism before World War I," in *Blaming the Victims*, Edward Said and
    Christopher Hitchens, eds. (New York: Verso, 1988).

7   Phil Marshall, *Intifada: Zionism, Imperialism and Palestinian Resistance*
    (London: Bookmarks, 1989), pp. 35–43.

8   Quoted in Schoenman, pp. 32–33.

9   Quoted in Maxime Rodinson, *Israel: A Colonial-Settler State?* (New York:
    Pathfinder Press, 1973), p.16. As Weinstock observes, "These words, it should
    be borne in mind, express the mentality of moderate 'Labour' Zionists" (Wein-
    stock, p. 154).

10 Quoted in Schoenman, pp. 31–32.

11 Quoted in Weinstock, p. 242. For a description by an Israeli historian of
    the massacre, see Simha Flapan, *The Birth of Israel: Myths and Realities* (New
    York: Pantheon Books, 1987), p. 94.

12 Quoted in Schoenman, p. 36. The massacres continued after the state of Israel
    was established, for example at Qibya in 1953 and at Kafr Qassem in 1956.
    Both of these attacks were commanded by Ariel Sharon, later Israel's defense
    minister and today prime minister. See Noam Chomsky, *Fateful Triangle: The
    United States, Israel, and the Palestinians* (Boston: South End Press, 1983),
    pp. 158–59, 383–85.

13 Quoted in Schoenman, p. 41.

14 John Rose, *Israel: The Hijack State* (Chicago: ISO, 1986), p. 42.

15 Schoenman, p. 59.

LANCE SELFA

Israel: The U.S. watchdog

THE ESTABLISHMENT of the state of Israel in 1948 coincided
with the rise of the Middle East as an oil producer and the displacement of Britain by the U.S. as the main imperialist power in
the region. Until the Second World War, imperialist strategists primarily considered the Middle East a passageway to trade in the
Far East. But in the 1930s and 1940s, according to a U.S. oil industry report prepared in that period, "The center of gravity of
world oil production is shifting from the Mexican Gulf and the
Caribbean area to the Middle East–Persian Gulf area and is likely
to continue to shift until it is firmly established in that area."[1]

The U.S. wasn't the only power to recognize the Middle East's
importance in the aftermath of the Second World War. So did the
other major superpower, the USSR. In 1947, the USSR voted with
the U.S. in the United Nations to approve the partition of Palestine. Later, in 1948, a shipment of Soviet Bloc arms from Czecho-
slovakia to the Zionist Haganah militia aided Israel's conquest of
Palestine.[2] In the geopolitics of the time, the U.S. and Russia competed to win allies in the Third World. Both the Russians and the
U.S. considered the loss of an ally an automatic gain for the other
side. Although it seems absurd today, some Zionists argued for
U.S. support on grounds that failure to aid Israel would drive the
Jewish state to seek support from the USSR. "The United States is
going to have to grant sufficient financial support to the present
Israeli regime to avoid seeing the country go bust and perhaps

First published in the International Socialist Review, *Spring 1998.*

swing into Communist hands," wrote Cyrus L. Sulzberger in the *New York Times* in 1948.[3]

Nevertheless, Zionist leaders such as David Ben-Gurion knew that the USSR could not provide the kind of financial and military aid to Israel that the U.S. and American Zionist organizations could. They continued to woo the U.S. to become Israel's chief patron. The U.S. took the first step toward underwriting the Israeli venture in 1949, when it extended a $100 million loan to Israel from the newly created Export-Import Bank. The U.S. justified its support for Israel as necessary to counteract "the Soviet threat" to Middle East oil fields. But its true enemy was rising nationalism in the region.

When Iran's moderate prime minister, Mohammad Mossadegh, announced his intention to nationalize Anglo-Iranian oil properties in 1952, the West responded with frenzied denunciations of Mossadegh as a communist. The CIA overthrew Mossadegh in 1953, installing the pro-U.S. Mohammad Reza Pahlavi as the Shah of Iran. During the Mossadegh crisis, the "moderate" Israeli newspaper *Ha'aretz* made an offer to the West:

> The West is none too happy about its relations with states in the Middle East. The feudal regimes there have to make such concessions to the nationalist movements...that they become more and more reluctant to supply Britain and the United States with their natural resources and military bases.... Therefore, strengthening Israel helps the Western powers maintain equilibrium and stability in the Middle East. Israel is to become the watchdog. There is no fear that Israel will undertake any aggressive policy towards the Arab states when this would explicitly contradict the wishes of the U.S. and Britain. But if for any reason the Western powers should sometimes prefer to close their eyes, Israel could be relied upon to punish one or several neighboring states whose discourtesy to the West went beyond the bounds of the permissible.[4]

In the first decade of Israel's existence, the U.S., France, and England took turns holding the watchdog's leash. Between 1948 and the early 1960s, France served as Israel's chief arms supplier and sponsor of Israel's nuclear power (and weapons) industry. In exchange for French patronage, Israel supported French colonialism in Algeria and Vietnam.

When a 1952 coup brought the Arab nationalist regime of Gamal Abdel Nasser to power in Egypt, Ben-Gurion worried that Nasser "raised [Arab] spirits, changed their character and turned them into a fighting nation."[5] To provoke Western intervention against Nasser, Israeli spies in Egypt set off bombs at the U.S. and British embassies in 1954. The plot backfired. Egyptian authorities arrested, tried, and executed the Israeli agents in 1955. In response, Israel attacked Gaza (then under Egyptian rule), killing 37. Subsequent revelations showed that Israel's military intelligence chief, most likely with the knowledge of Ben-Gurion's inner circle, ordered the bombings in Egypt. The resulting scandal, known as the "Lavon Affair" (because Ben-Gurion tried to pin the blame on Defense Minister Pinhas Lavon), forced Ben-Gurion from office.[6] Yet, as the Lavon Affair showed, terrorism and assassination have been central to Israel's foreign policy.

Despite Israel's best efforts, the U.S. wasn't yet convinced that Israel could serve as the main prop to U.S. power in the region. The U.S. maintained ties with Arab regimes, including Egypt, throughout the 1950s. When Israel, Britain, and France went to war against Egypt in 1956, the U.S. opposed the war and forced its allies to back down. The U.S. could afford to show this kind of independence because it knew that the influence of Britain and France in the region was waning. The U.S. thus positioned itself to assume full dominance in the region without its "allies" getting in the way.

In 1958, the U.S. sent marines to prop up the right-wing Christian regime of President Camille Chamoun in Lebanon. But U.S. efforts didn't stop the rise of Arab nationalists, who overthrew pro-Western regimes in Iraq in 1958 and in Yemen in 1962, or their courting of Russian support. The U.S. began to look more favorably on Israel's value as a strategic asset. A 1958 National Security Council document stated that the "logical corollary" of opposition to radical Arab nationalism "would be to support Israel as the only strong pro-West power left in the Near East."[7]

U.S. strategic doctrine relied on building a network of pro-Western states to hem in any Arab regime that bucked the West. Over the years, the U.S. relied on combinations of Turkey, the Shah's Iran, Israel, and the Gulf monarchies to forge this alliance.

But Israel became the first among these only after its quick victory in the 1967 war.

Following months of provocations against its Arab neighbors, Israel struck in June 1967, with an eye to throttling Nasserism and conquering the parts of Palestine it hadn't seized in 1948.[8] In six days, Israel crippled the Egyptian, Syrian, and Jordanian military forces. It seized the Golan Heights from Syria, the West Bank and East Jerusalem from Jordan, and the Gaza Strip and Sinai Peninsula from Egypt.

Nothing proved Israel's value to the U.S. better than its blitzkrieg through the Arab states. The U.S. was even willing to forgive and forget Israel's attack on a U.S. surveillance ship, the *Liberty,* anchored off the Sinai coast. Israeli planes bombed the *Liberty,* and naval vessels torpedoed it. Thirty-four U.S. sailors died in the attack.[9]

The payoff from the U.S. to Israel was immediate. Between 1967 and 1972, total U.S. aid to Israel jumped from $13.1 million per year to $600.8 million per year. U.S. loans for Israeli purchases of U.S.-made weapons jumped an average of $22 million annually in the 1960s to a yearly average of $445 million between 1970 and 1974. The U.S. Congress even allowed the Pentagon to hand weapons to Israel without expecting any payment. House Speaker John McCormack noted in 1971 that "Great Britain, at the height of its struggle with Hitler, never received such a blank check" in U.S. military aid.[10] Israel had finally gained its desired status as "strategic asset" to the U.S. in the Middle East.

Democratic Senator Henry "Scoop" Jackson, nicknamed the "Senator from Boeing" for his hawkish views, pronounced in May 1973 that "the strength and Western orientation of Israel on the Mediterranean and Iran on the Persian Gulf safeguards U.S. access to oil." They have "served to inhibit and contain those irresponsible and radical elements in certain Arab states, who, were they free to do so, would pose a grave threat indeed to our principle sources of petroleum in the Persian Gulf."[11]

Israel's role as regional enforcer for the U.S. fit the Nixon administration's post–Vietnam War policy of subcontracting U.S. foreign policy to local client states. Nixon and his errand boy,

National Security Adviser and later Secretary of State Henry Kissinger, assembled a "strategic triangle" of Saudi Arabia, the Shah's Iran, and Israel to guard U.S. interests in the Middle East. The Nixon administration remained "firmly committed to Israel's security and to her military superiority in the Middle East, for only Israel's strength can deter attack and prevent a call for direct American intervention," the pro-Zionist *New York Times* explained.[12] During the 1973 war between Egypt and Israel, Nixon put U.S. forces on nuclear alert. Nixon willingly risked nuclear war to protect this "strategic asset."

Doing the dirty work of the U.S.

Israel took to its newfound U.S. responsibilities with gusto. When King Hussein moved to crush Palestinian guerrillas in Jordan in September 1970, Syrian tanks invaded Jordan. Fearing that Palestinian and Syrian resistance would topple his regime, Hussein pleaded with the U.S. and Israel to intervene. Kissinger relayed this message to Israel's defense minister, Yitzhak Rabin: "King Hussein has approached us, describing the situation of his forces, and asked us to transmit his request that your air force attack the Syrians in northern Jordan. I need an immediate reply." Rabin objected to the U.S. acting as a "mailman" for Jordan, but he agreed to comply with the request. The Israel Defense Forces (IDF) mobilized, giving Jordan cover to attack the Syrians. Within a day, King Hussein had regained control of Jordan and proceeded to expel Palestinian guerrillas. The IDF never carried out its attack plans.[13]

The Jordanian crisis highlighted one of Israel's chief values to the U.S.—helping to prop up reactionary regimes in the Middle East. But Israel didn't confine its dirty work for the U.S. to the Middle East. Since 1948, every pro-U.S. repressive dictatorship in the world has received some kind of overt or covert Israeli aid. The U.S. funnels weapons and aid through Israel when it wants to evade congressional bans on aid to repressive regimes. The U.S. and the CIA subcontract the training of death squads and terrorists to Israel. Consider the following examples:

• Israeli military advisers helped to train the militaries and secret police agencies of such "friends of Israel" as the Shah of Iran, Mobutu Sese Seko in Zaire, Emperor Jean-Bedel Bokassa in the Central African Republic, General Idi Amin in Uganda, and Ian Smith of Rhodesia.

- In 1978, Israel sold U.S. jets and attack helicopters to Indonesia as that country's military carried out genocide against East Timor. Its relationship with the Suharto dictatorship continued, despite the fact that the Indonesian military had killed more than 200,000 Timorese by 1998.

- In the last year of the Somoza dictatorship in Nicaragua, Israel provided 98 percent of the arms that Somoza used to kill 50,000 Nicaraguans. In 1980, Israel supplied 83 percent of the arms to the genocidal military regime of Guatemala.[14]

- In the late 1970s and early 1980s, Israel earned more than $1 billion per year selling weapons to the military dictatorships in Argentina, Chile, and Brazil. "Thus while Jewish newspaper publisher [and human rights advocate] Jacobo Timerman was being tortured by the Argentine military in cells painted with swastikas, three Israeli generals, including the former armed forces chief of staff, were visiting Buenos Aires on a 'friendly mission' to sell arms."[15]

- In 1977, Israel's foreign minister, Moshe Dayan, announced that Israel would not abide by the international arms embargo against the racist South African apartheid regime. Even an Israeli newspaper conceded, "It is a clear and open secret known to everybody that in [South African] army camps one can find Israeli officers in not insignificant numbers who are busy teaching white soldiers to fight Black terrorists with methods imported from Israel."[16]

- Israel anchored an international terrorist network that ran guns, drugs, and other weapons between Panama's Noriega, the Contras in Nicaragua, Middle Eastern arms dealers, the Sultan of Brunei, and the CIA. The Reagan administration made use of this network during the "arms for hostages" Contragate affair in the mid-1980s.

Israel's aid to repressive regimes reflects more than a trade-off for U.S. dollars. To be sure, Israel's economy, one-fifth of which is devoted to the military, gains from military contracts and trade. But there is a more fundamental reason why Israel supports murderous dictatorships. As a state whose entire existence depends on an alliance with imperialism to suppress the Palestinian national liberation movement, it opposes in principle any movements for democracy or liberation in what was known as the Third World. In the Middle East, "[t]he Israeli establishment knows that an Arab democracy will be much stronger than any Arab autocratic regime," the radical Israeli human rights campaigner Israel Shahak explained. Israel wants an undemocratic Palestinian bantustan in the Occupied Territories because it knows that "democracy will strengthen the Palestinians while Israel wants to keep them weak."[17] From Rhodesia to apartheid South Africa to the Gulf monarchies, Israel has tied its interests not to the masses fighting for freedom, but with their jailers.

The nature of Israel's class society

As an outpost for imperialism in the Middle East, Israel depends for its survival on military, economic, and political support from outside its borders. The Zionist myth that Israeli "pioneers" made "the desert bloom" ignores the fact that massive economic subsidies from the West—in particular, from the U.S. Treasury—support Israel's European-like living standards.

Since Israel's establishment, funds flowing into Israel from a combination of sources—Zionist organizations outside Israel, post–Second World War reparations from West Germany, and grants and loans from the U.S. government—have regularly exceeded Israeli capital exports. "The importance of the United States as a source of capital imports (as well as of political support in general—not to mention defense goods!) can hardly be overemphasized," one academic study of Israeli society noted.[18] Between 1949 and 1996, the U.S. gave Israel about $62.5 billion in foreign aid—about the same amount it gave to all of the countries of sub-Saharan Africa, Latin America, and the Caribbean combined during the same period.[19] Israel remains the single greatest recipient of U.S. foreign assistance, pocketing more than $3 billion in aid each year. But even this figure underestimates the extent of U.S. assistance to Israel. When U.S. government tax breaks for donations to Zionist organizations, Israel bonds sold by U.S. firms, loans, and other forms of aid are taken into account, the yearly U.S. subsidy to Israel more than doubles. One estimate placed the aid level at nearly $1,400 per Israeli citizen.[20] The close relationship between the U.S. and Israel ensures that the Israeli military arsenal is the most advanced and deadly in the region.

U.S. and Western subsidies to Israel have distorted the country's development, producing a society with dynamics that differ from those of other capitalist societies. In any other capitalist society, the class struggle between workers and bosses contains the kernel for a challenge to the country's ruling class. Israel's dependence on external resources has blunted the impact of class struggle involving Jewish workers within Israel. "This means that although class conflicts do exist in Israeli society they are constrained by the fact that the society as a whole is subsidized from the outside," an Israeli revolutionary socialist explained. "This privileged status is related to Israel's role in the region, and as long as this role continues there is little prospect of the internal social conflicts acquiring a revolutionary character."[21]

In contrast, "all the Arab regimes are vulnerable to movements from below which express the interests of millions who have not shared in the oil boom, in the privileges of the ruling families and bureaucracies, or in the wealth of those who profit from the 'opening' to Western capital."[22] For this reason, Israel is the most stable and pro-American country in the region, which explains its privileged position among U.S. allies in the Middle East.

Much has changed in Israeli politics and society in the last decade. While the U.S. continues to underwrite Israel's economic and military infrastructure, Israel has established trade links with a wider range of countries. Between 1990 and 1995, the Israeli economy grew at an average of 7 percent per year. Since the 1993 Oslo accords were signed with the Palestine Liberation Organization (PLO), Israeli diplomats have been welcome in many countries from which they previously had been barred. The stronger Israeli economy and decline of Israeli isolation have even allowed Israel to pursue high-profile dealings with countries such as China and North Korea. These Israeli contacts certainly displease Washington.

In line with many of the world's governments in the 1990s, Israel's Labor and Likud parties have pushed free-market "reform." The right-wing government of Benjamin Netanyahu, elected in 1996, pushed through massive plans for privatization of state-owned firms and cutbacks to the country's welfare system. These attacks provoked weeks of general strikes in late 1997.

While these developments showed workers' discontent in Israel, they did not pose a challenge to the Zionist state—or even to its Zionist policies. The majority of Jewish workers still identify with the state of Israel, even if they disagree with government policies. This identification with the state stems from the creation of the Jewish working class as a product of the exclusion of Palestinian labor. This is true even for the poorest Jewish Israelis. Immigrants to Israel from Middle Eastern countries and their descendants face discrimination at the hands of the country's European-origin elite. Traditionally, these "Oriental" Jews are among the poorest Israelis. But they, who make up the Israeli right wing's base, also tend to be the most hawkish and racist toward the Palestinians.[23]

Many individual Israeli Jews have contributed heroic work to the struggle for Palestinian rights. The war in Lebanon and the first Palestinian Intifada, which began in 1987, stirred movements in Israel of deserters from the Israeli military and other dissidents. But the majority of Israeli workers continue to identify their interests with the state and its Zionist enterprise. As long as this situation persists, Jewish workers are weaker in their own confrontations with Israel's rulers. Israel's rulers can always claim that workers' selfish economic demands are imperiling the state's security. For Israel's Jewish working class, a political break from Zionism is the precondition for its emancipation as a class.

A large-scale challenge to Zionism and Israel is more likely to come from outside Israel. A serious challenge to Israel's role in the region would raise the issue of the nature of the Israeli state. Israeli revolutionaries have written:

[A] revolutionary breakthrough in the Arab world could change this situation. By releasing the activity of the masses throughout the Arab world, it would change the balance of power; this would make Israel's traditional politico-military role obsolete, and would thus reduce its usefulness for imperialism. At first Israel would probably be used in an attempt to crush such a revolutionary breakthrough in the Arab world; yet once this attempt had failed, Israel's politico-military role vis-á-vis the Arab world would be finished. Once this role and its associated privileges had been ended, the Zionist regime, depending as it does on these privileges, would be open to mass challenge from within Israel itself.[24]

The contradictions of U.S. support for Israel

U.S. Middle East policy rests on a dilemma. The U.S. maintains its special relationship with Israel because Israel is the most pro-Western and stable country in the region. Yet the U.S. realizes that it must also have support from some Arab regimes, the mass of whose populations resent U.S. links to Israel. The 3.4 million Palestinian refugees living around the region remain a destabilizing factor in countries such as Jordan and Lebanon. Thus, despite the fact that every person in the region is aware of the close links between the U.S. and Israel, the U.S. must sometimes try to play down those links. For example, as the U.S. assembled an Arab coalition to crush Iraq in the Gulf War of 1991, it couldn't make use of its most reliable ally. Knowing that Israeli intervention against Iraq would break up its alliances with Egypt, Syria, and the Gulf states, the U.S. kept Israel "on the sidelines." When Iraqi Scud missiles fell on Israel, the U.S. strong-armed its ally not to respond.

Nothing embodies the U.S. search for stability more than the seemingly never-ending peace process that Nixon and Kissinger initiated—and every American president since has continued. The peace process has nothing to do with bringing peace and justice for the Palestinians. On the contrary, "the 'peace process' undertaken under U.S. auspices was always aiming to peripheralize the centrality of the Palestine question and to advance the bilateral dimension of the Arab-Israeli conflict."[25] In other words, the U.S. has used the peace process to avoid dealing with the Palestinians and to entice Arab countries to cease hostilities with Israel. Be-

cause the peace process doesn't deal with the root cause of instability in the region—the Palestinians' dispossession—it can't bring
peace to the region.

The peace process did produce one sought-after result, when
Egypt became the first Arab country to conclude a formal peace
treaty with Israel in 1979. President Jimmy Carter hosted the signing of the Camp David accords between Egypt and Israel. The accords, signed by Israel's right-wing prime minister, Menachem
Begin, and Egypt's president, Anwar Sadat, stipulated a five-year
transition to Palestinian autonomy in all of the Occupied Territories. The accords also ceded back to Egypt the Sinai Peninsula,
which Israel occupied in 1967. Israel finally ended its occupation
of the Sinai in 1982.

For the Palestinians, the accords pledged only to allow them
"to participate in the determination of their future"—not to determine their future.[26] The Camp David accords didn't meet Palestinian demands, but they served Israeli, Egyptian, and U.S. aims. For
an investment of $3.5 billion per year in aid to Egypt, the U.S.
gained a new Arab ally. Egypt opened its doors to Western investment. In completing the peace with Egypt, Israel neutralized its
most powerful military rival in the region. This freed the Israeli
army to concentrate on its main enemy: the Palestinians.

After being driven from Jordan in 1970, the PLO, the representative of the Palestinian liberation movement, set up its headquarters in Lebanon. Three years after signing the peace accords
with Egypt, Israel launched an invasion of Lebanon. The invasion,
dubbed "Operation Peace in Galilee," had two purposes: to drive
the PLO out of Lebanon and to impose a right-wing pro-Israeli
government on the country. Israeli forces killed 19,000 civilians
and maimed 30,000 more in six weeks. Israeli warplanes dropped
cluster and phosphorous bombs on whole neighborhoods of
Beirut. Under its protection, Israeli allies in minority Christian
neofascist Phalange militias massacred more than 2,000 Palestinian refugees in the Sabra and Shatila refugee camps.[27] With U.S.
help, Israel forced the PLO out of Lebanon. The "peace" at Camp
David had set the stage for more war.

Toward a "new Middle East"?

The U.S. defeat of Iraq in the 1991 Gulf War eliminated the main Israeli adversary that had the military capability to pose even a minimal threat to Israel. The Gulf War severely weakened the PLO as well. Already reeling from its loss of financial and diplomatic support from the USSR and its Stalinist satellites in Europe, the PLO faced two more crises following the Gulf War. The Gulf monarchies cut off all financial support for the PLO. Also, they expelled more than 400,000 Palestinian workers, whose remittances to their families in the territories and refugee camps had been essential to Palestinian economic life. In the aftermath of the Gulf War, the U.S. saw its opportunity to foist a new "peace process" on the Middle East.

Israel's Labor government, elected in 1992, agreed to negotiate with the PLO for three main reasons. First, Israel was unable to stop the 1987 Intifada. The costs of maintaining the occupation of the West Bank and Gaza seriously taxed the Israeli economy. Before the Intifada, Israel patrolled the territories with 10,000 to 15,000 Israeli troops and an extensive network of Palestinian collaborators. The Intifada destroyed that network, requiring Israel to rule the territories directly by military force. At the uprising's height, 180,000 Israeli troops occupied the territories. Between 1987 and 1993, Israeli forces killed more than 1,200 Palestinians, including 344 children younger than 16, to crush the uprising.

The arrival of more than 525,000 Jewish immigrants from the former USSR accelerated the crisis. Faced with a massive increase in the demand for jobs, housing, and social spending for the immigrants, Israel could not continue to spend one-third to one-half of its budget on the military. Israel decided to cut the cost of repressing the Palestinians by handing over much of the job to PLO leader Yasser Arafat's Fatah wing of the PLO. As Israel's cynical prime minister, Yitzhak Rabin, explained in an interview with the Israeli newspaper *Yediot Aharonot*:

> I prefer the Palestinians to cope with the problem of enforcing order in Gaza. The Palestinians will be better at it than we were because they will allow no appeals to the Supreme Court and will prevent the [Israeli] Association for Civil Rights from criticizing the conditions there.

They will rule there by their own methods, freeing—and this is the most important—the Israeli Army soldiers from having to do what they will do.[28]

Second, Israel clearly saw Arafat's Fatah movement as a lesser evil to any other possible representative of Palestinian aspirations—especially the Hamas fundamentalists. Arafat, whose organization faced further disintegration, perceived the deal as his last chance to administer a small patch of Palestine. In grasping the Israeli offer, Arafat sold out Palestinian refugees, whose interests aren't addressed in the Oslo accords. Oslo deferred fundamental issues, such as the final status of Jerusalem—which both Israel and Palestine claim as their capital—to undetermined future talks.

Third, Israeli business hoped that the deal would open avenues to its domination of a Middle East free-trade bloc with the Arab states. Contrary to Israeli propaganda, states such as Jordan, Syria, and others desired normalized relations with Israel for years, but they held back, fearing domestic reaction to dealings with Israel while the Palestinians remained under occupation. Arafat's surrender let the Arab regimes off the hook.

Israel allowed Arafat to assume responsibility for some government functions in about 60 percent of the Gaza Strip and in only about 3 percent of the West Bank. In exchange for "autonomy" in the areas under Palestinian Authority (PA) jurisdiction, Arafat agreed to act as Israel's cop. Populating the PA with Fatah loyalists and building a security apparatus of nearly 50,000 police and paramilitary forces, Arafat used his authority to crack down on opponents—and even criticism—of the deal with Israel.

Ultimate authority in the PA still rests with Israel, which controls the PA's borders and can intervene militarily at any time it wishes in "autonomous" regions. Even candidates for the PA's Legislative Council, elected in 1996, had to pass Israeli approval. As a result, the majority of the council was composed of "Arafat clients, loyalists, and pro-Oslo people. And thus, 'The election campaign ended with a deepening feeling of an emerging ruling elite, whose economic interests are tied with Israel.'"[29]

Economically, Israel remains dominant over the PA. Not only does it retain full control over all of the region's resources (such as water) and trade, it imposes regulations that impede economic development in the autonomous areas. Also, Israel has brought economic misery to Palestinian workers with its repeated closures of the West Bank and Gaza. It envisions the PA as a source of cheap labor for its service industries—to be absorbed when needed and discarded and barred from working at other times. Between 1993 and 1996, Israel reduced the number of Palestinians working in Israel from 116,000 to 29,500. Since the PA took over formal rule of six West Bank towns and most of Gaza in 1994, the Palestinians living in those areas have seen their already miserable incomes decline by nearly 40 percent.

In truth, the Oslo peace process envisions the formation of a Palestinian bantustan, like the fake homelands run by African collaborators set up by the South African apartheid regime in the 1960s and 1970s. Radical scholar Norman Finkelstein argues that the language in the accords outlining the PA's powers matches nearly word-for-word the legislation setting up the Transkei bantustan in South Africa. Samih Farsoun and Christina Zacharia provide this assessment of the current peace process:

> We...believe that in the context of such an imbalance of power between the politically weak Palestinian Authority and a strong Israel, the [Oslo accords'] Declaration of Principles will not lead to Palestinian self-determination and independent statehood or to the restoration or compensation for the internationally codified rights of the Palestinian diaspora.[30]

Today, not much is left of the Israel-PLO peace process inaugurated with the 1993 Oslo accords. Since 1996, when the Netanyahu government was elected as an opponent of Oslo, Israel has backed off commitments made by the previous Labor Party government. In 1997, when Netanyahu announced that he would go ahead with the Har Homa settlement in East Jerusalem, he signaled that Israel wasn't simply trying to stall implementation of the Oslo accords—it was trying to rewrite them. From that point until August 1997, the PA broke off meetings between PA and Israeli security forces. Netanyahu's threats to reoccupy the PA autonomous areas marked the lowest point in relations between

Israel and the PA since September 1996 gun battles between PA police and Israeli soldiers.

The U.S. is trying to salvage at least the shell of the peace process because it fears the worst-case alternative. An adviser on Middle East affairs to several U.S. administrations spelled out one possibility: "A total breakdown of the peace process, combined with a hard-line Israeli government, could conceivably result in a more humane but very real form of 'ethnic cleansing.'"[31] Considerations of how "humane" Israeli ethnic cleansing would be aside, the U.S. cares little about the fate of the Palestinians. It is much more concerned that a total collapse of the peace process will set back its alliance with Arab regimes and, worse, radicalize the populations of Middle Eastern countries.

Still the watchdog state?

Israel remains the region's most dangerous threat. It is the only country in the region with a nuclear arsenal. It has started or participated in nearly every major war in the region in the last 50 years—in 1948, 1956, 1967, 1973, 1982, and 1991. It regularly conducts military operations outside its borders, such as the 1996 "Grapes of Wrath" bombardment of Lebanon, which drove 400,000 civilians from their homes. And it regularly carries out assassinations on its enemies drawn from a list prepared by the Israeli secret service, Mossad. "One of the first duties of any new Israeli prime minister is to read the execution list and to decide whether or not to initial each name on it," according to a former Mossad agent.[32] When Mossad agents botched an assassination attempt on a Palestinian Islamist leader in Jordan in September 1997, Netanyahu faced extensive criticism in the Knesset (parliament). Yet almost no one who criticized Mossad's failure questioned its right to kill opponents of the Israeli state. In February 1998, a government commission cleared Netanyahu of any responsibility in the assassination attempt.

Even after the Cold War rationale for supporting Israel—namely, "containing communism"—evaporated, Israel's role as protector of U.S. interests remained. In a 1992 article in the Israeli newspaper *Yediot Aharonot,* a retired Israeli general, Shlomo Gazit, former head of military intelligence and West Bank administrator, forthrightly spelled out Israel's valuable service to imperialism. It is worth quoting Gazit's article at length.

"[After the Cold War] Israel's main task has not changed at all, and it remains of crucial importance," Gazit wrote. "Its location at the center of the Arab Muslim Middle East predestines Israel to be a devoted guardian of the existing regimes: to prevent or halt the processes of radicalization and to block the expansion of fundamentalist religious zealotry."[33]

Gazit noted that Israel asserts its right to intervene militarily in any Arab state, particularly one facing threats of revolt, whether military or popular, that may end up bringing fanatical and extremist elements to power in the state concerned. The existence of such threats in Arab states has no connection with the Arab-Israeli conflict. They exist because the regimes find it difficult to offer solutions to their socioeconomic ills. But any development of the described kind is apt to subvert the existing relations between Israel and this or that state from among its neighbors.

This brings Gazit to the special role that Israel would continue to play for Western allies:

> In the aftermath of the disappearance of the USSR as a political power with interests of its own in the region, a number of Middle Eastern states lost a patron. A vacuum was thus created, leading to the region's instability. Under such conditions the Israeli role as a strategic asset guaranteeing a modicum of stability in the entire Middle East did not dwindle or disappear but was elevated to the first order of magnitude. Without Israel, the West would have to perform this role by itself, when none of the existing superpowers really could perform it, because of various domestic and international constraints. For Israel, by contrast, the need to intervene is a matter of survival.[34]

Almost five decades after *Ha'aretz* declared Israel the West's "watchdog," Israel still hasn't been muzzled. The names of its enemies have changed from "communism" and "Arab nationalism" to "Islamic fundamentalism," but the same dynamic holds. Israel remains the chief guarantor for the U.S. of "stability" in the Middle East. Preserving stability means preserving the region's status quo. And preserving the status quo means maintaining repressive conditions that can only be a catalyst for future wars.

1 Quoted in Tony Cliff, "The Middle East at the crossroads," *Neither Washington Nor Moscow* (London: Bookmarks, 1983), p. 13.

2 See Joel Beinin, *Was the Red Flag Flying There?* (Berkeley, Calif.: University of California Press, 1990), pp. 45–50, and Phil Marshall, *Intifada: Zionism, Imperialism, and Palestinian Resistance* (London: Bookmarks, 1989), pp. 65–69.

3 David Schoenbaum, *The United States and Israel* (New York: Oxford University Press,1993), p. 75.

4 Marshall, pp. 76–77.

5 Ben-Gurion quoted in Naseer Aruri, *The Obstruction of Peace: The U.S., Israel, and the Palestinians* (Monroe, Maine: Common Courage Press, 1995), p. 39.

6 Beinin, pp. 11–12.

7 Quoted in Noam Chomsky, *Fateful Triangle: The United States, Israel, and the Palestinians* (Boston: South End Press, 1983), p. 21.

8 See Norman G. Finkelstein's demolition of Israeli lies surrounding the 1967 war in "To live or perish," in *Image and Reality of the Israeli-Palestinian Conflict* (New York: Verso, 1996), pp. 123–49.

9 Schoenbaum, pp. 156–59.

10 Aid figures and the McCormack quote are from Marshall, pp. 82–85.

11 Jackson quoted in Noam Chomsky, "The Middle East settlement: Its sources and contours," in *Power and Prospects* (Boston: South End Press, 1996), p. 139.

12 Aruri, p. 45.

13 Andrew Cockburn and Leslie Cockburn, *Dangerous Liaison* (New York: Harper Collins, 1991), p. 167.

14 Israel Shahak, *Israel's Global Role: Weapons for Repression* (Belmont, Mass.: Association of Arab-American University Graduates, 1981), pp. 15–16.

15 Penny Lernoux, "Israeli arms sales imperil vital Latin friendships," in Shahak, *Israel's Global Rules,* p. 53. Timerman's story is recounted in his powerful *Prisoner Without a Name, Cell Without a Number* (New York: Vintage, 1988).

16 Cockburn and Cockburn, p. 300.

17 Israel Shahak, *Open Secrets* (London: Pluto Press, 1997), p. 162.

18 Michael Wolffsohn, *Israel, Policy, Society, and Economy, 1882–1986* (Atlantic Highlands, N.J.: Humanities Press, 1986), p. 264.

19 See Richard H. Curtiss, "True lies about U.S. aid to Israel," *Washington Report on Middle East Affairs,* December 1997, pp. 43–45.

20 Samih K. Farsoun and Christina E. Zacharia, *Palestine and the Palestinians* (Boulder, Colo.: Westview Press, 1997), p. 243.

21 Akiva Orr, Haim Hanegbi, and Moshe Machover, "The class nature of Israel," *New Left Review,* January–February 1971, p. 11.

22 Marshall, p. 203.

23 See the discussion of Oriental support for the right wing in Emmanuel Farjoun, "Class divisions in Israeli society," and Avishai Ehrlich's "The Oriental support for Begin—a critique of Farjoun," *Khamsin* (1983), pp. 29–46.

24 Orr, Hanegbi, and Machover, p. 11.

25 Aruri, p. 111.

26 Robert Fisk, *Pity the Nation* (New York: Touchstone Press, 1990), p. 142.

27 General Rafael Eitan congratulated the murderers on having "carried out good work" and offered an IDF bulldozer to help them out. Ariel Sharon, then defense minister, was forced to resign in the wake of the debacle in Lebanon and the massacre. Yet both Eitan and Sharon remain leading politicians in Israel today.

28 Rabin quoted in Aruri, p. 210.

29 Farsoun and Zacharia, p. 285.

30 Farsoun and Zacharia, p. 312.

31 Anthony H. Cordesman, *Perilous Prospects* (Boulder, Colo.: Westview Press, 1997), p. 152.

32 Victor Ostrovsky and Claire Hoy, *By Way of Deception* (New York: St. Martin's Press, 1990), pp. 25–26.

33 Gazit quoted in Chomsky, "The Middle East settlement," p. 165.

34 Gazit quoted in Shahak, *Open Secrets*, pp. 40–43.

PAUL D'AMATO

U.S. intervention in the Middle East: Blood for oil

"If Kuwait grew carrots, we wouldn't give a damn."
Lawrence Korb, assistant defense secretary under Reagan,
as the U.S. prepared its massive military assault on Iraq in 1991.

SINCE THE Second World War, the United States has been the
dominant world power in the Middle East. Every U.S. policy shift,
every military intervention, every CIA plot has been carried out to
secure one main aim: the cheap and plentiful flow of the world's
most important energy resource—oil. Despite new discoveries of
oil reserves in Central Asia, the Middle East still has two-thirds of
the world's proven oil reserves, and its oil is still the cheapest to
pump and produce. As Lawrence Korb's statement about Kuwait
and carrots makes clear, nothing that takes place in the Middle
East today can be understood without first understanding the
strategic and economic importance of "black gold."

The U.S. has relied on brutal, repressive regimes—Iran under the
Shah, Saudi Arabia, Israel—to do its dirty work. It has used the CIA
to foment coups against "unfriendly" regimes. When necessary, it
has intervened directly to punish regimes that have challenged its
dominance in the region, as it did to Iraq in 1991. To this day, the
U.S. spends billions annually to maintain a large military presence in
the region. It provides billions in military hardware to client states—

First published in the International Socialist Review, *December 2000–January 2001.*

particularly to Egypt, Saudi Arabia, and Israel, which the U.S. carefully maintains as the region's most formidable military power.

The prize

After the collapse of the Ottoman Empire, Britain and France drew the boundaries of the new states in the Middle East with absolutely no input from the people of the region. All promises of Arab independence made by the British to various local leaders during the First World War were scrapped. At the 1919 peace conference, when the victorious powers sat down to divvy up the spoils, foremost in their minds was the need to keep the region divided and thereby easier to control:

> Private oil concerns pushed their governments (in the national interest, of course) to renounce all wartime promises to the Arabs. For the oilmen saw only too well that oil concessions and royalties would be easier to negotiate with a series of rival Arab states lacking any sense of unity, than with a powerful independent Arab state in the Middle East.[1]

Britain took the areas that became Iraq, Kuwait, and Saudi Arabia. France took Syria and Lebanon. Each state was then handed to local kings and sheikhs who owed their position to British tutelage. Kuwait was handed to the al-Sabah family. After he was promised a united Arab republic, the Hashemite King Hussein was awarded Jordan. Britain gave Saudi Arabia—the only country in the world named after its ruling family—to Ibn Saud. France put Lebanon in the hands of the Christian minority.

Journalist Glenn Frankel describes how Britain's high commissioner, Sir Percy Cox, settled boundaries between Iraq, Kuwait, and Saudi Arabia at a 1922 conference in Baghdad:

> The meeting had gone on for five grueling days with no compromise in sight. So one night in late November 1922, Cox, Britain's representative in Baghdad, summoned to his tent Sheik Abdul-Aziz ibn Saud, soon to become ruler of Saudi Arabia, to explain the facts of life as the British carved up the remnants of the defeated Ottoman empire.
>
> "It was astonishing to see [Ibn Saud] being reprimanded like a naughty schoolboy by His Majesty's High Commissioner and being told sharply that he, Sir Percy Cox, would himself decide the type and general line of the frontier," recalled Harold Dickson, the

British military attaché to the region, in his memoirs.

"This ended the impasse. Ibn Saud almost broke down and pathetically remarked that Sir Percy was his father and mother who made him and raised him from nothing to the position he held and that he would surrender half his kingdom, nay the whole, if Sir Percy ordered."

Within two days, the deal was done. The modern borders of Iraq, Saudi Arabia, and Kuwait were established by British Imperial fiat at what became known as the Uqauir Conference.[2]

There was one unique exception to this arrangement. The 1917 Balfour Declaration had committed Britain to supporting the formation of a "national home for the Jewish people" in Palestine. When the postwar settlement made the country a British protectorate, Britain backed Jewish immigration to Palestine, hoping to create a "secure strategic outpost in an Arab world."[3] Though Lord Arthur Balfour was an anti-Semite, he and other members of the British ruling class could see the value of creating a colonial-settler outpost that, dependent on British support, could become a loyal protector of British interests in the area. The full significance of the role of such an outpost would not become apparent to or fully taken advantage of by the U.S. until several years after the formation of the state of Israel in 1948.

U.S. steps in

In the aftermath of the Second World War, the U.S. moved in quickly to establish itself as the number one power in the Middle East.

American policy in this period was chiefly concerned that countries in the region did not come under the control of nationalist regimes. They had their first taste of that threat in Iran, when the democratically elected president Mohammed Mossadegh, with mass popular support, nationalized the British-owned Anglo-Iranian Oil Company. In a coup engineered by CIA operative Kermit Roosevelt, Mossadegh was toppled and replaced by the Shah. The Shah's power was underwritten by massive infusions of American aid and upheld by the notoriously savage secret police, SAVAK.

The U.S. worried that Egypt, under Gamal Abdel Nasser—a nationalist military officer who had come to power, ironically, with the CIA's blessing after a 1952 coup—might become a pole of attraction for Pan-Arab movements.

U.S. interests in the region were couched in the Cold War terms of preventing Soviet domination, though it was clear that any regime attempting to leave the orbit of the U.S., whether it had ties to Russia or not, was considered a threat. Under the first of what would become a series of "doctrines" outlining U.S. policy in the Middle East, the 1957 Eisenhower Doctrine declared that the United States was "prepared to use armed forces to assist" any Middle Eastern country "requesting assistance against armed aggression from any country controlled by international communism."[4]

The Eisenhower Doctrine reflected Washington's anger over Nasser's turn to the Eastern Bloc for weapons. The U.S. refused to arm Egypt unless it agreed to join the U.S.-sponsored Baghdad Pact, a regional security agreement under U.S. auspices. The doctrine was quickly put to the test, as a series of developments in the region seemed to augur a wave of nationalism. In Jordan, King Hussein was threatened by a newly elected pro-Nasser parliament. In 1958, Egypt and Syria joined together to form the United Arab Republic. In Lebanon, Muslim Arab nationalists led a struggle against the minority Christian regime led by Camille Chamoun. More important to the U.S., a nationalist military coup in Iraq that same year overthrew pro-British dictator Nuri Said. This event was perceived as a severe blow to U.S. prestige in the region and a threat to American oil interests.

U.S. officials feared that the new Iraqi regime might reassert its historical claim to Kuwait, a tiny country created by British fiat in order to prevent any larger state from controlling what was then the biggest oil-producing area in the Gulf. A memorandum based on an emergency meeting between Secretary of State John Foster Dulles, Chair of the Joint Chiefs of Staff Nathan Twining, and CIA Director Allen Dulles asserted that unless the United States intervened, "the U.S. would lose influence," its "bases" would be "threatened," and U.S. credibility would be "brought into question throughout the world."[5] The U.S. was also concerned about the nationalist threat to what were very profitable oil concessions in Kuwait and Iraq.

Fearing that he was on the brink of losing power, Lebanon's

Chamoun asked the U.S. for assistance under the Eisenhower Doctrine. With its eye on Iraq, the U.S. seized this opportunity and declared a nuclear alert, mobilized a massive strike force ready to intervene when called on, and invaded Lebanon with 14,000 marines. When the new Iraqi regime announced its commitment to "respect its obligations," the U.S. withdrew its forces. "Thus what followed the coup in Iraq and the landing of troops in Beirut was a new understanding of the rules of the Middle East game," writes Micah Sifry. "Political changes were possible as long as economic interests were safeguarded."[6]

The "special relationship" with Israel

Since the late 1960s, Israel has been the most important ally of the U.S. in the Middle East, fulfilling the role laid out for it by the Israeli newspaper *Ha'aretz* as America's "watchdog" in the region. For this reason, Israel receives more economic and military aid from the U.S. than any other country in the world. "The U.S. relationship with Israel is singular," writes Stephen Zunes.

> Israel represents only one one-thousandth of the world's population and has the 16th highest per capita income in the world, yet it receives 40 percent of all U.S. foreign aid. In terms of U.S. aid to the Middle East, Israel received 54 percent in 1999, Egypt 38 percent and all other Middle East countries only about 8 percent. Direct aid to Israel in recent years has exceeded $3.5 billion annually and has been supported almost unanimously in Congress, even by liberal Democrats who normally insist on linking aid to human rights and international law.[7]

The basis on which Israel was formed—the mass expulsion of the local Arab population and the establishment of an exclusively Jewish state—makes Israel both the most reliable ally and a source of instability in the Middle East. The U.S. can rely on Israel's superior military might to help police the region because Israel's unique history makes the majority of its citizens zealous defenders of the Israeli state. In addition, Israel's dependence on American imperialism to pay for its massive military superiority over its neighbors makes Israel solidly pro-West. On the other hand, the forced expulsion of Palestinians by Israel has created a constant source of friction in the region that threatens to upset U.S. relations with Arab states.

In the early years following the Second World War, as the U.S. endeavored to extend its dominance over the Gulf states, Washington viewed Israel as an ally, but only as one among many. However, as the threat of Arab nationalism increased after the rise of Mossadegh and Nasser to power in the early 1950s, U.S. aid to Israel began to increase. Whereas, in 1951, the U.S. gave Israel only $100,000 in grants, the coup in Egypt the following year prompted the U.S. to give Israel $86.4 million.[8]

But the U.S. was still wary that stronger ties with Israel could sour relations with the Arab states. This was one of the reasons that the U.S. opposed Britain, France, and Israel's invasion of Egypt in 1956 over Nasser's nationalization of the Suez Canal. Yet the continuing growth of Arab nationalism and the fear of the growth of Soviet influence in the region prompted the U.S. to rely more closely on Israel's "watchdog" capabilities. "By 1958," writes Mark Curtis, "the U.S. National Security Council concluded that the 'logical corollary' of opposition to radical Arab nationalism 'would be to support Israel as the only strong pro-Western power left in the Middle East.'" He continues:

> During the "crisis" in the Middle East of 1958, when Britain landed troops in Jordan and the United States did likewise in Lebanon, President Eisenhower on several occasions considered the merits of "unleashing" Israel (along with Turkey) against Egypt. The Chairman of the Joint Chiefs of Staff, General Nathan Twining, proposed that Israel should seize the West Bank of Jordan as part of a regional offensive that would include British intervention in Iraq and Turkish intervention in Syria. In all, it has been little wonder that the building under British auspices of a national home in the region for Jews was regarded by Arabs as a "permanent imperialist bridgehead."[9]

By the 1960s, as aid to Israel increased, U.S. officials realized that Israel could be counted on to work, mostly covertly, to curb the expansion of Arab nationalism in the region. But it was with Israel's role in the June 1967 Six Day War, when the Israeli army proved itself superior to the combined forces of several other states and expanded its territory into the West Bank, the Golan Heights, and the Sinai Peninsula, that the U.S. cemented its special relationship with Israel. In fact, 99 percent of U.S. aid to Israel has come in the years since the Six Day War. That aid has been, in the eyes of U.S. imperialism, a very good investment.

Stephen Zunes recounts the importance of Israel to the United States:

> Israel has helped suppress victories by radical nationalist movements in Lebanon, Jordan, and Yemen, as well as in Palestine. The Israeli military has kept Syria, for many years an ally of the Soviet Union, in check, and its air force is predominant throughout the region. Israel's frequent wars have provided battlefield testing for American arms. Israel has also served as a conduit for U.S. arms to regimes and movements—such as apartheid-era South Africa, Iran, Guatemala, and the Nicaraguan contras—too unpopular in the United States for overt and direct military assistance. Israel's military advisors have assisted the contras, the Salvadoran Junta, and other governments allied with the United States; its secret service has assisted the United States in intelligence gathering and covert operations. Israel has hundreds of intermediate-range ballistic missiles and has cooperated with the U.S. military-industrial complex regarding research and development for new jet fighters, antimissile defense systems, and even the Strategic Defense Initiative. No U.S. administration wants to jeopardize such an important relationship.[10]

Benjamin Beit-Hallahmi makes a similar point:

> An American military expert—Major General George Keegan, a former air-force intelligence officer—has been quoted as saying that it would cost U.S. taxpayers $125 billion to maintain an armed force equal to Israel's in the Middle East, and that the U.S.-Israel military relationship was worth "five CIAs." There can be no doubt that from the U.S. point of view, the investment in Israel is a bargain, and the money well spent.[11]

Of course, the interests of Israel and the U.S. do not always exactly coincide. Sometimes, in fact, Israel's aggressive posture toward the Arab states must be curbed in order to foster closer relationships with the Arab ruling classes. George Bush, for example, during the 1991 Gulf War, had to restrain Israel from attacking Iraq for fear of upsetting Egypt and Saudi Arabia, two crucial regional anti-Iraq coalition members.

But it was Israel's military muscle in the Six Day War, and again in the 1973 war, which pitted Israel against Egypt and

Syria, that helped to bring Egypt into the U.S. fold. Under President Anwar Sadat, Egypt became the first country to recognize the state of Israel. Ever since, Egypt has become the second-largest recipient of U.S. aid after Israel.

In that sense, Israel *is* a watchdog, but like a watchdog, it must sometimes be kept on a short leash and sometimes tries to slip that leash. This has been a constant tension in U.S. policy toward the Middle East, and thus explains former President Bill Clinton's eagerness for the "peace process." The peace process is not aimed at securing justice for the Palestinians, but at bringing Palestinian Authority head Yasser Arafat under control, eliminating the "Palestinian problem," and thereby facilitating further cooperation between Israel and its Arab neighbors. As it stands, the resilience of the Palestinian movement continually upsets these calculations.

Surrogates

The U.S. debacle in Vietnam convinced U.S. planners in the late 1960s of the importance of securing control in the Middle East without direct military intervention. The new Nixon Doctrine looked to local powers to be America's regional police force. In the Middle East, Iran, Israel, and Saudi Arabia became the three "pillars" on which U.S. power rested in the region. Former U.S. Defense Secretary Melvin Laird explained, "America will no longer play policeman to the world. Instead we will expect other nations to provide more cops on the beat in their own neighborhood." As U.S. Senator Henry Jackson explained in 1973, Israel and Iran under the Shah were

> reliable friends of the United States [who] have served to inhibit and contain those irresponsible and radical elements in certain Arab states...who, were they free to do so, would pose a grave threat indeed to our principal source of petroleum in the Persian Gulf.[12]

The U.S. sold $8.3 billion worth of arms to the Shah between 1970 and 1979, and sent more than 50,000 U.S. advisers to train the Shah's army and secret police. Saudi Arabia has long been considered the most important Arab ally of the U.S. in the Gulf. Economically, it is the linchpin of Gulf oil production. If 65 percent of the world's proven oil reserves are in the Gulf region, 38 percent of those are in Saudi Arabia.[13] When oil was discovered there in

1938, U.S. oil companies such as Socal, Texaco, Mobil, and Standard Oil of New Jersey quickly gained lucrative concessions by forming the Arabian-American Oil Company (ARAMCO). A draft State Department memorandum in 1945 described Saudi Arabia's oil resources as "a stupendous source of strategic power, and one of the greatest material prizes in world history."[14]

To secure what was initially an impoverished and weak state, the U.S. gave Marshall Plan funds to Ibn Saud. Until the 1950s, when regional rulers began to assert more control over oil revenues, Ibn Saud and other local sheikhs sustained themselves from royalties handed to them by the oil companies. To give some sense of how this tremendous oil wealth was spent, while Ibn Saud spent $2 million in 1946 to maintain his garages, Saudi spending on education in the same year amounted to $150,000.[15] Today, the ruling Saud family, for whom Saudi Arabia is a piece of family real estate, consists of several thousand members. Of them, more than 50 are billionaires. The king's palace alone is estimated to be worth $17 billion, and the royal family's budget is $6 billion to $7 billion.

Protecting the Saudi Arabian "prize" became a chief aim of U.S. policy in the Gulf. President Truman wrote a letter to King Saud in 1950 in which he declared, "No threat to your kingdom could occur which would not be a matter of immediate concern to the United States."[16] After the oil-producing states, eager to gain a greater share of revenue from their oil, formed the Organization of Petroleum Exporting Countries (OPEC) in 1960, keeping Saudi Arabia in America's corner became even more important. As the world's largest oil producer, Saudi Arabia can be relied upon to use its leverage to ensure, among other things, that enough oil flows to keep prices down.

The U.S. has sold billions of dollars in military hardware to Saudi Arabia throughout its history, not only to protect Saudi oil from outside intervention, but also from internal dissent. The fact that Saudi Arabia is one of the most repressive societies in the world has not concerned U.S. officials one iota. Writes Saïd Aburish:

> Amnesty International, Middle East Watch, the Minnesota International Lawyers Association and other human rights organizations have documented endless cases of imprisonment, torture and elimi-

> nation within the kingdom. Solitary confinement for years on end is
> a regular happening..., kidnappings and disappearances are com-
> mon..., political executions without proper trial are frequent...and
> even women are not spared torture and humiliation.... In February
> 1996 a ten-year-old child was left in the sun tied to a rope in front
> of a police station. In six hours he was dead, the victim of the merci-
> less desert sun. The boy had criticized the House of Saud.[17]

Saudi Arabia's abysmal human rights record doesn't even appear
on the U.S. public radar, reflecting a longtime double standard
whereby enemies are demonized and friends are whitewashed.
U.S. military assistance helps to keep this reactionary, repressive
monarchy in power.

Though the U.S. now views Islam as a grave threat to its interests in the Middle East, and the U.S. press regularly pumps out
racist anti-Islamic stereotypes, Islamic Saudi Arabia remains completely unscathed. Ironically, at one time, the U.S. actively promoted Islamic fundamentalism as a counterweight to Arab
nationalism.[18] The CIA, for example, cooperated with the Muslim
Brotherhood in Nasser's Egypt and provided Muslim movements
with operating bases in Pakistan. Osama bin Laden is a former
U.S. ally, the product of U.S. efforts to arm and train Islamic fundamentalist forces fighting the Russians in Afghanistan in the
1980s. Even Israel once funded the Muslim Brotherhood and
Hamas in Palestine as a way of undermining the Palestine Liberation Organization's (PLO's) strength.

What is consistent in U.S. policy is its need to strengthen its
strategic, economic, and military control over the flow of oil.
How it does this changes with the times.

Rapid deployment

When the Shah of Iran was overthrown in 1979, U.S. policy in
the Middle East faced a severe crisis. It had lost one of its key pillars in the Middle East. Joe Stork and Martha Wenger describe
the problem:

> The revolution which overthrew the Shah in 1979 radically changed
> the strategic equation in the region. Sparsely populated Saudi Arabia
> was never a serious candidate to play a role comparable to Iran. The
> real "second pillar" of U.S. strategy in the Middle East was Israel, but
> Israel's political liabilities severely limited its usefulness in the Gulf.[19]

The Nixon Doctrine was now replaced by the Carter Doctrine, which emphasized the need to use direct military force if U.S. interests were threatened in the region. Accordingly, President Jimmy Carter promoted the idea of a U.S. "rapid deployment force" that could intervene quickly in the region. Such a strategy required the U.S. to line up local regimes to allow U.S. military bases on their territories. Saudi Arabia became the linchpin of this strategy. Unable to openly declare support for the U.S. and Israel for fear of alienating their own populations, Gulf rulers were forced to act discreetly, allowing U.S. air and naval forces limited use of military facilities. This forced the U.S. to depend heavily on more remote bases in Kenya and Diego Garcia in the Indian Ocean, as well as on the deployment of aircraft carriers.

The outbreak of the Iran-Iraq War in 1980 provided the U.S. with the perfect opportunity to bring Saudi Arabia into even closer military collaboration. As Stork and Wenger explain:

> Saudi fears of an expanded war gave the U.S. leverage to extract more intimate Saudi collaboration with U.S. military plans. The centerpiece of this effort was the sale of five AWACS planes and a system of bases with stocks of fuel, parts, and munitions. "No conceivable improvements in U.S. airlift or USAF rapid deployment and 'bare-basing' capability could come close to giving the U.S. this rapid and effective reinforcement capability," wrote military analyst Anthony Cordesman. An added advantage was that the Saudis paid for it all.
>
> Over the course of the decade, Saudi Arabia poured nearly $50 billion into building a Gulf-wide air defense system to U.S. and NATO specifications, ready for U.S. forces to use in a crisis. By 1988, the U.S. Army Corps of Engineers had designed and constructed a $14 billion network of military facilities across Saudi Arabia.[20]

U.S. policy during much of the eight-year Iran-Iraq War, which cost a million lives on both sides, was to encourage the war as a means to weaken both Iran and Iraq. Western powers and Russia each sold arms to both sides. But in 1987, when it appeared that Iran might win the war, the U.S. tilted toward Iraq, seeing an Iranian victory as the greater evil. The U.S. gave Iraq military aid, agricultural credits, and crucial intelligence information, and used the pretext of "freedom of navigation" in the Gulf to mobilize a massive armada to attack Iran's navy.

After Iran's defeat in 1988, U.S. support for Iraq's president, Saddam Hussein, increased. "Between 1985 and 1990," writes Lance Selfa,

> U.S. firms sold almost $800 million in "dual use" aircraft—ostensibly to be used for civilian purposes, but easily convertible to military use. In 1988 and 1989 alone, the U.S. government approved licenses to U.S. firms to sell biological products to the Iraqi Atomic Energy Agency and electronics equipment to Iraqi missile-producing plants. In July 1988—two months after Saddam used chemical weapons to wipe out the Kurdish village of Halabja—the California-based Bechtel Corp. won a contract to build a petrochemicals plant. Iraq planned to produce mustard gas and fuel-air explosives in the plant. The Bush administration doubled agricultural credits to Iraq to $1 billion a year.... U.S. business created a virtual "Saddam lobby" to press for greater ties with Iraq.[21]

The 1991 Gulf War

The 1991 Gulf War marked the first time since 1958 that the U.S. launched a full-scale invasion of the Middle East in order to protect its interests. Up to the day that Iraq invaded Kuwait, Saddam Hussein was under the impression that his actions would be acceptable to Washington. Bled dry by the war with Iran, Iraq was angry over Kuwait's insistence on dumping oil on the world market when Iraq needed better oil revenues to pay for the war. When Iraq began to threaten Kuwait, U.S. ambassador April Glaspie told Hussein, "We have no opinion on Arab-Arab conflicts like your border disagreement with Kuwait."[22] But when Iraq invaded Kuwait soon after, the U.S. completely reversed its position.

The U.S. could not allow Saddam Hussein to upset the balance of power by taking control of a quarter of the Gulf's oil. Saddam Hussein was a brutal military dictator long before he tried to get control of Kuwaiti oil. The only difference is that pre-invasion, he was a friend of the United States, whereas post-invasion, he had suddenly become the "new Hitler."

The collapse of the Soviet Union and the end of the Cold War created the unique conditions that allowed the U.S. to assert its dominance in the region more directly than it had in the past. Bush took the opportunity to cobble together a military coalition—under United Nations (UN) auspices—that included not only European powers such as Britain, France, and Germany, but also Middle Eastern states such as Saudi Arabia, Egypt, and Syria.

The U.S. freely used bribery and intimidation to create the anti-Iraq coalition. The U.S. pushed the Gulf states to give $4 billion to Russia; China, whose brutal suppression of the democracy movement in Tiananmen Square had left it isolated internationally, was now offered a place at the table; Egypt was forgiven $14 billion in debt; and Syria was given the green light to invade Lebanon. When Yemen voted against the UN resolution authorizing the use of force against Iraq, the U.S. cut off millions of dollars in aid, and Saudi Arabia promptly expelled 800,000 Yemeni "guest" workers.

Yet for all of the fanfare about the war pitting Iraq against the "international community," the war was overwhelmingly fought by U.S. forces, for U.S. aims, with some backup from Britain and Saudi Arabia. U.S. pilots flew 90 percent of all combat sorties. The UN was used purely as a fig leaf to cover what was an American-led and American-fought war.

The Bush administration deliberately sabotaged every effort made by European and Arab countries to work out a peace settlement—vetoing, for example, a four-point peace proposal put forward by France in the UN Security Council. The U.S. was itching to teach its former client a lesson. The month-long air war devastated Iraq's infrastructure. More than 90,000 sorties dropped 88,500 tons of cluster bombs, fuel-air explosives, and other ordnance, destroying Iraq's bridges, roads, power grid, and water processing capabilities, and killing tens of thousands of people.

Even though Saddam Hussein, after more than a month of bombing, agreed to accept the UN resolution calling for Iraq's withdrawal from Kuwait, the U.S. dismissed this gesture. Selfa describes Bush's brutal ground war that followed:

> Saddam had essentially cried "uncle," but the U.S. wanted to mount a ground offensive anyway. In six days, U.S. and coalition ground troops swept across Kuwait and southern Iraq, forcing Iraqi troops into a full-scale retreat. In the last 40 hours of the war, before Bush called a cease-fire on February 28, U.S. and British forces mounted a relentless assault against retreating and defenseless Iraqi soldiers. The road leading from Kuwait to Basra became known as the

"Highway of Death." Iraqi soldiers fled Kuwait in every possible vehicle they could get their hands on. Allied tank units cut the Iraqis off. U.S. warplanes bombed, strafed and firebombed the stranded columns for hours without resistance. In a slaughter that a U.S. pilot described as "like shooting fish in a barrel," thousands of Iraqi conscripts were killed on a 50-mile stretch of highway. So many planes filled the skies over southern Iraq that military air traffic controllers maneuvered to prevent mid-air collisions.[23]

The endgame to Bush's war was ironic. After calling on the Iraqi people to overthrow Saddam Hussein, U.S. forces stood by as Iraqi troops put down an uprising of Kurds in the North and Shiites in the South. General Norman Schwartzkopf gave Saddam Hussein's generals permission to violate the "no-fly" rule and use armed helicopters to put down the rebellion. Brent Scowcroft, who was national security adviser at the time, told Peter Jennings in 1998 that the U.S. wanted a military coup to oust Hussein, not a popular uprising: "I envisioned a postwar government being a military government."[24]

In the years following the war, the UN-imposed sanctions on Iraq have not only prevented Iraq from rebuilding its infrastructure, but have resulted in the deaths of thousands of children every month who suffer from diseases related to malnutrition. Thousands of others suffer from various cancers caused by depleted uranium shells used by U.S. tanks in the ground invasion during the Gulf War. Whereas the 1991 war killed upward of 200,000 Iraqis, the sanctions regime has since resulted in the deaths of more than 1 million Iraqis. In addition, the U.S. has engaged in ongoing bombings of Iraq, which have rarely been considered newsworthy in the U.S. press.

The U.S. secured a bloody victory in the Gulf War. At the cost of a few hundred American soldiers, the U.S. demonstrated that it will stop at nothing to exercise its imperial prerogatives and strengthen its hold over the Middle East. With Russia out of the picture, the sole remaining superpower seemed set to impose its "Pax Americana" over the region.

U.S. policy since the Gulf War

U.S. dominance over the region was now firmer than it had ever been. Iraq was destroyed and kept permanently weak, and the coalition allowed the U.S. to cement stronger ties with many of the Arab states. The success of the United States in the Gulf War sent the message, in Bush's words, that "what we say goes." As Michael Hudson, professor of international relations at Georgetown University, wrote in *Middle East Journal*:

> Even critics, such as the author, of U.S. Middle East policy must agree that the United States today stands astride this unhappy region like a colossus. A half century of regional involvement in every conceivable way—through diplomacy, aid, culture, education, espionage, subversion and (not least) the projection of military power—has secured the "holy trinity" of American interests: Israel, oil and anticommunism. Those who said it could not be done underestimated the U.S. ability to achieve contradictory goals. Today, the American president can summon the leaders of most Middle Eastern governments to endorse his regional (and domestic) political agenda. American financial officials can write the domestic economic policy for most governments in the region. The U.S. military enjoys unprecedented access and acceptance from North Africa to the Gulf.[25]

But the U.S. suffers from two Achilles' heels in its role as regional superpower. One, it has been unable to solve the Palestinian question, which again threatens to explode the delicate balance in the region. And, two, its massive military intervention has rendered the Gulf monarchies even more unpopular—and, with the crisis of declining oil revenues over the last decade as oil prices have plummeted, more unstable.

The policy of "dual containment" of Iraq and Iran pursued by the U.S. after the 1991 Gulf War has been more or less abandoned, but no policy has replaced it. The sanctions regime against Iraq has eroded, and Arab states' support for sanctions has weakened, while the changes in Iran have created an ambivalent relationship between it and the United States. The U.S. cannot decide whether to maintain a policy of sanctions against Iran or to shift to a policy of opening toward the country ("engagement"). Besides the U.S. lapdog Britain, other European states are no longer interested in maintaining the sanctions against Iraq. Eager to make oil deals, Russia has recently expressed its intention to work to bring an end to the bombing and sanctions against Iraq.

The increasing suffering of the Iraqi people has weakened the ability of the U.S. to justify the sanctions, particularly within the Middle East. Arab regimes have begun to resume political and economic relations with Baghdad. Taking advantage of resumed civilian flights to Baghdad by several states, dozens of Middle Eastern officials and celebrities have broken the "no-fly" rule to travel to Baghdad. For all intents and purposes, it seems that the new UN inspection team will never even set foot on Iraqi soil.

The problem that the United States faces, even after its success in the Gulf War, is that, outside Israel, it has no reliable "surrogates" in the Middle East, and Israel, as the Gulf War demonstrates, must sometimes be held at bay. Since the death of Nasser in 1970, the U.S. has successfully pulled Egypt into its orbit and neutralized it as a threat to Israel. But the U.S. cannot rely upon Egypt to discipline its Arab neighbors. The popularity of the Palestinian cause in Egypt has even compelled President Hosni Mubarak to withdraw Egypt's ambassador from Israel.

The U.S. has, it is true, armed Saudi Arabia to the teeth, but Saudi Arabia is in no position to successfully project its military power beyond its borders. That is why Saudi Arabia has pursued a policy of détente with Iran. The United States must spend massive amounts of money to arm what are undemocratic, illegitimate Gulf monarchies. Even so, it cannot rely on them to police the region in U.S. interests. These regimes are armed to cement them as allies and to create the military conditions in those countries to allow rapid deployment of U.S. troops.

The U.S. must keep an expensive military presence in and around the region in order to maintain its interests. This not only leaves American troops open to military attacks, such as the one recently in a Yemeni port against the USS *Cole,* but it also puts tremendous political strain on local rulers, whose own populations increasingly resent the U.S. imperial presence.

Conclusion

Hypocrisy has always permeated U.S. policy in the Middle East. While some regimes, such as those in Iraq, Iran, and Libya, are dubbed "rogue states," this has absolutely nothing to do with whether these regimes are repressive or invade their neighbors.

When Israel—the only nuclear power in the region—invaded Lebanon in 1982 and killed 40,000 people in its efforts to smash the PLO, it had the backing of Washington. Though lip service is paid to helping the oppressed Kurds in Iraq, U.S. ally Turkey is given weapons to attack its own Kurdish minority. While Saddam Hussein is certainly a tyrant, he was every bit as much of a tyrant when he was Washington's friend. While his invasion of Kuwait was condemned, the U.S. supports Israel's occupation of Palestinian land. The coalition lined up against Iraq in 1991 consisted of countries such as Kuwait, a monarchy that still does not grant women the right to vote; Saudi Arabia, which publicly executes its critics; and Egypt, which outlaws opposition parties, and sometimes murders their members when they protest.

U.S. imperialism in the Middle East has always been naked and brutal. It is primarily responsible for upholding backward, dictatorial regimes that, without its help, would have been overthrown long ago. Middle East specialist Dilip Hiro spelled it out:

> It is much simpler to manipulate a few ruling families (and to secure fat orders for arms and ensure that oil prices remain low) than a wide variety of personalities and policies bound to be thrown up by a democratic system.[26]

But such brutality always provokes a reaction—as the new Intifada shows. "If history is any guide," writes Michael Hudson, "hegemony by the United States or any other party in the Middle East tends to produce resistance."[27]

That resistance is back—not just in the Intifada in Palestine, but in the large sympathy demonstrations throughout the region. The struggle against U.S. imperialism in the Middle East is intimately tied up with the aspirations of the mass of Arab workers and peasants in that region, not only against the American "colossus," but against their own ruling classes.

---

1   Phillip Knightly, "Imperial legacy," *The Gulf War Reader*, Micah L. Sifry and Christopher Cerf, eds. (New York: Random House, 1991), p. 8.

2   Glenn Frankel, "Lines in the sand," *The Gulf War Reader*, p. 16.

3   Quoted in Mark Curtis, *The Great Deception: Anglo-American Power and World Order* (London: Pluto Press, 1998), p. 133.

4   Quoted in William Blum, *The CIA: A Forgotten History* (London: Zed, 1986), p. 96.

5   Micah L. Sifry, "U.S. intervention in the Middle East: A case study," *The Gulf War Reader*, p. 28.

6   Sifry, p. 33.

7   Stephen Zunes, "Continuing storm: The U.S. role in the Middle East," *Global Focus: U.S. Foreign Policy at the Turn of the Century*, Martha Honey and Tom Barry, eds. (New York: St. Martins Press, 2000), p. 248.

8   Phil Marshall, *Intifada: Zionism, Imperialism and Palestinian Resistance* (London: Bookmarks, 1989), p. 77.

9   Curtis, p. 133.

10 Zunes, p. 249.

11 Benjamin Beit-Hallahmi, *The Israeli Connection: Who Israel Arms and Why* (New York: Pantheon, 1987), pp. 196–98.

12 Quoted in Curtis, p. 129.

13 Anthony Cordesman, *The Gulf and Transition: U.S. Policy Ten Years After the Gulf War* (working draft), Center for Strategic and International Studies (CSIS), October 2000, p. 32.

14 Quoted in Joe Stork, *Middle East Oil and the Energy Crisis* (New York: Monthly Review Press, 1975), p. 34.

15 Saïd K. Aburish, *A Brutal Friendship: The West and the Arab Elite* (New York: St. Martins Press, 1997), p. 77.

16 Curtis, p. 159.

17 Aburish, pp. 242–43.

18 Aburish, pp. 60–61.

19 Joe Stork and Martha Wenger, "From rapid deployment to massive deployment," *The Gulf War Reader*, p. 35.

20 Stork and Wenger, p. 36.

21 Lance Selfa, "What we say goes," *International Socialist Review* 7 (Spring 1999), p. 23.

22 Selfa, p. 23.

23 Selfa, p. 25.

24 "How the U.S. helped keep Hussein in power," *International Socialist Review* 4 (Spring 1998), p. 32.

25 Michael C. Hudson, "To play the hegemon: 50 years of U.S. policy toward the Middle East," *Middle East Journal*, Summer 1996, p. 329.

26 Zunes, p. 251.

27 Hudson, p. 343.

LANCE SELFA

Standing up to Goliath: The new Intifada

THE PALESTINIAN uprising that began in late September 2000 marked the end of the "peace process" as we knew it. Israel, the U.S., and even the Palestinian Authority (PA) may try to restart it, but it has clearly lost any support it had in the occupied territories of the West Bank and Gaza. Even Hanan Ashrawi, a leading Palestinian moderate who supported the negotiations, declared that the "seriously flawed" peace process that began in 1993 "can't be resuscitated." She said, "There is no status quo ante to go back to."[1]

The uprising began September 29, one day after the leader of Israel's right-wing opposition, Ariel Sharon, stormed Al-Aqsa Mosque in East Jerusalem with more than 1,000 armed Israeli police. Sharon meant his "visit" to assert Israel's control over Muslim holy sites in occupied East Jerusalem. If this weren't provocative enough, Sharon chose to make his statement on the anniversary of the 1982 massacre of more than 2,000 Palestinians in the Sabra and Shatila refugee camps in Lebanon—a crime for which even the Israeli government held Sharon "indirectly responsible."

While even U.S. officials condemned Sharon's "provocation," he clearly had prior approval from Israel's prime minister, Ehud Barak. Sharon would not have had the military cordon that accompanied him without Barak's authorization. After Sharon departed, Israeli

First published in the International Socialist Review, *December 2000–January 2001.*

	Number	Percent
Live ammunition	1,448	18.7
"Rubber" bullets	3,314	42.8
Tear gas	2,389	30.9
Other	588	7.6
TOTAL	7,739	100

SOURCE: RED CRESCENT

PALESTINIANS INJURED, SEPTEMBER 29–NOVEMBER 10, 2000

soldiers and police remained. The stage was set for the following day's confrontation, when Israeli security forces opened fire on thousands of worshippers attending Friday prayers at Al-Aqsa. With Israeli forces under orders to shoot to kill, seven Palestinians died and 200 were wounded in the initial clashes. The Al-Aqsa Intifada quickly spread throughout the West Bank and Gaza.

As the struggle intensified, a pro-U.S., pro-Israel media focused on a few incidents of Palestinian violence, such as the sacking of Joseph's Tomb in Nablus and the lynching of two undercover Israeli cops. This media focus conveyed the desired message that Palestinians were laying siege to Israel. It may seem obvious that a confrontation between one of the world's strongest armies and stone-throwing youths isn't a fair fight. In the first six weeks of the uprising, Israeli forces killed more than 200 Palestinians. And, as the table above shows, almost 8,000 Palestinians in the Occupied Territories were injured during the same period. In comparison, during the first six weeks of the uprising, 49 Israeli civilians and 150 Israeli security police sustained injuries from rock throwers and gunfire.[2] By November 2, Israeli forces had killed 51 children.[3]

The Israeli military "locked down" the territories, preventing Palestinians from traveling to their jobs in Israel, leaving their towns, and, in some cases, even leaving their houses. Right-wing Israelis organized pogroms against Palestinian citizens of Israel in Nazareth and other towns as police stood by. Meanwhile, right-wing Israeli settlers carried out vigilante attacks. The Alternative Information Center, an Israeli-Palestinian human rights organization, documented settler attacks that bear all the hallmarks of Ku Klux Klan night riders in the Jim Crow South:

- On October 9, settlers killed Esam Joudeh, age 40, from Um Safa village, north of Ramallah. His body was partially burned.

- On October 12, settlers arrested three Palestinians for three hours on Almawasee Road near Khan Younis in the Gaza Strip. The Palestinians arrested were Jawad Ahmad Amin, 27 years old; Mohammed Khamees Akkawee, 25 years old; and Mahmoud Na'eem Lahman, 22 years old. During the arrest, the settlers physically attacked the three Palestinians, who sustained injuries to many parts of their bodies. They later received hospital treatment.

- On October 12, at 5 P.M., settlers shot Ibrahim Alami, a 25-year-old from Beit Omar in the district of Hebron. Alami was shot in the head and is now brain-dead. He was attacked on Bypass Road 60 while returning home.[4]

Back to 1987?

Today's uprising is similar to, but in many ways in advance of, the 1987–93 Intifada that pushed Israel to the negotiating table. The scenes of stone-throwing youths confronting armed Israeli soldiers recall images from the first Intifada. But the scale of the firepower being deployed—on both sides—is higher. Israel has dispatched tanks and helicopter gunships against the Palestinians. But unlike the 1980s Intifada, Palestinians are fighting back with more than rocks. Palestinian tactics include armed self-defense and attacks on Israeli military and settler targets in the territories. One indication of the intensity of the conflict has been the casualty rate. In its first six weeks, the Al-Aqsa Intifada has produced 15 percent of the casualties, almost all on the Palestinian side, that the 1987–93 Intifada produced in six years.

Palestinians clearly drew inspiration from the armed resistance that drove Israel out of Lebanon in May 2000. The Lebanese Hezbollah led a guerrilla resistance to Israel and its lackey, the South Lebanon Army (SLA), in the Israeli-occupied "security

zone" inside Lebanese territory. In May, Barak ordered an "or-
derly" Israeli withdrawal, with the aim of handing over the region
to the SLA. But Hezbollah-led resistance turned the withdrawal
into a rout. The SLA collapsed within days. For people around the
region, Hezbollah's armed resistance showed that Israel could be
beaten. "Hezbollah's heroic operations have had a fundamental
role in boosting the morale of our people and incited us to double
our efforts in our struggle against the occupier," Marwan Bargh-
outi, the general secretary of Arafat's Fatah movement, told a
Lebanese newspaper.[5]

The scale of solidarity between Palestinians in Israel (referred
to in the Israeli and U.S. press as "Israeli Arabs") and Palestinians
in the Occupied Territories marks another change from the previous Intifada. Palestinians inside Israel demonstrated in solidarity
with Palestinians in the Occupied Territories. Their spokespeople
clearly identified their struggle against second-class status in Israel
with the struggle of their brothers and sisters for independence.
The first Intifada produced an awakening of nationalist consciousness among Palestinians in Israel, but after an initial burst of
demonstrations in solidarity with Palestinians in the Occupied
Territories in 1987, Israel's Palestinian citizens retreated. For most
of the rest of the Intifada, they expressed their solidarity by raising
money and collecting food to ship to the territories.

Since the Israeli government began pursuing the "peace
process" with Palestinians, Palestinian citizens of Israel have voted
in overwhelming numbers for Labor candidates. But with Barak
sending tanks into the territories and police into Israeli Palestinian
towns, Palestinians in Israel organized demonstrations in their own
towns. Some even managed to cross the Green Line, the border between Israel and the Occupied Territories, to join the crowds fighting the Israelis. This new assertiveness followed on incidents last
summer in Galilee towns when thousands of Palestinian Israeli citizens fought off Israeli military attempts to demolish their homes.[6]

Palestinians on both sides of the Green Line were demonstrat-
ing against the apartheid conditions that Israel enforces. Seven
years ago, Palestinians were willing to give the peace process a

chance. If it could contribute to lifting the worst excesses of the Israeli occupation of their land, it was worth a try, they thought.
But seven years later, it's clear that none of the developments that
Palestinians hoped for have come to pass. In fact, in many ways,
life for ordinary Palestinians in the Occupied Territories is worse
today than it was in 1993. For years, public opinion surveys have
indicated Palestinian disillusionment with the peace process. The
Al-Aqsa Intifada turned that disillusionment into mass action.

From Camp David to Haram al-Sharif

Crucial to the media case against the Palestinians is the notion
that the PA's Yasser Arafat is chiefly to blame for the breakdown
in the peace process. After all, they say, Barak had gone the "extra
mile" in proposing unprecedented concessions at the July 2000
U.S.-sponsored summit at Camp David. Arafat walked away from
the deal. And no wonder. Had he signed it, he would have gone
down in history as the biggest traitor to the Palestinian cause.

Barak and the U.S. sought Arafat's signature on a document
that would end the "transition period" envisioned in the proposals
signed on the White House lawn in 1993. Arafat's signature would
allow him to proclaim a "state" in the Occupied Territories
(crowning himself president). In exchange for U.S. and Israeli
recognition of this "state," Arafat was asked to sign away long-
standing and historically just Palestinian claims on three major issues: Jerusalem, Palestinian refugees, and sovereignty over their
land.

Israel offered to hand the PA the dusty village of Abu Dis, on
the outskirts of Jerusalem (known as "al-Quds" in Arabic). Abu
Dis would be renamed al-Quds, allowing the Palestinians to claim
it as their historic capital. Meanwhile, Israel would retain control
over the real Jerusalem. For the refugees, the U.S. offered to as-
semble a fund of billions of dollars to resettle them within the borders of the Palestinian state or within the Arab countries where
they currently reside. In exchange, the U.S. and Israel demanded
that Arafat renounce the refugees' internationally recognized right
to return to their homeland inside the Green Line. Israel also required the Palestinians to renounce their demand that Israel recog-

nize its responsibility for creating the "refugee problem," even though Israel's armies expelled nearly one million Palestinians from their homes in 1948. Finally, the state that Arafat would be forced to accept would divide Palestine into three unconnected sections (or "cantons"), over which the PA would have strictly limited authority. Jewish settlement in historic Palestine would continue, and Israel would retain its right to invade the Palestinian state at any time. In other words, Israel was only willing to grant the PA civil (not military) administration over 65 percent of the Palestinian land that Israel seized in 1967. Again, Arafat's agreement to this term would effectively ratify Israel's occupation.

In return for Arafat's agreement to these terms, according to Scott Burchill:

> Barak demanded two things.... First, [Arafat] must formally termi- nate all Palestinian claims against Israel. Second, the PLO [Palestine Liberation Organization] head had to sell the deal to his people. Ul- timately, Arafat couldn't do either, and used the pretext of holy sites in Jerusalem as his escape clause.

Arafat's refusal to swallow the U.S.-Israel ultimatum at Camp David led President Clinton to condemn Arafat while praising Barak. If anyone doubted whether the U.S. was truly the "honest broker" it claimed to be, Clinton's blast should have clarified it. As it stood, Burchill likened the U.S. role to that of a cop. "Camp David was like sitting down with the thief and the police to be told by both how much of your stolen property they think you should get back," he concluded.[7]

The U.S. failure at Camp David contributed to the unraveling of Barak's already shaky government. In 1998, Barak's Labor Party defeated the corrupt, right-wing government of Benjamin Netanyahu by a landslide. Promising to negotiate a final compre- hensive peace with the Palestinians, Barak assembled a broad coalition government that spanned the Zionist political spectrum, from the secular "left" to the religious "right."

But Barak's plan for peace hardly differed from Netanyahu's stonewalling. Baruch Kimmerling wrote:

> The fact is that since Barak came to power, not one agreement on any basic issue has been reached with the Palestinians, and Barak

has accommodated them even less than Netanyahu (who implemented the Hebron agreement).[8]

Yet every Barak move to push the negotiations along brought
more condemnation from the right. The conservative religious
Shas Party abandoned Barak's government on the eve of the failure at Camp David. Only one "no confidence" vote in the Israeli
Knesset stood between a Barak government and new elections.
Barak's collaboration with Sharon's storming of Haram al-Sharif
may have been a lame effort to prepare for that eventuality.

Barak openly proclaimed his interest in forming a "national
unity" government with the right-wing Likud Bloc (led by Sharon)
if new elections were called. Palestinians announced that any
Barak attempt to include the war criminal Sharon in the government would end any planned negotiations.

Death of Oslo

Israel seized the West Bank, East Jerusalem, and Gaza in the
1967 Six Day War. At the time, no country or international body
recognized Israel's sovereignty over the Occupied Territories.
Even the U.S. approved the pivotal United Nations (UN) Security
Council Resolution 242 that emphasized "the inadmissibility of
the acquisition of territory by war." Resolution 242, approved in
1967, explicitly called for the "[w]ithdrawal of Israeli armed
forces from territories occupied in the recent conflict."

The 1973 Security Council Resolution 338, passed within days
of the end of the 1973 Arab-Israel war, reaffirmed Resolution 242
"in all its parts." It called for "negotiations...between the parties
concerned under appropriate auspices aimed at establishing a just
and durable peace in the Middle East." All international diplomacy aimed at ending the Israeli occupation was supposedly built
on the foundation of these two "land for peace" resolutions.

The point of recounting this diplomatic history is to contrast
the clear statements ordering Israel's withdrawal from the Occupied Territories with subsequent developments under Oslo. When
the George Bush Sr. administration convened the Madrid conference between Israel, Syria, Jordan, and a Palestinian delegation, it
allowed "each party" to bring its own interpretation of Resolu-

tion 242 into the negotiations. The Clinton administration moved even further into Israel's camp. In June 1993, then-Secretary of State Warren Christopher proposed a "Declaration of Principles" that referred to the West Bank and Gaza as "disputed" rather than "occupied" territories. In one fell swoop, the U.S. government repudiated a stack of UN resolutions—and its own official diplomatic position. If the territories were merely "disputed," then Israel had as much right to control them as the Palestinians did. What's more, Christopher's declaration acknowledged Palestinian authority over people rather than territory. The Clinton administration radically shifted the terms of negotiation. Justice for the Palestinians wasn't on the agenda. Only the terms of Palestinian surrender were up for discussion.

The U.S. move reflected not only the worldview of the most pro-Israel U.S. government ever, but a calculation of the balance of forces in the region. The crushing U.S.-led victory over Iraq in the Gulf War of 1991 made the United States the unchallenged imperial power in the Middle East. The Soviet Union's collapse removed any other rival power in the area, causing the Arab regimes to scramble to win U.S. favor. The PLO's support of Iraq during the war isolated it from all but a few supporters in the region. The Gulf states expelled hundreds of thousands of Palestinian workers from their countries. Arab states and the Soviet Union cut off aid to the PLO. The Israel-U.S. side was never stronger and the Palestinians never weaker than they were in 1993. Palestinian weakness offered Israel an opportunity to repackage the occupation. Israel would deputize Palestinians to carry out repression on Israel's behalf.

Israel's motive for seeking negotiations was clear. Years of military repression had failed to stem the Intifada. At the height of the uprising, Israel used 180,000 troops to suppress it—more than 10 times the number before the Intifada. As then-Prime Minister Yitzhak Rabin put it:

> I prefer the Palestinians to cope with the problem of enforcing order in the Gaza. The Palestinians will be better at it than we were because they will allow no appeals to the Supreme Court and will prevent the [Israeli] Association for Civil Rights from criticizing the conditions there.... They will rule by their own methods, freeing—

and this is most important—the Israeli Army soldiers from having to do what they will do.[9]

At the time when nearly half a million Jewish immigrants were arriving in Israel from Russia, suppressing the Intifada was diverting necessary resources. Israeli business supported the deal as a way to open Israeli trade to the world. If Israel could be perceived as seeking peace with the PLO's help, countries that had boycotted Israel to protest its treatment of Palestinians could open up trade relations with it.

The "breakthrough" came in secret negotiations between Arafat and a handful of his inner circle with Israeli negotiators, held under the cover of academic research discussions in Oslo, Norway. The product of these discussions, the Declaration of Principles signed on the White House lawn in September 1993, marked a turning point—but not a turning point toward peace.

As Naseer Aruri explained:

> For the first time in history, the Palestinian leadership endorsed a settlement which kept the Israeli occupation intact on the premise that all the outstanding issues in the conflict would be subject to negotiations during a period of three to five years hence.[10]

In exchange for Palestinian recognition of Israel (already granted in 1988) and a renunciation of "terrorism," the U.S. and Israel would recognize Arafat's PLO as the chief bargaining agent for the Palestinians. The Palestinians would receive municipal government authority over the Gaza Strip, Jericho, and a handful of other villages on the West Bank. All of the fundamental issues that had driven the Israeli-Palestinian conflict for half a century—the occupation, the status of Jerusalem, the status of Palestinian refugees—were to be deferred to future negotiations. Arafat ceded the moral and political high ground on all of the core issues so that the U.S. and Israel would treat him as a "partner in peace."

Why did Arafat sign on to this humiliation? With the PLO bureaucracy in Tunis crumbling and Arafat losing support to other forces in the Occupied Territories, he became sufficiently pliable. Israel and the U.S. gambled that Arafat would accept a minimal deal. And he did. Arafat and his cronies were desperate to get hold of some territory they could rule. "Clearly the PLO has transformed itself from a national liberation movement into a kind of small-town government, with the same handful of people in command," wrote Arafat critic Edward Said in September 1993.[11] In fact, most of the organizations in the PLO—a coalition of organizations—rejected the deal. Arafat consulted none of the official Palestinian representative bodies, from the PLO's national executive to the Palestine National Council (the Palestinian parliament-in-exile).

The Declaration of Principles opened the way for a series of agreements to lay down the precise terms of the surrender of Palestine. Rather than set the course to a Palestinian state, the successive agreements—1994's Cairo I and II and Oslo II, the Wye River memorandum of 1998—merely codified Israel's domination. Of these, the most important was Oslo II. This 400-page document established in minute detail the workings of the Palestinian Authority and its relations with Israel. It envisioned the gradual "redeployment" of Israeli military forces to the outskirts of clusters of Palestinian villages. The PA would take over "civil administration" of things like garbage collection and police powers over Palestinians in these areas. Israel would retain full rights to intervene to "protect" Jewish settlements in the West Bank and Gaza. The PA would have no power over any Israeli citizens living in or near Palestinian towns. Moreover, the PA accepted Israel's right to control all major resources in the Occupied Territories. "The deal kept the following in Israeli hands: 73 percent of the lands of the territories, 97 percent of security, and 80 percent of the water," said Shimon Peres, Israel's chief negotiator at the Oslo II negotiations.[12]

The implementation of the Oslo accords depended on "both parties" to carry out their ends of the bargain. Yet it soon became clear that Israel had no intention of upholding any of its paper pledges. And the U.S. had no intention of forcing Israel to comply. The U.S. and Israel put a magnifying glass on any Palestinian violation or "failure" to guarantee Israel's "security"—real or imagined. When the right-wing government of Benjamin Netanyahu took power in 1996, it refused to follow through on the previous government's commitment to redeploy troops from Hebron. A band of 400 fanatical Jewish settlers—most of them born in the U.S.—provided the excuse for Israel's continued occupation in

Hebron, a Palestinian city of more than 200,000.

Characteristically, Israel used the delay to extract even more concessions from the Palestinians with Washington's help. At the Washington-sponsored summit held at the Wye River Plantation in Maryland in October 1998, Netanyahu went back on an earlier agreement to withdraw fully from West Bank towns. Instead, he split up the pledged redeployment into two phases—only one of which he carried out. At Wye, Israel and the PA agreed to allow the CIA to oversee Palestinian police forces, tasked with repressing any opposition to the colonial administration. A year later, the "peace candidate" Barak reversed even Netanyahu's pledge to pull back from 41 percent of the West Bank.

Since 1993, Israel's stonewalling has followed a familiar pattern. Israel reneges on a paper pledge, bringing the "peace process" to the verge of collapse. Washington intervenes to get the process back on track. A high-level summit produces a patched-together agreement that hands Israel even more concessions. Then the cycle begins again.

This pattern describes only Israeli evasion of official commitments under the peace process. Far more egregious have been Israel's actions outside the letter of the Oslo accords. Violating even the Geneva convention's bar on settling territory under military occupation, since 1993, Israeli governments—both Labor and Likud—have built settlements for more than 400,000 Jews, housing 200,000 in the West Bank and Gaza, and 200,000 in East Jerusalem. As it has always done, Israel uses its settlements to "create facts on the ground"—to expand Israel's control over the Occupied Territories.

The settlements concentrated in East Jerusalem aim to "Judaize" this traditionally Arab area, blocking the assertion of Palestinian sovereignty over the Palestinian capital. When completed, the Ma'ale Adumim settlement will stretch from Jerusalem to the Jordan River, covering an area larger than Tel Aviv. Meanwhile, according to Amnesty International, as of late 1999, Israel had demolished 1,100 Palestinian homes for reasons such as failure to obtain building permits. These permits are nearly impossible for Palestinians to obtain from the Israeli-controlled Civil Administration in the territories.[13]

Israel links settlement expansion to a more ambitious master plan to assure Israeli control over the territories. Since 1993, Israel has invested $1.2 billion, mostly from U.S. aid, in building a massive highway system crisscrossing the Occupied Territories. The highways link Jewish settlements and bypass Palestinian villages. When the highways are completed, Jewish Israelis will be able to travel through the territories without interacting with Palestinians at all. The highways accomplish in physical terms what the Oslo accords did in political terms—they enforce the dismemberment of Palestine. PA-controlled cities and towns exist as 227 islands surrounded by Israeli settlements and military outposts. Palestinian critics describe the post-Oslo map of the territories as "Swiss cheese," with Palestinian-controlled areas likened to the holes. A Palestinian from one village must make a Herculean effort to negotiate checkpoints, avoid armed settlers, and obtain transportation to visit a family member living in another town only a few miles away.

Under the cover of Oslo, Barak prepared a far-reaching "final solution" to the Palestinian question—an arrangement described in Israel as "Us Here, Them There." As Roger Normand explains:

> Palestinians are to be separated from Israel politically and geographically, linked only economically in the form of cheap labor and captive markets. Arafat will be anointed president of his cherished state on 90 percent of the West Bank and Gaza. But the population will remain confined in territorially non-contiguous Bantustans, encircled by and controlled through a network of Israeli settlements, roads and military checkpoints, and subject to repressive PA security forces. In return for Israeli sovereignty over the settlements, the Barak camp has even floated the possibility of ceding sovereignty over Arab areas in northern Israel, thereby ridding the state of 300,000 Palestinian citizens. As the final element in this plan, over three million Palestinian refugees will be denied their internationally recognized human right to return to homes within Israel, and instead given some cash and the "choice" of involuntary resettlement in either the new statelet of Palestine or surrounding Arab countries.[14]

Barak's government, like the Labor governments before it, viewed the solution to the "Palestinian problem" as apartheid—the separation of Jew and Arab. In fall 2000, the only question for Barak was whether to win "Us Here, Them There" at the negotiating table or to impose it by force of arms.

The Palestinian Authority

The Palestinian Authority created under the Oslo accords possesses many of the trappings of an independent state—security forces, a flag, postage stamps, an airport, and a legislative body. But it is a state in the same sense that the African bantustans were. In apartheid South Africa, the white minority regime put Black collaborators such as Chief Gatsha Buthelezi in charge of bantustans, or African "homelands." South Africa labeled these "homelands" as independent countries, allowing the apartheid regime to deny citizenship to Blacks. The Black collaborators, with the full backing of the South African military, would police the bantustan population to root out any anti-apartheid activity.

Under the Oslo accords, the Palestinian Authority acts as a subcontractor of the Israeli army in the task of repressing the Palestinians. To the U.S. and Israel, that's virtually the only task the PA is accorded. It's no wonder, then, that Arafat controls nine different police and security operations, accounting for as many as 50,000 cops. These security forces work hand-in-glove with the Israeli security forces and the CIA, which provides "training" to Arafat's police. When Israeli undercover police arrested Palestinians accused of lynching two Israeli cops (in a well-publicized October 2000 incident), Arafat's police were said to have fingered the arrestees.[15]

In this way, the former leaders of the Palestinian liberation movement have been transformed into collaborators with Israel's colonial-settler state. This degeneration took root long before the PA set up shop in Gaza in 1994. According to Naseer Aruri:

> For many in the ruling faction, the "revolution" has become, over the years, a source of employment and livelihood, when ruling used to mean no more than running a bureaucracy whose function was to arbitrate conflicts and cater to the needs of organized constituencies. The many factions of the revolution were kept in the fold by a system of patronage over which Arafat presided almost alone.[16]

Inside the PA, a small number of Arafat loyalists attend to two tasks: repressing opponents and making themselves rich. To take one example, 27 public and private monopolies control the import into Gaza of fuel and basic foodstuffs. Controlled by a handful of PA officials with particularly close ties to Israel's security and business establishments, the political purpose behind the monopolies is to generate revenues for the bureaucracy and so consolidate the PA's rule. But the economic impact on Gaza residents has been disastrous, with the monopolies causing spiraling prices, destroying local firms, and creating a lawless climate that discourages private investment.[17]

In the years since the Palestinians embarked on the peace process, conditions for ordinary Palestinians have only worsened. Living standards in PA-controlled areas have dropped by one-third from where they stood under direct Israeli occupation. Israeli closures—which the PA is powerless to stop—represent a form of economic warfare against the Palestinians. Israel uses the closures to enforce another aspect of its policy of "separation"—replacing Palestinian workers who commute into Israel with Jewish Israelis. Of the nearly 120,000 Palestinian workers who commuted to jobs in Israel before Oslo, more than half have lost their jobs. Nearly one in three Palestinians living in the PA's area is unemployed. Forty percent of Gaza residents and 12 percent of West Bank residents live in poverty.[18]

In the first two years of the PA's existence, Palestinians were willing to grant it some leeway. But in the run-up to the 1996 Israeli elections, when Islamists launched a campaign of suicide bombings in Israel, the PA showed its true colors:

> The unprecedented Israeli siege of the Occupied Territories imposed in the wake of the suicide bombings constituted a turning point for Palestinian public opinion. The hermetic closure of the West Bank and Gaza Strip and the policy of "separation" removed any remaining ambiguities about the nature of post-Oslo Israeli-Palestinian relations. Equally, this period—which saw an unprecedented PA campaign against anyone and anything currently or formerly Islamist—left little to the imagination regarding the PA's own role within this relationship.[19]

Since 1996, most Palestinians place little faith in the PA. Many, if not most, see it as corrupt, dictatorial, and existing largely at Israel's sufferance. That's why the Al-Aqsa Intifada is not only a revolt against Israel's occupation. It is also a revolt against the PA, Israel's subcontractor.

Palestinian politics

The new Intifada began spontaneously, but Arafat's Fatah movement quickly asserted its leadership over events. Fatah's *tanzim* (Arabic for "organization"), composed of cadre from the 1987–93 Intifada and of fighters in the PA's security forces, provide on-the-ground leadership, according to journalist Graham Usher.[20] Despite Fatah's leadership, the new Intifada has forged an unprecedented unity between factions inside the PLO and Islamists outside the PLO. These forces recently issued a joint statement in support of the uprising.

The Islamic organizations Hamas and Islamic Jihad are the largest forces in the territories opposed to the peace process. To the U.S. and Israel, the Islamists represent the all-purpose "opponents of peace," and they constantly urge the PA to crack down on them. Until early November 2000, when Islamic Jihad exploded a car bomb in Jewish West Jerusalem, the Islamists had taken actions consistent with the tactics of the mainstream PLO:

> [The Islamists] have not challenged Fatah's leading role on the political, diplomatic, or military levels, and, like Fatah, have mobilized their supporters mainly in defense of Palestinian civilian areas. They have granted the PA/PLO unprecedented legitimacy by, for the first time, attending sessions of its leadership and joining the National and Islamic Forces (NIF), an umbrella body that sets the calendar of the protests.[21]

Arafat even repaid the Islamists for their support, releasing 85 Hamas and Islamic Jihad activists from PA jails.

Tanzim activists have organized mass civilian protests, many of them youths too young to have participated in the first Intifada. They have also mounted military attacks on Israeli and settler outposts. This more militant strategy—departing from negotiations—helped the *tanzim* to move to the front ranks of the Palestinian opposition. Mouin Rabbani characterizes the *tanzim* as

> that wing of the movement which while ultimately loyal [to Arafat
> and the Fatah leadership] has long sought to distance Fatah from
> the PA and establish it as a mass-based political party. This wing
> has become increasingly critical of if not hostile to the Oslo
> process.[22]

The actions of *tanzim* have helped Fatah to regain support on the
Palestinian streets.

While the Islamists are estimated to have the support of 20–40
percent of Palestinians, their deference to the mainstream secular
nationalists is consistent with their action under the PA administration. From its founding in 1988, Hamas has refused to confront the
PLO directly and has operated alongside the PLO to pose an alternative leadership to the struggle. Hamas's charter calls the PLO
"the father, brother, relative or friend" and recognizes, "Our nation is one, plight is one, destiny is one, and our enemy is the
same."[23]

Despite this posture, the PA has also targeted the Islamists for
the harshest repression. In 1994, confrontations between the PA
authorities and Hamas activists escalated into the shootings of 14
Hamas activists. In 1996, on the eve of the Israeli election that
Netanyahu won, Islamic Jihad and Hamas suicide bombers
mounted several attacks in Tel Aviv and Jerusalem. The PA
rounded up hundreds of Islamist activists. Islamist-PA relations
have settled into a certain mutual accommodation.

The leadership group, the Nationalist and Islamic Forces in
Palestine, has agreed on a platform of mass action against the occupation. Armed action inside the territories is approved, but the
PA opposes attacks on civilians inside the Green Line. Yet it remains to be seen if Palestinian political unity displayed in the earliest weeks of the Al-Aqsa Intifada can be maintained. Israel
possesses a huge firepower advantage over the Palestinians. And
Arafat's remaining legitimacy (at least in Western eyes) will impel
him back to the bargaining table. If Arafat accepts another rotten
deal, there may be no holding back the opposition to his rule.

As this article was being written, Arafat and senior Israeli negotiator Shimon Peres concluded an agreement to stop the violence. Israel agreed to withdraw military hardware from positions occupied

during the uprising. Arafat pledged to call a halt to the protests in the Occupied Territories. The Peres-Arafat agreement received good press in the West, but events since then have shown that such agreements are unlikely to stop the uprising or Israel's escalation of force.

The Peres-Arafat agreement is of a piece with all of the other short-term agreements cobbled together when the peace process collapsed. It views the conflict as primarily an issue of "security." It seeks to reestablish a status quo that virtually all Palestinians have rejected. It establishes an agreement between two parties that have little room to maneuver.

Barak's government was hanging by a thread. To save himself, he considered entering into an all-party "national unity government" with Sharon. Sharon's likely price for that agreement would be Barak's repudiation of Oslo. On the other side, Arafat risked throwing away his newfound support if he moved to wind down the struggle. And there is no guarantee that he could deliver. Huge crowds in the Occupied Territories demonstrated against Arafat's attendance at the October 2000 Sharm al-Sheik summit in Egypt. The Islamists have no reason to hold back suicide bombings. The uprising—directed primarily against conditions of life in the territories during the peace process—won't stop. It would likely continue "under more militant leadership, including presumably a substantial number of ex-Fatah cadres."[24]

Which way forward?

The Al-Aqsa Intifada is the most significant development in Palestinian politics since the 1993 Oslo accords. Palestinians' initial hopes that the peace process would lift the Israeli occupation came to nothing. Meanwhile, all of the worst aspects of occupation— erecting of settlements, house demolitions, closures, and curfews— increased. Many observers described the mass of Palestinians as increasingly opposed to Oslo but lacking the confidence to do anything about it. The Al-Aqsa Intifada broke this sense of resignation. A new generation of fighters, drawing inspiration from Hezbollah's liberation of Southern Lebanon, have moved to the fore.

Even if the Intifada escalated to an armed uprising in the Occupied Territories—a war of liberation—Palestinians would still have to confront the overwhelming firepower of Israel and its patron, the United States. This would raise the cost of the occupation to Israel, but it would be unlikely to force Israel's retreat.

Likewise, Palestinians lack the kind of social power that Black South Africans, the majority of the country's workforce, exercised to force an end to apartheid. And with its closures and increased employment of Jewish immigrants, Israel is trying to further dampen the impact of Palestinian labor.

Therefore, Palestinians must fight for their liberation, but they can't win it on their own. They must look to the region's working classes, where massive sympathy and solidarity exists with the Palestinian cause. In the earliest weeks of the Intifada, huge demonstrations in solidarity with the Palestinians took place in Egypt, Jordan, Morocco, and Iraq. There were even demonstrations in the Arab Gulf states and in Saudi Arabia. Sentiment ran so deep that Arab regimes that largely accommodate to Israel and the U.S. agenda in the region felt compelled to issue statements of support. This force—the Arab working class—has the power to challenge U.S. designs in the region.

A new strategy would have to emphasize building class solidarity between Palestinians and other Arab workers. Such a strategy would be based on connecting workers' struggles in the region to the fight for a secular, democratic state in Palestine. Until that state is won, there will be no peace in the Middle East.

---

1   Center for Policy Analysis on Palestine, "Oslo cannot be resuscitated, declares Ashrawi; new approach to peace process needed," November 3, 2000. See www.palestinecenter.org.

2   These figures are posted on the Web site of the Israeli human rights organization B'Tselem at www.btselem.org.

3   "Total of children martyrs reaches 51," *Middle East News Online*, November 2, 2000, available online at www.MiddleEastWire.com.

4   Alternative Information Center, available online at www.alternativenews.org/intifadah2000/settlers_violence/report_no_1.htm.

5   Agence France Presse, "Intifada will continue until Palestinian state," October 27, 2000.

6   See Center for Policy Analysis on Palestine, "Israel's 'apartheid policy' toward Palestinian citizens," report from a CPAP briefing with Basel Ghattas, October 12, 2000, available online at www.palestinecenter.org.

7   Scott Burchill, "Israel's plan for Palestine, a la Pretoria," *The Age* (Australia),
    October 18, 2000.

8   Baruch Kimmerling, "Blame Barak, not Sharon," *Ha'aretz*, October 4, 2000.
    The "Hebron agreement" refers to the Wye River agreement.

9   Rabin quoted in *Yediot Aharonot*, September 7, 1993.

10 Naseer Aruri, *The Obstruction of Peace: The U.S., Israel, and the Palestinians*
    (Monroe, Maine: Common Courage Press, 1995), p. 209.

11 Edward Said, "Arafat's deal," *The Nation*, September 20, 1993, p. 269.

12 Samih K. Farsoun with Christina E. Zacharia, *Palestine and the Palestinians*
    (Boulder, Colorado: Westview Press, 1997), p. 267.

13 Center for Policy Analysis on Palestine, "Israel's matrix of control in
    Palestine," February 14, 2000.

14 Roger Normand, "The iron fist in the peace process," MERIP Press
    Information Note 33, October 4, 2000, available online at www.merip.org.

15 See Tanya Reinhart, "Green light to slaughter," available online at
    www.llbs.org/meastwatch/green_light.htm.

16 Aruri, p. 240.

17 *Middle East International,* June 27, 1997, p. 4.

18 Figures from Allegra Pacheco, "Closure and apartheid: Seven years of 'peace'
    through separation," Center for Policy Analysis on Palestine, March 3, 2000.

19 Mouin Rabbani, "Palestinian Authority, Israeli rule," *Middle East Report*, Fall
    1996, available online at www.merip.org.

20 Graham Usher, "The unifying impact of the Al-Aqsa Intifada," Information
    Brief Number 51, Center for Policy Analysis on Palestine, November 3, 2000,
    available online at www.palestinecenter.org.

21 Usher, "The unifying impact of the Al-Aqsa Intifada."

22 Mouin Rabbani, "The Peres-Arafat agreement: Can it work?" MERIP Press
    Information Note 34, November 3, 2000, available online at www.merip.org.

23 Farsoun and Zacharia, p. 238.

24 Rabbani, "The Peres-Arafat agreement."

NASEER ARURI

Oslo: Cover for territorial conquest

NASEER ARURI is Chancellor Professor of Political Science at the University of Massachusetts at Dartmouth. He is the author of The Obstruction of Peace: The U.S., Israel, and the Palestinians. *He formerly served as a member of the Palestine National Council and the Palestine Liberation Organization Central Committee. He has lectured and written widely on the politics and history of the Middle East. He spoke to* International Socialist Review *editor Anthony Arnove about the Oslo accords and the Al-Aqsa Intifada.*

WHAT HAS the peace process begun at Oslo in 1993 meant for ordinary Palestinians?

OSLO HAS become a symbol of diplomatic paralysis for the Palestinian people. It is an instrument to prolong and consolidate the Israeli occupation of Palestine by pseudo-diplomatic means.

More Jewish settlements have been built since the start of the Oslo process in 1993 than at any other period in the past. Palestinians simply sat and watched the expropriation of their land for settlements and bypass roads—built for Israelis only—to connect the settlements to each other and to Israel proper, while at the same time atomizing Palestinian society. Oslo provided a cover for these conquests, as people around the world watched a diplomatic charade that was packaged by the U.S. media and Israel's propaganda apparatus as peace negotiations.

First published in the International Socialist Review, *December 2000–January 2001.*

For Palestinians everywhere, Oslo has meant the voluntary re-nunciation of internationally recognized rights in favor of agreeing to engage in talks during which they would have to convince the Israelis that they have rights. This is almost unprecedented in the annals of diplomatic history.

The Palestinian people have been plagued by having one of the most stupid leaderships in modern history—and one of the most militarily powerful and ruthless enemies. That combination is one of the factors in the present uprising, Al-Aqsa Intifada.

HOW DID Oslo come about?

THE U.S. endeavor to impose its hegemony on the Middle East, which predates the 1967 [Six Day] War, reflects the consensus of U.S. politicians on all sides of the spectrum. With the departure of the former colonial powers—the United Kingdom and France—U.S. planners decided the Middle East would have to be recolo-nized by the United States. In an era of decolonization, Arab nationalist ideas and concepts—such as Arab unity, Arab social-ism, nonalignment, return and restitution for Palestinian refugees, and indeed Arab-Israeli parity—were considered anathema in Washington and Tel Aviv.

The various U.S. doctrines for the Middle East—starting with the Truman Doctrine all the way up to the Carter Doctrine and Reagan Codicil—were part of the U.S. policy of containment. That policy was intended to contain Arab nationalism just as much as it was directed against the Soviet Union. The Arab world had to be kept at bay and subordinated to Israel, which was as-sured of a "margin of technological and military superiority over all of her Arab neighbors combined." That assurance, which was made by President Richard Nixon, who was widely considered to be an anti-Semite, was kept by every succeeding president and has been upheld by presidential candidates from the two major parties all the way through to George W. Bush and Al Gore. That is how powerful the U.S. consensus on Middle East policy is.

For four decades, U.S. administrations were able to hold tight to this consensus, but there were adaptations and stylistic changes along the way, meant as a sort of cosmetic surgery to make the

policy less objectionable to conservative Arabs. This is the significance of the numerous "plans" presented by and named for either
presidents or secretaries of state, most of which adhered to an Israeli consensus that rejected withdrawal from occupied Arab territories, the right of return for refugees, Palestinian independence,
and the concept of parity.

Oslo represents a departure from the past insofar as the Arabs
yielded on their consensus and the Palestinian leadership accepted
a peace process outside the framework of international legality.

Given that Iraq, a contender for strategic deterrence vis-à-vis
Israel, had just been crushed, and given that the Palestine Liberation Organization had lost the support of the Gulf countries and
their financial backing because of its support for Iraq in the Gulf
War, the United States was able to impose its will and agenda—
together with Israel's agenda—on the Arabs and the Palestinians.

When 18 months of negotiations between West Bank and Gaza
leaders and the government of Israel failed to yield any results, the
road was paved to Oslo. Israel had rejected any framework in
which it acknowledged it was an occupier and refused to make any
commitment to withdraw and to stop building settlements.

The impasse was broken only when Yasser Arafat—whose organization was stricken by a crisis of legitimacy, of finance, of ideology, and of leadership—stepped in and agreed to negotiate with
Israel without any conditions and in an open-ended process. That
was viewed by Israel as a crowning achievement—a vindication of
its policy of no compromise. It was also a major victory for the
U.S. government, which now looks at a strategic region that it has
coveted for decades where there is virtually no opposition at the
official level to its policy and designs for the area.

The United States now has unimpeded military access and
bases throughout the Gulf region and naval forces stationed in the
surrounding seas, with hardly any rivals in international diplomacy. George Bush Sr.'s famous statement, "What we say goes,"
sums up these developments.

Oslo was the diplomatic equivalent of the military destruction
of Iraq.

WAS THE recent collapse of Oslo unexpected?

THE RECENT collapse of the so-called peace process was predictable. At the Camp David II talks in August [2000], Israelis and Palestinians had to face a moment of truth. The "final status issues"—Jerusalem, refugees, borders, water, and statehood—were suddenly on the table.

Oslo was based on the theory that the two parties needed two stages of negotiations in order to get used to each other and to develop the necessary confidence-building measures before they could move on to the intractable issues, such as Jerusalem. The interim period was allegedly needed to work out plans for Palestinian self-governance and to smooth the way for the more difficult issues.

The whole process was to take five years, so it should have been over by 1998. Instead, by 1998, Benjamin Netanyahu had reneged on previous commitments to redeploy Israeli forces. When Ehud Barak assumed power, he pledged to have peace within a year, but at the end of 1999, [he] was insisting on negotiating what he called a "framework agreement" as a necessary condition for making another redeployment in accordance with previous agreements.

Barak also insisted on going directly to the final status negotiations, while the Palestinian Authority (PA) was demanding the redeployment that Israel was obligated to undertake. Not unexpectedly, President Bill Clinton and Secretary of State Madeleine Albright maneuvered Arafat into Camp David under the pretext that Israel would be generous. Arafat had to simply have faith in the "honest broker."

The oxymoronic nature of the phrase "honest broker" was never comprehended by Arafat, who was flattered to have numerous invitations to the White House after years of being snubbed by the United States. After all, he was the quintessential "terrorist," and even the United Nations in New York City was out of bounds for him in 1988.

Had Arafat resisted the notion of a framework agreement and stood by Oslo's call for the completion of Israeli redeployments prior to final status talks, he would not have been cornered at Camp David. True to pattern, though, Palestinian concessions never seem to bottom out. At Camp David, Barak was able to outmaneuver Arafat with Clinton's help.

Selective reporting and biased editorializing seemed to convince public opinion that Barak had offered Arafat 94 percent of the West Bank, Palestinian sovereignty over the Muslim holy places in Jerusalem, and a sharing of power in East Jerusalem. In fact, that was a plain and simple lie.

Most people are not aware that Israel arbitrarily tampered with the borders of Jerusalem after the 1967 conquest and that 20 percent of the West Bank is annexed Jerusalem territory. So, in fact, the Palestinians were offered about 65 percent of the West Bank, itself only 22 percent of what Palestine was in 1948, when Israel was established on land that was 94 percent owned, farmed, and used by Palestinians.

Palestinian refugees were also given short shrift at Camp David: no right of return and no restitution. With regard to Jerusalem, Barak offered Arafat sovereignty over the structures of the Dome of the Rock and the Al-Aqsa Mosque, but not over the land on which these structures are built—not far different from the right-wing Zionist dictum of sovereignty for the people, not the land. When Arafat couldn't accept this deal and Clinton blamed him publicly on Israeli television for the failure, it became obvious that an explosion was imminent.

Anyone reading the Israeli press at that time would have noticed the number of editorials and opinion pieces predicting that such a daring act—to turn down the president of the United States and mighty Israel, particularly coming from someone like Arafat, who is closer to a mayor than a president—could not be allowed. Arafat had to be taught a lesson. He and his people must be given a taste of what the Middle East's superpower can deliver.

Israel has never had difficulty finding pretexts for its military adventures—not in 1948, 1956, 1967, 1976, 1982, or now. This time, Ariel Sharon, who ought to be afraid to be caught—like the Chilean dictator Augusto Pinochet—and tried for war crimes, made a triumphant entry to the compound of al-Haram al-Sharif (known to Jews as the Temple Mount) to provoke the Palestinians. Israel's newly trained sharpshooters, with orders to kill, went into action and their massacre is ongoing.

URI SAVIR, chief Israeli negotiator at Oslo, told the New York Times, "I think we'll end up concluding that we need more Oslo, not less Oslo." What's your reaction to that?

ISRAEL WANTS more Oslo because it is the single most important instrument in the realization of strategic Israeli and Zionist goals. It is cost-effective, sufficiently deceptive, and rather disarming. It has been simply indispensable for Israel—left, right, and center.

Historically, colonial-settler movements relied mostly on military conquests, population expulsion, land alienation, and even genocide to accomplish their goals of ethnic cleansing. While Israel has been no exception, having tried most of these reprehensible methods, Oslo is the first diplomatic arrangement that has permitted it to make tangible colonial achievements with minimum reliance on its armed forces.

In fact, Oslo has enabled [Israel] to recruit its victims to police the natives and keep them under control. Oslo provided for the dirty work to be transferred to Israel's new subcontractor—the Palestinian Authority.

Moreover, Oslo has opened markets for Israeli exports, after having transformed Israel from a pariah state to a legitimate and rather influential state that is now considered the Middle East Silicon Valley. Had it not been for Oslo, many Arab, Islamic, African, and Asian states would not have opened their doors either to Israeli diplomats or salesmen.

Uri Savir, who conceptualized Oslo and sold it to Arafat, knows the exact worth of this. It is not surprising that he wants "more Oslo."

THE MAINSTREAM media here have called the current uprising "Arafat's war" and have suggested that he deliberately provoked it.

THE ROLE of the U.S. media borders on that of an information office in the Israeli Foreign Ministry and the U.S. State Department. They parrot the Israeli accusation that Palestinian parents send their children to the street to throw stones and get killed in order to score a propaganda victory.

Such racist attitudes are based on the premise that Palestinians don't value human lives as do Israelis and Westerners—a well-known and well-documented phenomenon in Western discourse about Third World societies challenging colonialism.

Moreover, the accusation assumes that Arafat is directing the uprising by remote control. Not only does this defy simple logic—since the uprising is in part being waged against his own regime—but it's racist in that it assumes that the Palestinian people have no independent judgment or critical faculties.

This isn't the first time that the U.S. media have misunderstood the essence of a popular revolution among oppressed people. South Africans, the Vietnamese, Central Americans, and African American activists in the 1960s were portrayed as being driven by "external" forces whenever they challenged the oppressive status quo.

Moreover, Arafat is an easier target than the "Palestinian people." Demonizing individual leaders like Saddam Hussein has proven rather effective in the arena of public opinion. Arafat is also regarded in the U.S. as a former terrorist, and thus makes an easy target.

What the media fail to—or refuse to—understand is that all these struggles and the popular discontent throughout the Arab world are really a consequence of the efforts of the imperial powers and their regional collaborators to restructure and rearrange the political systems of the region to suit their interests.

ARAFAT SEEMS to be in a bind. He'll lose legitimacy if he makes further compromises on Palestinian rights, yet he has gone so far down the road of concessions to Israel.

NEGOTIATIONS BETWEEN Israel and the PA are like an encounter between the wolf and the chicken. Having traded the Palestinian people's legitimacy for U.S. and Israeli legitimacy, Arafat has placed himself in a no-win situation. He has placed himself in the untenable position of being unable to deliver either to Israel and its U.S. patron, or to his own constituents, who were ready to scale down their aspirations but not to surrender their fundamental rights.

Arafat's denunciations of "terror" and vows to eradicate violence under repeated urging by the United States and Israel over the past seven years have been seen in the Palestinian streets as an ominous attack on civil liberties and the right of dissent.

By expecting Arafat to agree to a cease-fire, Clinton and Barak seem to miss a new reality: that Arafat's commitments may have been made on the Palestinian people's behalf but without their consent. The people are asserting their legitimate right of resistance, and they are paying an exceedingly high price for it—with their lives and children's lives, with their homes and property, and with their livelihood. As long as this Intifada continues, the old rules of the division of labor between the PA, Israel, and the United States will be obsolete, discredited, and illegitimate.

The Intifada has penetrated the conscience of the Arab masses, the Islamic community, and numerous constituencies around the world who came to recognize Israel's acts as a form of war crimes.

The Intifada is directed just as much against Arafat and his PA as it is against the entire Oslo process and its sponsors.

HADAS THIER

Ariel Sharon: War criminal

JUST DAYS after he was sworn in as prime minister of Israel, Ariel Sharon tightened the Israeli grip on Ramallah, a community of 60,000 people. The Israeli military sealed off the town with trenches and barricades. Hundreds of Palestinian protesters faced live ammunition, tear gas, and rubber-coated bullets. The blockade on Ramallah kept food shipments out of shops and teachers out of schools. It left nurses and doctors unable to reach hospitals. A *New York Times* reporter talked to one man who had been waiting for hours to take his infant out of Ramallah to a doctor. "This is difficult, difficult, extremely difficult," said one Palestinian taxi driver. "It will lead to an explosion. People will do anything to feed their children."[1] Sharon's election means a declaration of war.

In September 2000, in what is widely accepted as the provocation that set off the new Palestinian Intifada, Ariel Sharon descended on the Muslim holy site al-Haram al-Sharif during prayer services. More than 1,000 armed police flanked him. Palestinian frustration with a stalled peace process had already been mounting, but Sharon's storming of al-Haram al-Sharif represented the last straw.

Sharon, nicknamed "The Bulldozer" for his preference for clearing Palestinians off their land, has one of the most extensive and brutal records of war crimes, spanning more than 50 years. To Palestinians, Sharon represents massacres at refugee camps,

---

First published in the International Socialist Review, *April–May 2001.*

bulldozed homes, and a complete disregard for the rights and lives of Arabs in the region.

While the Bush administration calls for the heads of Iraq's Saddam Hussein and Serbia's Slobodan Milosevic, it has promised "rock solid" support for Sharon. And, instead of reporting on Sharon's bloody history, the mainstream media have conducted a whitewashing campaign, trying to portray Sharon as a legitimate politician. The *New York Times* assured us that "in private, the combative rightist is known as a charming raconteur and a gentleman farmer with a love of classical music."[2] Another *Times* article explains:

> Despite a professional history that makes him a reviled figure in the Arab world, Mr. Sharon repeats often that he has never offended the Palestinians in his personal meetings with them. This is an important point for him, that he deals respectfully with "the other."[3]

Some in the Israeli press are even more delusional. *Ha'aretz* columnist Doron Rosenblum pondered, "Perhaps the elderly Sharon, who is making no promises, will leave a garden behind him? It's always good to have hope."[4] And, Israeli "dove" Shimon Peres assured us that the new prime minister does not "wish to see the country covered with blood."[5] The Nobel Peace Prize winner Peres joined the war criminal's cabinet as foreign minister.

In an effort to remake his image, Sharon is talking about peace and watching his words more carefully today. However, some might recall his advice for dealing with demonstrators in the West Bank: "Cut off their testicles."[6] Sharon's base of popular support among the most right-wing and racist elements in Israeli society expresses his strategy in a more uncensored form than Sharon does himself. "Death to the Arabs!" and "The only good Arab is a dead Arab!" are their favorite chants.

War Crimes 101

During the pre-state days of Israel, Sharon joined the Haganah, the underground military organization formed by the Labor wing of the Zionist movement. In 1953, he was given command of the infamous Unit 101, whose mission was to lead "retaliatory" strikes against Arab terrorism. In reality, these missions took the form of indiscriminate violence aimed at civilians, not at direct sources of terrorism.

Unit 101's first documented assault took place in August 1953, on the el-Bureij refugee camp, south of Gaza. The reasoning given for the attack was "retaliatory," despite no evidence of provocation.[7] An Israeli historian reported 50 refugees killed. United Nations (UN) commander Major General Vagn Bennike described the scene: "[B]ombs were thrown through the windows of huts in which the refugees were sleeping and, as they fled, they were attacked by small arms and automatic weapons."[8]

In October 1953, Unit 101 descended on the Jordanian village of Qibya. This time the "reprisal" was for the killing of a mother and two children in an Israeli village. Jordan condemned the murders and offered to help in the investigation. No connection between the murders and Qibya was suspected. Nevertheless, Unit 101 showed no mercy on the people of Qibya. The unit blew up 45 houses, a school, and a mosque, and killed 69 civilians, including dozens of women and children.

UN military observers who arrived two hours after Sharon's commandos had left the scene reported:

> Bullet-riddled bodies near the doorways and multiple bullet hits on the doors of the demolished houses indicated that the inhabitants had been forced to remain inside until their homes were blown up over them.... Witnesses were uniform in describing their experience as a night of horror, during which Israeli soldiers moved about in their village blowing up buildings, firing into doorways and windows with automatic weapons and throwing hand grenades.[9]

Time reported that Sharon's soldiers shot "every man, woman and child they could find. The cries of the dying could be heard amidst the explosions."[10]

In his autobiography, *Warrior,* Sharon makes the outrageous claim that he was not aware that people were in the houses they were blowing up. "But," says the warrior,

> while civilian deaths were a tragedy, the Qibya raid was also a turning point.... [I]t was now clear that Israeli forces were again capable of finding and hitting targets far behind enemy lines. What this

means to army morale can hardly be exaggerated.... [W]ith Qibya a
new sense of confidence began to take root.[11]

He also describes a meeting with Prime Minister David Ben-
Gurion, who told Sharon that the raid on Qibya would "make it
possible for us to live here."[12]

The actions of Unit 101 were part of Israel's overall strategy to
provoke armed conflict along the borders of UN-partitioned Palestine. The strategy had two goals. One was aimed at the Palestinian
population directly: to instill terror, further disperse the refugees,
and destroy emerging political and military structures. Particularly
targeted was Yasser Arafat's Fatah, later the core group in the
Palestine Liberation Organization (PLO). The second was directed
toward the surrounding Arab countries: to force the Arab states
into confrontations in order to further expand Israel's territory.[13]

Loose cannon?

The Israeli military handpicked Sharon for this role because he
had a reputation as a "loose cannon." He talked a great deal about
his insubordination to his superiors. How true this was is debat-
able, but it certainly made it easier for the government to distance
itself from Sharon's actions. When Unit 101 was disbanded, it was
not because the experiment had failed; rather, it was to further in-
tegrate the model into the rest of the Israel Defense Forces (IDF).

Sharon was a major player in the IDF throughout all of Israel's
wars. In the 1956 Suez War, he led the initial attack through the
Sinai Desert, capturing the Mitla Pass. The overall casualties of
the war: 2,000 on the Egyptian side and nearly 1,000 civilians in
Port Said, as compared to 160 or so Israelis. During the 1967 Six
Day War, in which Israel captured the West Bank, East Jerusalem,
the Sinai Desert, and the Golan Heights, Sharon commanded
brigades that seized Umm-Kateif, blasting an opening into the
Sinai. The overall casualties of that war: 759 Israelis and as many
as 30,000 Arabs. Refugees from Syria, the West Bank, and the
Sinai numbered more than 300,000.[14]

After the 1967 war, Israel succeeded in furthering the territorial goals of a "Greater Israel," but not without resistance. The
highest level of Palestinian organization against the occupation

was in Gaza. As head of the IDF's southern command, Sharon was charged with the task of "pacifying" the Gaza Strip. Phil Reeves wrote in the *Independent* newspaper in 2001:

> [T]he old men still remember it well. Especially the old men on Wreckage Street.... The street acquired its name after an unusually prolonged visit from Mr. Sharon's soldiers. Their orders were to bulldoze hundreds of homes to carve a wide, straight street....
>
> "They came at night and began marking the houses they wanted to demolish with red paint," said Ibrahim Ghanim, 70, a retired laborer. "In the morning they came back, and ordered everyone to leave. I remember all the soldiers shouting at people, 'Yalla, yalla, yalla, yalla!'
>
> "They threw everyone's belongings into the street. Then Sharon brought in bulldozers and started flattening the street. He did the whole lot, almost in one day. And the soldiers would beat people, can you imagine? Soldiers with guns, beating little kids?"

Reeves continues:

> In August 1971 alone, troops under Mr. Sharon's command destroyed some 2,000 homes in the Gaza Strip, uprooting 16,000 people for the second time in their lives.
>
> Hundreds of young Palestinian men were arrested and deported to Jordan and Lebanon. Six hundred relatives of suspected guerrillas were exiled to Sinai. In the second half of 1971, 104 guerrillas were assassinated.[15]

In 1977, a newly formed right-wing Likud party, led by Menachem Begin, won the national elections. Begin and Yitzhak Shamir led the pre-state terrorist armies Irgun and Lehi, which carried out massacres of civilians at Deir Yassin and other Arab villages.[16]

The Likud government set to work furthering the clampdown on Palestinian resistance and continuing the drive to settle the Occupied Territories. The previous Labor-led government had already increased spending on "security" to 11 percent of the gross national product. Zionist historian Howard Sachar pegged military spending at 14 percent or more.[17] Ariel Sharon, serving as minister of agriculture, was put in charge of settlement policy.

The government and the World Zionist Organization created a commission to devise plans to "incorporate Judea and Samaria" (the Israeli right's Biblical label for the West Bank) into Israel. The commission's purpose flouted international law and numerous UN resolutions. Sharon was put in charge of finding a way to confiscate Palestinian land for Israeli use. His solution? To redefine private property and state land. Between 1980 and 1981, Israeli authorities surveyed land titles in the area. Families that had not completed the proper paperwork were denied rights to their homes, despite the fact that they had lived there for generations. By 1981, Sharon had acquired 31 percent of land in the West Bank. Forty new settlements were built, tripling the Jewish population to 18,000.

Settlers were given a high level of autonomy in legal, economic, and military matters. They had their own councils and tax systems, and IDF Chief of Staff Rafael Eitan authorized each town to accept responsibility for its own defense. Settlers were able to transfer from their army units to the settlements, creating militias with an "extensive array of government issue weaponry."[18]

Horror stories of the settlers' brutality abound. Noam Chomsky writes of one Israeli soldier's account:

> A soldier reports that 30 12–13-year-old boys were lined up facing a wall with their hands up for five hours in Hebron one very cold night, kicked if they moved. He justified the punishment because they are not "all innocent lambs as they look now, with their hands up and their eyes asking pity.... They burn and they throw stones and participate in demonstrations, and they are not less harmful than their parents."[19]

Murders of Palestinians by settlers were recorded, but not punished.[20] In fact, soldiers were given instructions to "harass the West Bank population in general, not just those involved in anti-Israeli demonstrations." Soldiers involved in the Peace Now movement prompted one investigation that found that Sharon had "urged Israeli soldiers to beat Arab schoolchildren in the West Bank."[21]

"The Bulldozer"

Begin promoted Sharon to defense minister in 1981, giving Sharon the platform to enact his grand visions for Israel in the region. These included "Operation Peace for Galilee" to crush the PLO, as well as the Syrian presence in Lebanon, and "Operation Big Pines" to set up a "responsible" government in Lebanon. Sharon planned to hand Lebanon's government to Bashir Gemayal's Phalange, a fascist political-military mafia composed of members of the Maronite Christian sect. The "responsible" government would represent a small minority answerable to Israel in an overwhelmingly Muslim country.[22]

With plans for Operation Peace in Galilee and Operation Big Pines laid out, and with approval from U.S. Secretary of State Alexander Haig obtained, Israel looked for an excuse to invade Lebanon. The instigating act was the attempted assassination of the Israeli ambassador to Britain—never mind that his attackers were from the Abu Nidal–led Palestine National Liberation Movement, which organized in opposition to the PLO. Begin declared, "They're all PLO,"[23] and the following day the Israeli air force launched a massive bombardment, killing at least 45 Palestinians and Lebanese (210 according to Lebanese police) and wounding 150 to 200. The PLO shelled settlements in northern Israel, wounding eight.

Israeli forces then launched into a full-scale war with 80,000 troops, 1,240 tanks, 1,520 armored personnel carriers, and heavy air bombardments with napalm. Sharon told officers that Palestinian neighborhoods in Beirut should be "utterly destroyed," even though they contained some 85,000 civilians.[24] The American Red Cross counted 10,000 dead and 100,000 homeless by the sixth day of the attack. Thousands of these deaths occurred in Palestinian refugee camps and Shiite Lebanese villages. For more than three months, Sharon led the IDF, working with the Phalangists, in slaughtering 30,000 to 40,000 Lebanese and Palestinians, with 100,000 seriously wounded and half a million homeless.[25]

The IDF and its allies demolished and bulldozed Palestinian camps. The children's hospital in the Sabra refugee camp and the Gaza Hospital were attacked. When a *New York Times* reporter asked an IDF official why houses where women and children lived were bulldozed, the answer was simply, "They're all terrorists."[26]

By far the most barbaric episodes of the war occurred at its end. Israel, armed to the teeth by Western powers, had easily crushed the PLO in Lebanon. But Bashir Gemayal wasn't as grateful to Israel as Begin had hoped. On September 14, Gemayal died in a huge explosion in his headquarters. Speculation fingered a more pro-Israeli Phalange faction, who may have assassinated Gemayal with Israel's help. Nevertheless, Gemayal's supporters looked for revenge against the Palestinians. Sharon insisted that the Sabra and Shatila refugee camps harbored 2,000 to 3,000 "terrorists," and he and Eitan met with Phalange leaders on September 15 to discuss a plan. Israeli forces would enter West Beirut under the pretext of preventing Christian reprisals (but really to attack Muslim militias), and the Phalange would enter the camps to search for "terrorists." Sharon himself gave the order to allow the Phalange into the camps.

Israeli forces surrounded the camps, as the Phalange, with Israeli equipment, killed every man, woman, and child they could find. On September 17, two days into the slaughter, IDF officers met with Phalangist officers. The IDF officers "knew that Phalangists would be in the camps (again) all night and that they were using bulldozers (to dispose of corpses); they also knew about the flight of panic-stricken civilians."[27] About 3,000 Palestinian civilians were butchered in three days. Two Israeli reporters gave the following description:

> In addition to the wholesale slaughter of families, the Phalangists indulged in such sadistic horrors as hanging live grenades around their victims' necks. In one particularly vicious act of barbarity, an infant was trampled to death by a man wearing spiked shoes. The entire Phalangist action in Sabra and Shatilla seemed to be directed against civilians....
>
> We have had many accounts of women raped, pregnant women, their fetuses cut out afterward, women with hands chopped off, earrings pulled.[28]

The Kahan Commission, an official Israeli board of inquiry into Israeli complicity in the massacre, found Sharon "indirectly responsible" and urged his resignation. Even though the testimony produced in the 1983 commission report would lead any reasonable person to conclude that Sharon and Eitan directly collaborated in the massacre, the commission still sought to whitewash Sharon's role. No "responsibility should be imputed to the Defense Minister [i.e., Sharon] for not ordering the removal of the Phalangists from the camps when the first reports reached him about the acts of killing being committed." Assessing this cowardly excuse, Noam Chomsky wrote: "One might ask...whether the IDF would have taken a similarly casual attitude, with the support of the distinguished Commission, had it learned that PLO terrorists were killing hundreds of Jews."[29] Sharon took the Kahan Commission's advice to resign as defense minister. However, instead of disgrace and banishment from government, he took a position as "minister without portfolio."

Sharon has never been brought to justice for the atrocities he has committed. The Israeli public, the American government, and the mainstream media want to paper over his past. On the eve of Sharon's election as prime minister, journalist Robert Fisk—one of the first journalists to enter Sabra and Shatila after the massacre—wrote:

> Yes, those of us who got into Sabra and Shatilla before the murderers left have our memories. The flies racing between the reeking bodies and our faces, between dried blood and reporter's notebook, the hands of watches still ticking on dead wrists. I clambered up a rampart of earth—an abandoned bulldozer stood guiltily nearby—only to find, once I was atop the mound, that it swayed beneath me. And I looked down to find faces, elbows, mouths, a woman's legs protruding through the soil. I had to hold on to these body parts to climb down the other side. Then there was the pretty girl, her head surrounded by a halo of clothes pegs, her blood still running from a hole in her back. We had burst into the yard of her home, desperate to avoid the Israeli-uniformed militiamen who still roamed the camp; coming in by back door, we had found her body as the murderers left by the front door....
>
> And so today, in this fetid, awful place, where Lebanese Muslim militiamen were—three years later—to kill hundreds more Palestinians in a war which produced no official inquiries, where scarcely 20 percent of the survivors still live, where brown mud and rubbish now covers the mass grave of 600 of the 1982 victims, the Palestinians wait to see if their tormentor will hold the highest office in the state of Israel.[30]

With a bona fide war criminal leading Israel today, some might be tempted to look favorably on the Labor governments that pursued the "peace process" with Palestinians. Yet this would be wrong. Not only are leading Labor politicians from previous "pro-peace" administrations sitting in Sharon's cabinet, but they and their Labor forebears have plenty of Palestinian blood on their hands. As frightening as Sharon's record may be, it is perfectly in sync with the rest of Israeli history and Zionist ideology. This is why the *New York Times* can speak of Sharon and Peres as "two old friends" who disagree more on "tone and attitude" than content.[31]

The only true justice for Palestinians will come with an end to Israel's terrorist state.

---

1 Joel Greenberg, "Sharon blockades a Palestinian center in the West Bank," *New York Times*, March 13, 2001.

2 William A. Orme Jr., "Warrior who confounds—Ariel Sharon," *New York Times*, profile, February 7, 2001.

3 Deborah Sontag, "They agree on one thing: Barak was all wrong," *New York Times*, March 9, 2001.

4 Doron Rosenblum, "Hope never hurts," *Ha'aretz,* March 7, 2001.

5 Sontag, "They agree on one thing."

6 Noam Chomsky, *The Fateful Triangle: The United States, Israel and the Palestinians* (Cambridge, Mass.: South End Press, 1999), p. 144.

7 Baylis Thomas, *How Israel Was Won: A Concise History of the Arab-Israeli Conflict* (Lanham, Md.: Lexington Books, 1999), p. 107.

8 Uri Milshtein, cited in Chomsky, p. 384.

9 E. H. Hutchison, cited in Chomsky, p. 383.

10 James Ron, "Is Sharon a war criminal?" *Chicago Tribune*, February 8, 2001.

11 Ariel Sharon, *Warrior: The Autobiography of Ariel Sharon* (New York: Simon & Schuster Inc., 1989), p. 88.

12 Sharon, p. 98.

13 This strategy included, but was by no means limited to, the actions of Unit 101. By early 1995, between 2,700 and 5,000 refugees (mostly unarmed civilians) had been blown up by Israeli mines or shot. Chapter 10 of Thomas's *How Israel Was Won* provides a good account of Israel's border actions between 1948 and 1955.

14 Thomas, pp. 127–84.

15 Phil Reeves, "Sharon's return puts Wreckage Street in fear," *Independent*, January 21, 2001.

16 On April 9, 1948, the Irgun and Lehi slaughtered 254 men, women, and children in Deir Yassin. Some villagers were taken by truck for a victory parade in Jerusalem and then returned and shot against a wall. This event terrorized other Palestinians and convinced them to flee for their lives.

17 Howard Sachar, *A History of Israel: From the Rise of Zionism to Our Time* (New York: Alfred A. Knopf, 1996), p. 637.

18 Sachar, p. 869.

19 Quoted in Chomsky, p. 125.

20 Howard Sachar's book goes into some of these accounts on pp. 894–96.

21 From the *Jerusalem Post*, December 12 and 24, 1982, cited in Chomsky, pp. 128–29.

22 The Phalange was an interesting bedfellow for Israel. Founded by Pierre Gemayal (Bashir's father), it was an openly fascist militia. "Phalange" literally means "fascist," and Gemayal modeled the group accordingly. In 1936, he visited Berlin and met with Hitler. The Phalange relationship with Israel originated under the previous Labor administration. Rabin met with Gemayal, and both Labor and Likud governments armed the Phalange over the years.

23 Thomas, p. 222.

24 Ron, "Is Sharon a war criminal?"

25 Thomas, pp. 222–29.

26 Chomsky, p. 217.

27 Ze'ev Schiff and Ehud Ya'ari, *Israel's Lebanon War*, Ina Friedman, ed. and trans. (New York: Simon and Schuster, 1984), p. 113.

28 Schiff and Ya'ari, pp. 118–19.

29 Chomsky, pp. 405–06.

30 Robert Fisk, "The legacy of Ariel Sharon," *Independent*, February 6, 2001.

31 Sontag, "They agree on one thing."

RANIA MASRI

The Al-Aqsa Intifada:
A natural consequence of the military occupation, the Oslo accords, and the "peace process"

WE'VE SEEN the pictures of the Al-Aqsa Intifada, the second popular uprising in the occupied Palestinian lands. We've seen the pictures of children throwing stones at armed Israeli military occupiers and of Israeli occupying soldiers armed with U.S.-supplied weaponry. We may still remember the pictures of Rami Mohammad al-Durra, the child who was killed in his father's arms by Israeli occupying soldiers on September 30, 2000. As of May 3, 2002, 1,531 Palestinians had been killed and 19,172 injured in the West Bank and Gaza Strip since September 29, 2000. Palestinian cities and towns have been completely under siege, with no access to ambulances and medical teams.[1] In addition, 400 Israelis have been killed during the same period. All of their deaths are due to one simple fact: the 35-year military occupation of Palestinian land.

The mainstream media and political viewpoint is that this Intifada resulted from the breakdown of the peace process. However, the Al-Aqsa Intifada is a direct and natural consequence of the military occupation, an occupation that remains nearly nine years into the "peace process." To seek an end to the current violence, we must seek an end to the occupation.

This is an expanded version of an article published in the International Socialist Review, *November–December, 2001.*

The Oslo accords, signed in 1993, were thought to construct a framework of negotiations and a gradual schedule that would effectively end the human rights abuses in the Occupied Territories and build a just path for peace. Quite the contrary. The Oslo accords did not end the illegal Israeli military occupation, but rather, as noted by freelance writer Laurie King-Irani of the Electronic Intifada, "enabled it to continue by other means."[2]

Oslo effectively undercut the significance and applicability of international legal principles and key United Nations (UN) resolutions related to the situation on the ground in the West Bank and Gaza Strip (such as UN Security Council Resolution 242, passed in 1967, which demanded that Israel end the military occupation by withdrawing to within its 1967 borders).

Effects of the Oslo accords on the ground

From its inception, Oslo has enabled and exacerbated Israeli abuses of Palestinians' legal, social, political, and economic rights in the occupied West Bank and Gaza Strip. These accords have, as planned, clearly created an apartheid situation in the Occupied Territories (similar to the apartheid situation already present within Israel). Yes, apartheid. As explained by Mouin Rabbani, director of the Palestinian American Research Center in the West Bank town of Ramallah, according to the relevant UN convention, which defines apartheid as a crime against humanity, the defining characteristic of the phenomenon is (as the literal meaning, "separateness," of the term implies) the separate administration of persons within a single territorial unit on the basis of race or ethnicity. Explicitly racist laws that confirm such policies and the institutionalized forms of discrimination that result from such administrative separation are thus consequences of apartheid.

Israel's consistent claims since 1967 that it subjects the Palestinian civilian and Jewish settler populations in the territories to separate legal regimes and issues them distinct identity cards, vehicle license plates, and so on, for purely "administrative" reasons, therefore, provide formal confirmation of its practice of apartheid. Israeli human rights activist Jeff Halper further notes that there are several essential elements of apartheid: exclusivity, inequality, separation, control, dependency, violation of human rights, and suffering. All of these characteristics have been strengthened since the inception of the Oslo accords.

During the eight-plus years since the signing of the Oslo accords, Israel has exploited Oslo's legal and political ambiguity to limit Palestinians' freedom of movement, to increase illegal Jewish-only settlement building, to construct an elaborate network of Jewish-only access roads that link Jewish-only settlements, to intensify the bureaucratic and "legal" limitations placed upon Palestinian life, and to intensify the suffering of life under military occupation. Contrary to popular perception—influenced directly by misleading reports from the mainstream media—Israel remains clearly in control of the Occupied Territories and of the lives of the Palestinians who live in those lands.

Israel's closure policy and its effects on the economy

For the past eight years, Israel has imposed a policy of closure on the Palestinians in the West Bank and Gaza Strip. This closure policy at times restricts, and at other times bans, the movement of labor and goods from the occupied West Bank and Gaza Strip to each other, to Israel, and to external activity and Palestinian life in general. Israel first imposed closure on the Occupied Territories in March 1993, before signing the first Oslo accord in September of that year, and it has never once lifted this siege.[3]

As noted by B'Tselem, a leading Israeli human rights monitoring organization, this closure constitutes a destructive form of collective punishment, bringing Palestinian economic, medical, and educational life to a virtual halt. Collective punishment, in and of itself, is a violation of international law and of the Geneva convention. Amnesty International (AI), in a July 18, 2001, report, called on the international community to act to end Israel's policy of closures. As Philippe Hensmans, an AI delegate, reported:

> Almost every road to every village we passed south of Jerusalem was blocked by mountains of earth or concrete blocks. The main north-south road between Nablus, the area's largest city, and Jenin is empty of vehicles other than army vehicles for many stretches. Army checkpoints consistently turn back Palestinian vehicles. In a number of cases, Palestinians requiring urgent medical attention have died.

AI concluded, "In all cases the closures deny the right to freedom of movement and suffocate economic life."[4] In a later AI report, the organization again urged an end to this policy, quoting delegates who observed:

> The closures represent the punishment of all Palestinians in the Occupied Territories in the name of security. Basic foodstuffs and water are not getting through and Palestinians have died as access to hospitals becomes increasingly difficult. The closures are...simply increasing poverty and despair and creating a population which sees no future and no possibility for a better life.[5]

This constraint on movement severely affects Palestinians' economic well-being, as well as their access to proper health care and educational and professional opportunities. In addition, this draconian policy forbids Palestinians the freedom to travel easily, *if at all,* between various occupied areas of the West Bank, between the West Bank and Gaza, and between the West Bank and Gaza into Jerusalem and Israel to pursue work, education, and medical care, and to meet with family members. Consequently, the Palestinian economy and Palestinian life in general have been further crippled.

Palestinian families are undergoing significant economic hardships, living in much worse straits than they did during the days before the Oslo accords. In Gaza, for example, 40 percent of all households are living below the poverty line. According to the World Bank, the direct cost of Israel's closure to the Palestinian economy is more than $5 million per day. According to a World Bank study completed before the outbreak of the Al-Aqsa Intifada, Yemen is now "the only country in the MENA [Middle East and North Africa] region that has a lower average income than the [West Bank and Gaza Strip]."[6]

During these so-called peace process years, the Palestinian economy has been devastated further. According to the World Bank, the average unemployment rate increased more than ninefold between 1992 and 1996, rising from 3 percent to 28 percent, one of the highest unemployment rates among nearly 200 countries and political entities. As revealed by Sara Roy, author of *The Gaza Strip: The Political Economy of De-Development,* "poverty, especially among children, is now visible in a manner not seen for at least twenty-five years." As Roy explains,

> The "peace process" not only failed to ameliorate, let alone end, Palestinian economic decline or the terms upon which it is based; it accelerated that process by introducing into the Palestinian economy new dynamics that further attenuated an already diminished socioeconomic base. Arguably, there never has been a period since the imposition of Israeli control in 1967 when the Palestinian economy has been so vulnerable. When measured against the advances made by other states in the region, the Palestinian economy is weaker now than in 1967.

The consequences of this permanent closure system include, as revealed by Roy's research,

> high and fluctuating unemployment, permanent unemployment for a growing segment of the labor force, the declining mobility of labor, diminishing trade, weakening agricultural and industrial sectors and declines in domestic production, reduced investment in needed export-oriented industries, low levels of infrastructural development, rising levels of poverty and child labor, and increasing demand for relief and social assistance.

Are these accidental consequences of the closure policy? Is the closure a policy unrelated to the Oslo accords? Quite the contrary. The continuation of preexisting power relations between Israel and the Palestinians, and the structures that underlie them, is a characteristic feature of the Oslo agreements! It is not any action by any Israeli government that obstructs "the peace"; rather, it is the agreements that allegedly claim to be "the process of peace" that are the obstacles to peace.

Increase of Jewish-only illegal settlements

Illegal settlements, as with borders, refugee rights, and Jerusalem, were to be discussed in the "final status negotiations." Consequently, with the aim of creating "facts on the ground," thus building a stronger "negotiating" position with the Palestinians (i.e., "We're already here, so how can you expect us to leave, even though our building of settlements was—and remains—an illegal venture?"), Israel, since the start of Oslo, has significantly expanded its settlement building. According to Israeli data there are

141 settlements in the West Bank and Gaza. However, satellite images show 282 built-up Jewish areas in the West Bank, including East Jerusalem, and 26 in Gaza. This is excluding military sites. These built-up areas cover 150.5 kilometers.[7] Israeli sources consider those Jewish built-up areas in East Jerusalem to be neighborhoods of municipal Jerusalem and not settlements.

These exclusively Jewish settlements house some 400,000 Israelis sprinkled across the Occupied Territories—about 200,000 settlers in the West Bank; 200,000 in East Jerusalem; and 6,000 in Gaza Strip (the latter occupying one-fourth of the land, including most of the coastline). According to the *Report on Israeli Settlement in the Occupied Territories,* 110,000 Jews lived in illegal settlements in Gaza and the West Bank before Oslo; the number has since increased to approximately 200,000—a figure that doesn't include those Jews (200,000) who have taken up residence in Arab East Jerusalem (see Table 1). In addition, in recent years, smaller settlements have been consolidated into settlement blocs of 50,000 settlers or more. These settlement blocs divide Palestinian communities and control strategic corridors.

Contrary to the perception propagated by the mainstream press, Israel's former prime minister, Ehud Barak, was a more avid settler than Benjamin Netanyahu. According to the *Report on Israeli Settlement in the Occupied Territories,* during Barak's first year in office in 1999, his "peace cabinet" authorized 1,924 housing starts across the Green Line, a full 65 percent more than the 1,160 approved by the Netanyahu government in 1997. According to Miftah,

> Since 1967, the Israeli authorities have confiscated large areas of Palestinian land in East Jerusalem as green areas, only to be changed later to yellow areas for exclusive Jewish use. The settlements of Neve Ya'cub, Pisgat Zeiv, Ma'ale Adumim, Gilo, the French Hill, Giva'at Shabira, and Har Homa are all built on land previously classified by the Israeli authorities as "Green Zones."
>
> The discovery of archeological sites doesn't stop Israeli colonialist activities, as long as the discovered places are non-Jewish. This policy is very well manifested in Rachis Shu'fat colony, where Canaanite, Roman, Byzantine, and Islamic excavations have been discovered. Nevertheless, Israeli bulldozers continued to destroy these sites to make room for new Jewish construction.[8]

Year	1997	1999	2000	2001	
Settlement area (square km)	108.9	147.8	150.5	222.2	SOURCE: MIFTAH
Percent of the West Bank	1.9	2.6	2.7	4.0	

TABLE 1: THE GROWTH OF SETTLEMENT AREA IN THE WEST BANK

It is important to recognize that these settlements are houses constructed only for Jews. Palestinians living in the Occupied Territories cannot reside in these houses, and Palestinians with Israeli citizenship within Israel (i.e., non-Jewish, Palestinian residents of Israel) cannot live there either. In addition, the Israeli Jews who choose to live in these settlements are illegally occupying Palestinian land.

Furthermore, the construct of these settlements is in violation of international law. The *very existence* of these settlements is a direct violation of internationally binding agreements and regulations. International humanitarian law explicitly prohibits the occupying state to make permanent changes that are not, in the first place, intended to benefit the population of the *occupied*. Rene Kosirnik, head of the International Committee of the Red Cross delegation to Israel and the Occupied Territories, stated at a press conference on May 17, 2001,

> The transfer, the installation of population of the occupying power into the occupied territories is considered as an illegal move and qualified as a "grave breach." It's a grave breach, formally speaking, but grave breaches are equal in principle to war crimes.

These settlements fragment and diminish the living space of the Palestinians, increase the confiscation—the theft—of Palestinian land, and interfere with the ultimate possible definition of borders. In addition, significant portions of the Jewish settlers are armed, and all of the settlements are "protected" by scores of Israeli military occupying soldiers. Thus, through increasing Israeli occupying forces, these settlements, in addition to stealing the land of the Palestinians, directly increase the tension in the region and pose a direct risk to the lives of the Palestinians.

The violence committed by the armed Jewish settlers typically goes unreported. As Nigel Parry, of the Electronic Intifada, reports:

> For two-and-a-half days, since it began on the night of Saturday, October 7, 2000, large groups of settlers were rampaging through Palestinian villages and towns in the West Bank and 1948 areas/inside the Green Line, attacking Palestinians and their property. In many cases they were protected and even aided by the Israeli military.
>
> Tanks, heavy artillery, and helicopters were deployed around all Palestinian cities in Gaza, and tanks were deployed around Gilo settlement near Bethlehem, and the Pisgot settlement on Jebal Al-Tawwl in Ramallah. During the night, literally thousands of Israeli settlers (in many cases together with Israeli soldiers) attacked Palestinian villages and towns in the West Bank and 1948 areas (Nazereth, Bidya, Sourif, Salfit area) and East Jerusalem neighborhoods (Shufat, Al Azeriyeh, Anata, and Sheik Jarrah). Attacks included the use of live ammunition and beatings, and acts of serious vandalism included the burning of shops, cars, and olive groves.[9]

The Christian Peacemaker Team in Hebron reported on December 9, 2000:

> All day the settlers moved about the Baqa'a [Valley, east of Hebron] with impunity, attacking homes and terrorizing Palestinians. One Palestinian boy was shot by a settler through the abdomen, IDF [Israel Defense Forces] soldiers have transferred him to a hospital. Settlers are still occupying the home of Atta and Rodeina Jabber, they have been damaging the home, and the settlers have now brought a bulldozer to the site.
>
> The Israeli military and police have allowed all this to happen as they watched. The military on the site told witnesses that they were ordered to allow the settlers to take over Atta's house; at first the police said they intended to remove the settlers after Shabbat—now past—but now they say they intend to remove the settlers tomorrow.[10]

The settlers behave as a free arm of the Israeli military occupying forces—violently acting, with impunity, to seize further Palestinian land and terrorize Palestinian communities.

The Mitchell Commission Report, made public on May 20, 2001, called for a complete freeze in settlement expansion and suggested that Israel consider the evacuation of some settlements for security reasons (the "security" of the well-protected Jewish settlers, not the security of the Palestinians). The report states:

> [T]he GOI [Government of Israel] should freeze all settlement activ-

ity, including the "natural growth" of existing settlements. The kind of security cooperation desired by the GOI cannot for long co-exist with settlement activity.[11]

The government of Prime Minister Ariel Sharon (akin to the Barak government) insists that the Israeli settlement policy will continue to support further settlements. Since Sharon's election in February 2001, his government has established 25 new settlement sites in the West Bank. At the present time, there are 9,500 empty houses in the settlements, and Israel's housing minister, Natan Sharansky, proposes to add some 7,000 more.

Jewish-only road systems

These illegally constructed settlements on confiscated Palestinian land are linked together by an intricate system of highways and bypass roads, creating additional barriers and limitations between Palestinian areas and further incorporating the occupied West Bank into Israel. The very term "bypass roads" was not present before the Oslo accords. They are called "bypass roads" because they are meant to bypass (circumvent) Palestinian communities. These roads are completely under Israeli control and are built on stolen Palestinian land.

Currently, there are two major Israeli road construction projects: the Trans-Israeli highway and the massive system of bypass and "security" roads being built throughout the West Bank. In 2000, $198 million in road projects were under construction across the Green Line. The emerging grid of bypass roads is closely integrated with the Trans-Israeli highway plan and fully incorporates the West Bank into Israel. Already, approximately 29 bypass roads link settlements to each other and to Israel, and further divide the Palestinian communities. The Jerusalem Ring Road also intensifies Israel's control of municipal Jerusalem (including occupied Jerusalem).

These roads are not simple two-lane roads, but are actually quite massive in scale. The "security" highways are approximately 50 meters wide with 100–150 meters of fenced-in "sanitary" margins on each side, for a total width of three to four football fields. Within these 100–150 meter margins, no Palestinian construction or Palestinian agriculture is allowed. Specifically, according to reports by LAW, the Palestinian Society for the Protection of Human Rights and the Environment, every 100 kilometers of colonial road require 10,000 dunams of land (2,500 acres).

More than 40 percent of lands expropriated in 1999 (16,657 dunams or 4,164 acres) were dedicated to road construction, spelling a rootless end for approximately 15,000 trees. [12] As Jeff Halper explains, "Placed over the West Bank, an area the size of Delaware but with triple the population, these highways have a major impact on Palestinian freedom of movement, the fragile and historic environment, and Palestinian agriculture" (see Table 2). These colonial roads not only ease the lives of the illegal colonizers and occupiers, but also bolster and perpetuate the encirclement of the several dozen Palestinian enclaves. Consequently, it has become impossible to drive more than a few kilometers without entering Israeli-controlled territory and encountering military checkpoints manned by soldiers dedicated to systematically brutalizing and humiliating Palestinians.

As with the settlements, these roads serve only Jews. Palestinians in the Occupied Territories have different license plates on their vehicles and cannot utilize these roads. And, as with the settlements, the construction of these roads divides the Palestinian communities, further isolating them from each other—an isolation that intensifies the harsh economic situation in which they live. And, as with the settlements, these roads are constructed on stolen Palestinian land and their construction is a violation of international law and of UN Security Council Resolution 242.

Divisions

What of the withdrawals from the occupied lands? What about the return of the land to its rightful owners, the Palestinians? As Edward Said explained, "The Oslo strategy was to redivide and subdivide an already divided Palestinian territory into three subzones, A, B, and C, in ways entirely devised and controlled by the Israeli side." [13]

The West Bank is divided into four areas (A, B, C, and D), Al-Khalil/Hebron is divided into two areas (H-1, under Palestinian Authority control; and H-2, under Israeli rule), and the Gaza Strip

	Existing roads	Under construction	Total
Total length (km)	316.7	24.1	340.8
Area (square km) includes 75m buffer zone	47.5	3.6	51.1

SOURCE: MIFTAH, 2001

TABLE 2: LENGTH AND BUFFER AREA OF BYPASS ROADS IN THE WEST

is divided into four areas (Yellow, Green, Blue, and White areas). Area A is where the Palestinian Authority (PA) has been allowed to take over the large population centers; in Area B, Israel allowed the PA to help police the main village areas, near settlements that were constantly under construction. Despite joint patrols of Palestinian and Israeli officers, Israel held all the real security of Area B in its hands. In Area C, Israel has kept all the territory for itself (60 percent of the West Bank) in order to build more settlements, open up more roads, and establish military areas—all of which were intended to set up a "matrix of control," in Jeff Halper's words, from which the Palestinians would never be free.

The various parts of Area A are separated from each other and surrounded by Area B, and, more importantly, Area C. In other words, the closures and encirclements that have turned the Palestinian areas into besieged spots on the map have been long in the making. In October 2000, Amira Hass, the *Ha'aretz* correspondent in the Palestinian territories, wrote:

> More than seven years have gone by, and Israel has security and administrative control of 61.2 percent of the West Bank, and about 20 percent of the Gaza Strip (Area C), and security control over another 26.8 percent of the West Bank (Area B).
>
> This control is what has enabled Israel to double the number of settlers in 10 years, to enlarge the settlements, to continue its discriminatory policy of cutting back water quotas for 3 million Palestinians, to prevent Palestinian development in most of the area of the West Bank, and to seal an entire nation into restricted areas, imprisoned in a network of bypass roads meant for Jews only. During these days of strict internal restriction of movement in the West Bank, one can see how carefully each road was planned: So that 200,000 Jews have freedom of movement, about 3 million Palestinians are locked into their Bantustans until they submit to Israeli de-

mands.[14]

There is no freedom of movement between these disconnected bantustans. Palestinians cannot travel freely, if they are permitted to travel at all, to and from the areas in West Bank, Gaza Strip, Al-Khalil/Hebron, and Jerusalem. Thus, since the Oslo accords, the Palestinians' living space has drastically decreased, and their state of siege has increased. Furthermore, from the 1993 Oslo accords until the start of the Al-Aqsa Intifada in September 2000, Israel had only withdrawn its occupying military from 18 percent of the West Bank and Gaza Strip.

Bureaucratic limitations and home demolitions

Another set of control mechanisms imposed upon the Palestinians may, at first, sound rather benign, since it is of a "legal" nature. However, these laws are deliberately designed to be destructive. A system of "permits" intensifies the state of siege in which the Palestinians are living. Palestinians are not allowed to build on their own land without a permit, and permits to build homes are generally rejected. The building permits are enforced by daily harassment, fines, arrests, and home demolitions. Palestinians also cannot plant crops on their own land without permission, which is restricted. Israel further controls the licensing and inspection of Palestinian businesses.

The reasons given for land confiscation, home demolition, and environmental destruction include building without a permit, the Absentee Law (which states that land not in use for three continuous years is subject to Israeli confiscation), and security purposes.[15] In occupied East Jerusalem, the vast majority of homes are destroyed for the benefit of neighboring (illegal and occupying) Jewish settlements/colonies.

The destruction of Palestinian land has left many peasants in destitute economic conditions. The clearing of land for settlements is destroying crops on which Palestinian peasants are dependent. This Israeli policy has led to a significant loss of income to an already deprived Palestinian peasant community. Furthermore, this decrease in agriculture-generated income has caused a significant transformation of many Palestinian peasants into cheap labor for

Israeli industry.

Since 1967—the start of the occupation of the West Bank, Gaza Strip, and East Jerusalem—Israel has demolished more than 7,000 Palestinian homes. In the first Intifada (1987–93), Israel completely destroyed 770 Palestinian homes. During the first six months of 1999 alone, Israel confiscated 2,500 acres of land for the purpose of settlements and their infrastructure, and a total of 3,500 acres were leveled in order to facilitate the further expansion of settlements and bypass road construction. Furthermore, 2,265 trees were uprooted during that period, and a total of 34 Palestinian homes were illegally and unjustly demolished in the West Bank, including Jerusalem.

In these "peace process" years, from the signing of the Oslo accords until August 2001 (before the start of the Al-Aqsa Intifada), more than 675 homes had been destroyed, more than 70,000 acres of land confiscated, and more than 282,000 trees uprooted *in the West Bank alone.* In the first six months of this continuing Al-Aqsa Intifada, Israel destroyed 226 Palestinian homes, and the destruction of homes continues. For example, on July 9, 2001, at 5 A.M., thousands of Israeli military troops stormed Shu'fat refugee camp from all directions, destroying 25 residential flats and making more than 120 people homeless.[16]

On January 10, 2002, after four Israeli military soldiers were killed in an attack by Hamas on a military post on the border between Israel and the Gaza Strip (a people struggling for freedom attacking their military occupiers), Israeli military troops entered Rafah with tanks and bulldozers and demolished houses. According to an AI news story:

> "Six hundred people, most of them children, were left homeless in this raid against quarters that had no relationship with the attack on the military post," said Amnesty International.
>
> "Over the past 16 months, at least 250 homes have been demolished in Rafah making more than 1,500 people homeless, the vast majority of them children," Amnesty International said, adding that in the past four days, in the middle of winter, hundreds more men, women and children have been forced to live in donated tents....
>
> "Israel should cease this policy which has been universally condemned," the organization added, recalling that the United Nations'

Committee against Torture concluded as recently as last November that house demolitions may amount to cruel, inhuman or degrading treatment or punishment, in breach of the UN Convention against Torture....

Sometimes Palestinians, who have been given no notice of the demolitions, have been killed or wounded as their homes are destroyed. More than 250 Palestinian homes have been destroyed in Rafah since the beginning of the Intifada at the end of September 2000; the families made homeless live with relatives or in tents. Over the past weeks the weather in the Gaza Strip has been extremely cold. A week ago, on January 7, five Palestinian children aged between two and 11 from one family made homeless by the Israeli demolition of their home in Khan Yunis in the Gaza Strip died in a blaze caused by a candle in their tent. [17]

Daily suffering

On top of all the "administrative" forms of siege imposed on them, Palestinians also endure the daily trauma of life under military occupation: anger and frustration, humiliation, beatings, torture, detentions and imprisonments, harassment, loss of home, and loss of life. Sara Abu Khreik, a 43-year-old mother in Gaza, describes how she awoke to the destruction of her own house:

We were sleeping in our houses. At around 11:30, the Israelis started shooting at us with the tanks and machine guns and their big shells. At around 12, we found the tanks and bulldozers coming at us and they started to demolish the home on top of us. At that moment, we grabbed the children. We had about 30 seconds. The planes were flying overhead and from every direction the guns were working on us. We left without our scarves, without any covering. It came as a surprise, just like that.

In the night, the kids have nightmares of shooting. In the day, they have nightmares of shooting. When you sit and listen to what the children are talking about, they are saying to each other, "Today they shelled; today they shot guns; today they demolished; today they bulldozed." How much are our people supposed to endure? [18]

Through this strategic system of economic, geographic, and administrative choke points, Israel controls nearly every aspect of life in the Occupied Territories. This control has only been strengthened by the Oslo accords and the so-called peace process. As Jeff Halper explains,

A Palestinian state carved into small, disconnected enclaves, surrounded and indeed truncated by massive Israeli settlement blocs,
subject to Israeli military and economic closures, unable to offer justice to its dispersed people and without its most sacred symbols of
religion and identity, can hardly by called a viable state.[19]

Yet this is the most that Oslo grants the Palestinians.

Effects of the Oslo accords on the U.S. media

On June 6, 2001, an editorial in a major national newspaper
commented about the uprising in this fashion:

After some 35 years of occupation, exploitation, uprooting and
degradation, the Palestinian people have the right to use force to oppose the Israeli occupation, which, in itself, is the brutal exercise of
force. Millions of people cannot be forced today to remain under
the subjugation of a foreign occupier. Anyone who thinks otherwise
is merely indulging in pipe-dreams.

This editorial was not published in the *New York Times,* the
Washington Post, USA Today, or any other U.S. paper. Rather,
this editorial was published in *Ha'aretz,* the mainstream Israeli
daily newspaper.[20] It would be extremely rare to see such an editorial in the U.S. press.

Since the 1993 signing of the Oslo accords, the mainstream U.S.
media have generally replaced references to Israel's military occupation of the Gaza Strip, the West Bank, and East Jerusalem with references to the "dying peace process." Concurrently, the media have
removed images of Palestinian civilian life from the overwhelming
majority of reports. Instead, the media have presented images of
stone-throwing Palestinians, without any context for their anger—
no discussion of the historical, political, legal, or moral roots of the
Intifada, and no discussion of the clashes in their present context: a
resistance against 35 years of Israeli military occupation.

Amid the flow of erratic media footage that shows confrontations between Palestinian civilians and Israeli occupying soldiers, almost all network TV coverage has failed to present the central fact
of the conflict: The West Bank and Gaza Strip are occupied territories—illegally occupied for 35 years. As Nigel Parry explains, "This
is tantamount to reporting on Black South African protest in the
1980s without mentioning the context of apartheid."[21] It is tanta-

mount to reporting on the civil rights protests in the U.S. in the 1960s without mentioning segregation. It is tantamount to reporting on the antiwar protests in the U.S. in the 1960s without mentioning the Vietnam War.

Does the mainstream media typically fail to present context when it reports on news, or this is a solitary case? How did the media in the U.S. report on another occupation—the Iraqi occupation of Kuwait in 1990? As documented by Fairness and Accuracy in Reporting (FAIR):

> During Iraq's seven-month occupation of Kuwait in 1990-91, TV journalists had little difficulty recognizing [the principle of occupation and resistance]. On ABC, Peter Jennings forthrightly referred to the country as "Iraqi-occupied Kuwait." "Tell us about the resistance to the Iraqi occupation," Jennings asked in an interview with a Kuwaiti living under Iraqi rule (*World News Tonight*, 9/6/90).
>
> On CBS, Dan Rather reported that Westerners who had left the emirate "are bringing back stories of an occupied but still unconquered nation" (*CBS Evening News*, 9/11/90), while his correspondent in the Persian Gulf reported on Kuwaitis who "have vowed to return to resist the Iraqi occupation" and reports of "attacks and ambushes on Iraqi soldiers by a fledgling Kuwaiti resistance" (*CBS This Morning*, 8/23/90).
>
> Yet in the Israeli-occupied territories, CBS correspondents today talk of "Israeli soldiers under daily attack"; "Israel…again feeling isolated and under siege"; and, in one case where Israeli occupation troops abandoned a fortified position in the West Bank, "Israelis have surrendered territory to Palestinian violence" (*CBS Evening News*, 10/4/00, 10/8/00, 10/7/00).

FAIR noted that of the 99 Intifada stories broadcast on the evening news by the three major U.S. networks between September 28 and November 2, 2001, only four made reference to the Israeli occupation. Even more disturbing:

> Some outlets have even taken the step of referring to occupied Palestinian land as part of Israel. Tom Brokaw (*NBC Nightly News*, 10/2/00) introduced a report about "the ever-widening eruptions of violence in Israel." He then went to NBC correspondent Martin Fletcher, who explained that Palestinians were "storming an Israeli army outpost in Gaza" and "setting siege to another army post in the West Bank." [22]

The fact that Israel is conducting a military occupation—an illegal military occupation funded by the United States—is entirely missing. Without this context, without the discussion of the very heart of the problem, how can this second popular uprising, the Al-Aqsa Intifada, be understood?

From the signing of the Oslo accords in 1993 to the start of the Al-Aqsa Intifada in September 2000, Israel

- withdrew its illegal military from only 18 percent of the occupied West Bank and Gaza Strip;

- increased the number of Jewish occupying settlers in the West Bank and Gaza Strip by 77 percent, from about 110,000 to about 195,000 (in absolute terms, the annual rate of implantation of Jewish settlers in illegal West Bank and Gaza Strip colonies averaged 4,200 between 1967 and 1993; 9,600 between 1986 and 1996; and more than 12,000 between 1994 and 2000);

- increased housing construction of Jewish-only settlements in the Occupied Territories by 52 percent;

- continued its discriminatory policy of cutting back water quotas for 3 million Palestinians (75 percent of the water in the occupied West Bank and Gaza Strip is used by Israel);

- prevented Palestinian development (even the building of homes) in most of the West Bank and Jerusalem;

- paved more than 400 kilometers of roads on confiscated Palestinian land, thereby imprisoning the Palestinians in a network of Jewish-only bypass roads;

- illegally arrested or detained more than 13,000 Palestinians;

- imposed complete closure on the Occupied Territories for more than 300 days during those "peace process" years, which inflicted billions of dollars of losses on Palestinians;

- demolished hundreds of Palestinian homes and made thousands of people homeless;

- consistently broke its written agreements with the

Palestinians.

Series of broken promises

From the start, Israeli governments (both Labor and Likud) have signed agreements with the Palestinian Authority, violated those agreements, then renegotiated their previous agreements, and so forth. As Mouin Rabbani explains,

> A simple comparison of the September 1993 Declaration of Principles ("Oslo"), the September 1995 Interim Agreement ("Oslo II"), the January 1997 Hebron Protocol, the October 1998 Wye River Memorandum, and the September 1999 Sharm el Sheik agreement reveals a clear pattern in which Israel first refuses to implement its own commitments, seeks and obtains their dilution in a new agreement, subsequently engages in systematic prevarication, and finally demands additional negotiations, leading to a yet further diluted agreement.

"Oslo's fatal flaw," Rabbani argues,

> is that it is neither an instrument of decolonization nor a mechanism to apply international legitimacy to the Israeli-Palestinian conflict, but rather a framework that changes the basis of Israeli control over the Occupied Territories in order to perpetuate it. As such, the process is simply incapable of producing a viable or durable (let alone, just) settlement, and will ultimately result in further conflict, further bloodshed....
>
> [W]hereas the lion's share of Palestinian concessions historically demanded by Israel were made in the letters or recognition exchanged pursuant to Israel's demand prior to ratification of Oslo, the relevant agreements never refer to the West Bank and Gaza Strip as occupied territories; do not explicitly commit Israel to desist from illegal activities—such as settlement expansion or grave breaches of the 1949 Fourth Geneva Conventions—designed to further consolidate Israeli rule over Palestine and the Palestinians; and make no attempt either to resolve the core issues that collectively define the Israeli-Palestinian conflict (for example, borders, refugees, and Jerusalem) or establish unambiguous guidelines for their settlement. Instead, the latter are shunted aside under "final-status issues" and postponed for negotiation at the end of the process.

In addition, in a 1993 letter to Israel's prime minister, Yitzhak Rabin, and in a separate letter to Norway's foreign minister, Johan Jorgen Holst, then Palestine Liberation Organization Chairman Yasser Arafat essentially promised that the PLO would end the Intifada. In response, Israel commits "in light of the PLO commitments...to recognize the PLO as the representative of the Palestinian people and commence negotiations with the PLO and within the Middle East process."

The "peace process" never was a process toward peace, but rather one through which Israel would retain possession of the West Bank and Gaza Strip's strategic assets (land, water, borders, Jerusalem), and the Palestinian Authority would police the indigenous population. It is, as Rabbani described it,

> a process that necessarily leads to separation within the occupied territories under continued Israeli hegemony, as opposed to the partition of Palestine through a comprehensive Israeli withdrawal from the West Bank and Gaza Strip. In doing so it formalizes arrangements tantamount to apartheid.[23]

This "peace process" basically locks the Palestinian Authority in, as described by Edward Said, a "fruitless arrangement via security committees made up of Mossad, the CIA and the Palestinian security services." The justifications of further concessions and further Palestinian sacrifices are always based on Israel's need for security—no one speaks of Palestinian security. As Said commented, "Clearly we must conclude, as Zionist discourse has always stipulated, that the very existence of Palestinians, no matter how confined or disempowered, constitutes a racial and religious threat to Israel's security."[24]

How could there, then, not have been an Intifada, an uprising, to this continual, 35-year occupation and to the 10 years of consistently broken promises? The Al-Aqsa Intifada is not only a revolt against occupation, not only a response to the structures of Oslo, but also a rising up against the Israeli campaign of violence (in all its forms) initiated to draw further and further concessions from the Palestinians.

Israel's reaction to the uprising?

The occupied territories of the West Bank, Gaza, and Jerusalem are not under a state of occupation as much as an institutionalized colonization, an institutionalized state of apartheid. This is not a policy of occupying a people, but more akin to a policy of removing and sequestering the native people of the land and replacing them with another group of people. As King-Irani explains:

> Israeli occupation is a strange survival of colonialism in the 21st century. Where else in the world do we hear of 'settlements' and 'settlers'? Where else in the world do soldiers and armed civilian groups take over hilltops, uproot trees and crops, steal water reserves, and block access to an indigenous population's freedom of movement and right to earn a living, go to school, get to the doctor, or visit family and friends? The last place we witnessed human rights violations on this scale was in South Africa before the end of apartheid. If it wasn't right there, it isn't right here.[25]

And why should we expect that Palestinian land stolen in 1967 be regarded differently by Israeli leaders than Palestinian land stolen in 1948...if there is no uproar from the international community, from the U.S.? Joseph Weitz, head of the Jewish Agency's Colonization Department in 1940, said:

> Between ourselves it must be clear that there is no room for both

PALESTINIAN HUMAN AND MATERIAL LOSSES INFLICTED BY ISRAEL DURING THE INTIFADA, SEPTEMBER 29, 2000–JANUARY 16, 2002

Number of Palestinians killed by Israeli military occupying soldiers and settlers	
In the West Bank, Gaza Strip, and east Jerusalem	913
In Israel	14
In southern Lebanon (killed in clashes on Israel's northern borders)	2
Total (including 195 deaths inflicted among children aged 18 and below)	929
Gender distribution of Palestinian deaths:	
Number of males killed (including 195 children aged 18 and below)	887
Number of females killed (including two three-year-olds, one two-year-old, and one four-month-old)	42
Number of Palestinians injured by Israeli security forces and settlers	
Live ammunition	3,616
Rubber bullets	5,318
Tear gas	4,850
Miscellaneous	3,315
Total (including 6,000 injuries inflicted among children below the age of 18)	17,099

Permanent disabilities among injured
(including 25 cases of total blindness)   1,500

Palestinians arrested by Israeli authorities for political reasons

Within Israeli territories (the vast majority have been released)   1,189
Within Palestinian territories (1,000 have been released)   1,787
Total   2,976

Residential Palestinian buildings destroyed by Israeli attacks

Gaza Strip   226
West Bank   333
Total of buildings destroyed   559

Total of residential buildings shelled   3,669

Number of olive trees uprooted form Palestinian land   112,900

Area of Palestinian cultivated land destroyed
                                            3,669,000 square meters

**Palestinian homes demolished by Israeli authorities since
September 29, 2001**   809

Israeli attacks against doctors and ambulance drivers

Number of ambulance drivers killed: 3
Number of doctors killed: 1
Number of doctors and ambulance drivers injured   160
Number of ambulances hit   135

Number of Palestinian schools shut down due to Israeli siege 174

**Number of Palestinian students
deprived from attending school**   90,000

Impact of Israeli closures on Palestinian economic life

Number of Palestinians unemployed due to the closures   257,000
Average unemployment rate in the West Bank
    and the Gaza Strip   57 percent
Income losses for Palestinian workers
    previously employed inside Israel: $ 3.6 million/day
Shortfall in gross national product (September 2000–March 2001) $1.5 billion
Decrease in per capita income   47 percent
Percentage of Palestinians living below poverty line   53 percent
Estimated loss from closures in 2001 $1.7 billion
Daily overall economic losses $11 million

Sources: Palestine Red Crescent Society; World Bank (West Bank and Gaza Strip); Office of
the United Nations Special Coordinator (UNSCO)–Gaza; Ramallah Hospital; Palestinian
Central Bureau of Statistics; Miftah; Al-Shifa Hospital, Gaza; PECDAR; UNICEF; B'Tselem.

peoples together in this country. We shall not achieve our goal if the Arabs are in this small country. There is no other way than to transfer the Arabs from here to neighboring countries—all of them. Not one village, not one tribe should be left.[26]

More than 40 years later, in 1983, the same sentiments were echoed by Rafael Eitan, chief of staff of the Israel Defense Forces:

We declare openly that the Arabs have no right to settle on even one centimeter of Eretz Israel.... Force is all they do or ever will understand. We shall use the ultimate force until the Palestinians come crawling to us on all fours.[27]

In early 1997, four years after the start of the so-called peace process, this position was further formalized by an agreement entitled "National [Labour-Likud] agreement regarding the negotiations on permanent settlement with the Palestinians," signed between former (Labor) minister Yossi Beilin and Likud's parliamentary faction head Michael Eitan. This agreement revealed the Israeli consensus on the so-called final status negotiations with the Palestinian Authority:

- no to withdrawal to the borders of June 1967;

- no to division of Jerusalem or sharing sovereignty over the city;

- no to dismantling the settlements; and

- no to the return of the refugees.[28]

Nothing, then, remains open for negotiation in the "final status" talks except for minor, superficial changes.

What can you do?

While attempting to present itself as an "honest broker," the U.S. government (both Republican and Democrat) has consistently supported Israel—through billions of dollars in aid, through support at the United Nations, and through opposition to Palestinian and Arab resistance. The U.S. has given Israel at least $81.9 billion in aid, the vast majority ($50.8 billion) for the Israeli military.[29] Recently, the U.S. Senate overwhelmingly passed the fiscal year 2002 Foreign Aid Appropriations bill by a 96–2 vote. The Senate version of this bill, similar to the version passed earlier this year in the

House, contains $2.04 billion in military aid and $720 million in economic aid for Israel. The bill has important provisions that enable Israel to maximize the benefits of the aid, such as payment of the money in a lump sum at the beginning of the fiscal year.

In addition to funding Israeli apartheid and Israeli occupation, the U.S. government has also condemned Palestinian resistance. Last year, for example, Representative Gary Ackerman (D-N.Y.) introduced a bill (H.R. 1795, ironically cited as the "Middle East Peace Commitments Act of 2001") that would apply sanctions on the Palestinian Authority. The bill would also designate the PLO, one or more of its constituent groups, or groups operating as arms of the Palestinian Authority as foreign terrorist organizations, and would prohibit virtually all U.S. economic assistance to the Palestinians. Currently the bill has 84 cosponsors.

Earlier in 2001, coinciding with Sharon's inaugural trip to the U.S. as Israel's prime minister, nearly 300 members of Congress signed a letter that placed exclusive blame on the Palestinians for the ongoing violence and urged President Bush to downgrade U.S. relations with the Palestinian Authority. Since then, members of Congress have become more outspoken in their one-sided criticism of the Palestinians.

The U.S. has also vetoed UN resolutions condemning Israeli violence and resolutions asking for international peace monitors in the Occupied Territories. The Bush administration has continued President Clinton's policy of unconditionally supplying arms and funds to Israel, thus directly fueling the conflict and supporting the occupation. Also like Clinton, the Bush administration vetoed a UN Security Council resolution that would have put observers on the ground in the Occupied Territories, because Israel doesn't like the idea.

Long-standing U.S. policy has been to oppose the building of settlements, with various administrations referring to them as "illegal," as "provocations," and as "obstacles to peace." Yet U.S. policy effectively funds and protects these settlements, since U.S. economic aid helps to build them, and U.S. military aid pays for the Israeli occupation forces that protect them and crush any Palestinian resistance to the further seizure of their land.

We need to reveal Israeli policy for what it is—apartheid and "ethnic cleansing." We need to effectively organize, and to demand both corporate and governmental divestment from Israeli apartheid. We also need to talk about this uprising clearly and reject the mainstream media's approach of blaming the oppressed.

To understand the Al-Aqsa Intifada, we must understand the context—a people fighting for liberty from military occupation. To seek an end to the violence—the vast majority of which is perpetrated against Palestinians—we must first seek an end to the occupation. To seek justice for both the Palestinians and Israelis, we must oppose Israeli apartheid.

1   Figures from the Palestine Red Crescent Society, available online at
    www.palestinercs.org.
2   Laurie King-Irani, "How Oslo promoted human rights violations," Electronic
    Intifada, available online at www.electronicintifada.net.
3   Sara Roy, "Decline and disfigurement," in *The New Intifada: Resisting Israel's
    Apartheid*, Roane Carey, ed. (New York and London: Verso Press, 2001).
    This book is an excellent review and illustration of the Intifada, as it traces
    the origins of the uprising, its consequences, and its possible impact on peace
    in the region.
4   Amnesty International, "The international community must act to end Israel's
    policy of closures and house demolitions," July 18, 2001, available online at
    www.amnesty.org.
5   Amnesty International, "An end to closures and the introduction of international human rights observers are a vital necessity," September 21, 2001.
6   World Bank Group, *West Bank and Gaza Update*, April 2000.
7   Geographical Information System database, Applied Research Institute of
    Jerusalem, 2000.
8   "Home demolition and land confiscation," Miftah, the Palestinian Initiative
    for the Promotion of Global Dialogue and Democracy, October 15, 2001,
    available online at www.miftah.org.
9   Nigel Parry, "Widespread settler violence unreported," Electronic Intifada,
    coverage trends.
10 Parry, "Violence unreported."
11 The full text of the Mitchell Report is available online at
    www.mideastweb.org/mitchell_report.htm.
12 "1999 annual report," LAW: The Palestinian Society for the Protection of
    Human Rights & the Environment, available online at www.lawsociety.org.
13 Edward Said, "Palestinians under siege," *London Review of Books*, December 14, 2000.

14 Amira Hass, "Israel has failed the test," *Ha'aretz,* October 18, 2000.

15 "Home demolition and land confiscation." The document explains, "Demolition or sealing of a house is performed in accordance with a military order signed by the military commander of the region, issued pursuant to regulation 119 of the Defense (Emergency) Regulations 1945. (B'Tselem)"

16 "Sharon's demolition campaign in Shu'fat camp," Applied Research Institute of Jerusalem, July 2001, available online at www.poica.org/casestudies/ Shufat-camp10-7-01/index.htm.

17 Amnesty International, "Israel/Occupied Territories: Demolition of houses is an act of collective punishment," January 14, 2002.

18 Charmaine Seitz, "Faces of Gaza," *Palestine Report Online,* April 25, 2001, available online at www.jmcc.org/media/reportonline.

19 Jeff Halper, "The 94 percent solution: A matrix of control, *Middle East Report,* Fall 2000.

20 Baruch Kimmerling, "The basic assumptions have not collapsed," *Ha'aretz,* June 6, 2001.

21 Parry, "The 'peace process' vs. the military occupation," Electronic Intifada, coverage trends.

22 "Missing from Mideast coverage: Occupied territories no longer 'occupied' on TV news," FAIR, action alert, November 3, 2000.

23 Mouin Rabbani, "A smorgasbord of failure: Oslo and the Al-Aqsa Intifada," in *The New Intifada,* pp. 72, 75, 76.

24 Said, "Palestinians under siege."

25 King-Irani, "While we wait for the other shoe to drop...," Electronic Intifada, features.

26 Quoted in Maxime Rodinson, *Israel: A Colonial-Settler State?* (New York: Pathfinder Press, 1973), p. 16.

27 *New York Times,* April 14, 1983.

28 The full text of the agreement is available online from the Jewish Virtual Library at www.us-israel.org/jsource/Peace/beilin_eitan.html.

29 Jewish Virtual Library, "U.S. Assistance to Israel, FY1949–FY2001," available online at www.us-israel.org/jsource/US-Israel/U.S._Assistance_to_Israel1.html. For more information on U.S. aid to Israel, visit the SUSTAIN (Stop U.S. Tax-funded Aid to Israel Now!) Web site at www.sustaincampaign.org.

TANYA REINHART

Evil unleashed

IN MAINSTREAM political discourse, Israel's recent atrocities
are described as "retaliatory acts"—answering the last wave of
terror attacks on Israeli civilians. But, in fact, this "retaliation"
had been carefully prepared long before.

In December 2001, Israel just made official what had been in
the air for many months—that it is aiming, eventually, at a total
destruction of the Palestinian Authority (PA), Arafat's rule, and
the process of Oslo, which is by now dominantly considered "a
historical mistake." As Sharon declared in October, "Oslo is not
continuing; there won't be Oslo; Oslo is over."[1]

Since March 2001, the Israeli media have discussed openly the
plans to reestablish full military control of the territories. The
army's daily activities in the territories were viewed as necessary
steps in implementing the plans: isolating the Palestinian communities from each other, in preparation for the full takeover.

Alex Fishman, senior security correspondent in *Yediot
Aharonot*, explained that since Oslo, "the IDF [Israeli army] regarded the Occupied Territories as if they were one territorial cell,"
and this placed some constraints on the IDF and enabled a certain
amount of freedom for the PA and the Palestinian population. The
new plan is a return to the concept of the military administration
during the pre-Oslo years: The Occupied Territories will be divided

---

*This is a revised version of an article published December 19, 2001, on ZNet
Mideast Watch (www.zmag.org/meastwatch/meastwat.htm).*

into 64 isolated territorial cells, each of which will be assigned a special military force, "and the local commander will have freedom to use his discretion" as to when and who to shoot. The IDF has completed already the division of Gaza into territorial cells, "but so far there has only been isolation, and not yet treatment inside the cells."[2]

The preparations for toppling Arafat and the Palestinian Authority started much earlier. Already, in October 2000, at the outset of the Palestinian uprising, military circles were ready with detailed operative plans. This was before the Palestinian terror attacks started. (The first attack on Israeli civilians was on November 3, 2000, in a market in Jerusalem.) A document prepared by the security services on October 15, 2000, at the request of then-Prime Minister Barak, stated that "Arafat, the person, is a severe threat to the security of the state [of Israel] and the damage which will result from his disappearance is less than the damage caused by his existence."[3] The operative plan, known as "Fields of Thorns," had been prepared back in 1996, and was then updated during the Intifada.[4] The plan includes everything that Israel has been executing lately, and more.[5]

The political echelon (Barak's circles), for its part, worked on preparing public opinion for the toppling of Arafat. On November 20, 2000, Nahman Shai, then public-affairs coordinator of the Barak government, released in a meeting with the press a 60-page document titled "Palestinian Authority and PLO non-compliance with signed agreements and commitments: A record of bad faith and misconduct." The document, informally referred to as the "White Book," was prepared by Barak's aid, Danny Yatom.[6]

According to the "White Book," Arafat's present crime, "orchestrating the Intifada," is just the last in a long chain of proofs that he has never deserted the "option of violence and 'struggle'":

> As early as Arafat's own speech on the White House lawn, on September 13, 1993, there were indications that for him, the DOP [declaration of principles] did not necessarily signify an end to the conflict. He did not, at any point, relinquish his uniform, symbolic of his status as a revolutionary commander.[7]

This uniform, incidentally, is the only "indication" that the report cites of Arafat's hidden intentions on that occasion.

A large section of the document is devoted to establishing Arafat's "ambivalence and compliance" regarding terror:

> In March 1997 there was once again more than a hint of a "Green Light" from Arafat to the Hamas, prior to the bombing in Tel Aviv.... This is implicit in the statement made by a Hamas-affiliated member of Arafat's Cabinet, Imad Faluji, to an American paper.[8]

No further hints are provided regarding how this links Arafat to that bombing, but this is the "green light to terror" theme which the Military Intelligence (Ama'n) has been promoting since 1997, when its anti-Oslo line was consolidated. This theme was since repeated again and again by military circles, and eventually became the mantra of Israeli propaganda—Arafat is still a terrorist and is personally responsible for the acts of all groups, from Hamas and the Islamic Jihad to Hizbollah.

Jane's Foreign Report of July 12, 2001, disclosed that the Israeli army (now under Sharon's government) had updated its plans for an "all-out assault to smash the Palestinian authority, force out leader Yasser Arafat and kill or detain its army." The blueprint, titled "The destruction of the Palestinian Authority and disarmament of all armed forces," was presented to the Israeli government by chief of staff Shaul Mofaz, on July 8. The assault would be launched, at the government's discretion, after a big suicide bomb attack in Israel, causing widespread deaths and injuries, citing the bloodshed as justification.

Many in Israel suspected that the assassination of the Hamas terrorist Mahmoud Abu Hanoud in November 2001, just when the Hamas was respecting for two months its agreement with Arafat not to attack inside Israel, was designed to create the appropriate "bloodshed justification," at the eve of Sharon's visit to the U.S. Alex Fishman noted at the time that

> whoever decided upon the liquidation of Abu Hanoud knew in advance that would be the price. The subject was extensively discussed both by Israel's military echelon and its political one, before it was decided to carry out the liquidation.[9]

Israel's move to destroy the PA, thus, cannot be viewed as a spontaneous "act of retaliation." It is a calculated plan, long in the making. The execution requires, first, weakening the resistance of the Palestinians, which Israel has been doing systematically since October 2000, through killing, bombarding of infrastructure, imprisoning people in their hometowns, and bringing them close to starvation. All this, while waiting for the international conditions to "ripen" for the more "advanced" steps of the plan.

In December 2001, the conditions seem to have ripened. In the power-drunk political atmosphere in the U.S., anything goes. If at first it seemed that the U.S. would try to keep the Arab world on its side by some tokens of persuasion, as it did during the Gulf War, it is now clear that they couldn't care less. U.S. policy is no longer based on building coalitions or investing in persuasion, but on sheer force. The smashing "victory" in Afghanistan has sent a clear message to the Third World that nothing can stop the U.S. from targeting any nation for annihilation. They seem to believe that the most sophisticated weapons of the 21st century, combined with total absence of any considerations of moral principles, international law, or public opinion, can sustain them as the sole rulers of the world forever. From now on, fear should be the sufficient condition for obedience.

The U.S. hawks, who push to expand the war to Iraq and further, view Israel as an asset. There are few regimes in the world like Israel, so eager to risk the lives of their citizens for some new regional war. As Professor Alain Joxe, head of the French CIRPES (peace and strategic studies), put it in *Le Monde* on December 17, 2001, "The American leadership is presently shaped by dangerous right-wing Southern extremists, who seek to use Israel as an offensive tool to destabilize the whole Middle East area." The same hawks are also talking about expanding the future war zone to targets on Israel's agenda, like Hizbollah and Syria.

Under these circumstances, Sharon got his green light in his trip to Washington in December. As the Israeli media kept raving, "Bush is fed up with this character [Arafat]," and "Powell said that Arafat must stop with his lies."[10] Since December, Arafat has been, practically, under house arrest, surrounded by Israeli tanks. As Israeli F-16 bombers plough the sky and Israel's brutality is generating, every day, new desperate human bombs, the U.S., accompanied for a while by the European Union, keep urging Arafat to "act" from his prison. From then on, there was nothing Arafat could do to please Sharon, backed by the United States.

On December 17, from his bunker, he issued a televised call to all organizations to refrain from any terror or armed activities. The various Palestinian organizations complied, understanding the gravity of the situation, and a relative calm was maintained. Sharon, apparently, needed another "bloodshed justification" to advance further the reoccupation plan. On January 14, the Israeli army assassinated another Palestinian leader—Raed Karmi, head of a Tul Karem militia belonging to the mainstream Fatah organization. The horrible revenge at a Bat Mitzvah celebration in Hadera did not take long to follow.

"Disappointment" with Arafat?

What is the rationale behind Israel's systematic drive to eliminate the Palestinian Authority and undo the Oslo arrangements? It certainly cannot be based on "disappointment" with Arafat's performance, as is commonly claimed. The fact of the matter is that from the perspective of Israel's interests in maintaining the occupation, Arafat did fulfill Israel's expectations all these last years.

As far as Israeli security goes, there is nothing further from the truth than the fake accusations in the "White Book," or in subsequent Israeli propaganda. To take just one example, in 1997—the year mentioned in the "White Book" as an instance of Arafat's "green light to terror"—a "security agreement" was signed between Israel and the Palestinian Authority, under the auspices of the head of the Tel Aviv station of the CIA, Stan Muskovitz. The agreement commits the PA to take active care of the security of Israel—to fight "the terrorists, the terrorist base, and the environmental conditions leading to support of terror" in cooperation with Israel, including "mutual exchange of information, ideas, and military cooperation."[11] Arafat's security services carried out this job faithfully, with assassinations of Hamas terrorists (disguised as accidents), and arrests of Hamas political leaders.[12]

Ample information was published in the Israeli media regarding these activities, and "security sources" were full of praises for Arafat's achievements. For instance, Ami Ayalon, then head of the Israeli secret service (Shab'ak), announced, in the government meeting on April 5, 1998, that "Arafat is doing his job—he is fighting terror and puts all his weight against the Hamas."[13] The rate of success of the Israeli security services in containing terror was never higher than that of Arafat; in fact, it was much lower.

In left and critical circles, one can hardly find compassion for Arafat's personal fate (as opposed to the tragedy of the Palestinian people). As David Hirst writes in the *Guardian*, when Arafat returned to the Occupied Territories in 1994,

> he came as collaborator as much as liberator. For the Israelis, security—theirs, not the Palestinians'—was the be-all and end-all of Oslo. His job was to supply it on their behalf. But he could only sustain the collaborator's role if he won the political quid pro quo which, through a series of "interim agreements" leading to "final status," was supposedly to come his way. He never could.... [Along the road], he acquiesced in accumulating concessions that only widened the gulf between what he was actually achieving and what he assured his people he would achieve, by this method, in the end. He was Mr. Palestine still, with a charisma and historical legitimacy all his own. But he was proving to be grievously wanting in that other great and complementary task, building his state-in-the-making. Economic misery, corruption, abuse of human rights, the creation of a vast apparatus of repression—all these flowed, wholly or in part, from the Authority over which he presided.[14]

But from the perspective of the Israeli occupation, all this means that the Oslo plan was, essentially, successful. Arafat did manage, through harsh means of repression, to contain the frustration of his people and guarantee the safety of the settlers, as Israel continued undisturbed to build new settlements and appropriate more Palestinian land.

The repressive machinery—the various security forces of Arafat—were formed and trained in collaboration with Israel. Much energy and resources were put into building this complex Oslo apparatus. It is often admitted that the Israeli security forces cannot manage to prevent terror any better than Arafat can. Why, then, was the military and political echelon so determined to destroy all this already in October 2000, even before the terror waves started? Answering this requires some look at the history.

Two conceptions of Oslo

Right from the start of the "Oslo process," in September 1993, two conceptions were competing in the Israeli political and military system. The one, led by Yosi Beilin, was striving to implement some version of the Alon plan, which the Labor party has been advocating for years. The original plan consisted of annexation of about 35 percent of the territories to Israel, and either Jordanian rule, or some form of self-rule for the rest—the land on which the Palestinians actually live. In the eyes of its proponents, this plan represented a necessary compromise, compared to the alternatives of either giving up the territories altogether, or an eternal bloodshed (as we witness today). It appeared that Rabin was willing to follow this line, at least at the start, and that in return for Arafat's commitment to control the frustration of his people and guarantee the security of Israel, he would allow the PA to run the enclaves in which the Palestinians still reside, in some form of self-rule, which may even be called a Palestinian "state."

But the other pole objected even to that much. This was mostly visible in military circles, whose most vocal spokesperson in the early years of Oslo was then chief of staff, Ehud Barak. Another center of opposition was, of course, Sharon and the extreme right wing, who were against the Oslo process from the start. This affinity between the military circles and Sharon is hardly surprising. Sharon—the last of the leaders of the "1948 generation," was a legendary figure in the army, and many of the generals were his disciples, like Barak. As Amir Oren wrote,

> Barak's deep and abiding admiration for Ariel Sharon's military insights is another indication of his views; Barak and Sharon both belong to a line of political generals that started with Moshe Dayan.[15]

This breed of generals was raised on the myth of redemption of the land. A glimpse into this worldview is offered in Sharon's interview with Ari Shavit, which appeared in the weekend supplement of *Ha'aretz* on April 13, 2001. Everything is entangled into one romantic framework: the fields, the blossom of the orchards, the plough, and the wars. The heart of this ideology is the sanctity of the land.

In a 1976 interview, Moshe Dayan, who was the defense minister in 1967, explained what led, then, to the decision to attack Syria. In the collective Israeli consciousness of the period, Syria was conceived as a serious threat to the security of Israel and a constant initiator of aggression toward the residents of northern Israel. But according to Dayan, this is "bull-shit"—Syria was not a threat to Israel before 1967:

> Just drop it.... I know how at least 80 percent of all the incidents with Syria started. We were sending a tractor to the demilitarized zone and we knew that the Syrians would shoot.

According to Dayan (who at the time of the interview confessed some regrets), what led Israel to provoke Syria this way was the greediness for the land—the idea that it is possible "to grab a piece of land and keep it, until the enemy will get tired and give it to us."[16]

At the eve of Oslo, the majority of Israeli society was tired of wars. In their eyes, the fights over land and resources were over. Most Israelis believe that the 1948 Independence War, with its horrible consequences for the Palestinians, was necessary to establish a state for the Jews, haunted by the memory of the Holocaust. But now that they have a state, they long to just live normally with whatever they have.

However, the ideology of the redemption of land has never died out in the army, or in the circles of the "political generals," who switched from the army to the government. In their eyes, Sharon's alternative of fighting the Palestinians to the bitter end and imposing new regional orders—as he tried in Lebanon in 1982—may have failed because of the weakness of the spoiled Israeli society. But, given the new war philosophy established in Iraq, Kosovo, and Afghanistan, they believe that with the massive superiority of the Israeli air force, it may still be possible to win this battle in the future.

While Sharon's party was in the opposition at the time of Oslo, Barak, as chief of staff, participated in the negotiations and played a crucial role in shaping the agreements—and Israel's attitude to the Palestinian Authority. I quote from an article I wrote in February 1994, because it reflects what anybody who read carefully the Israeli media could see at the time:

> From the start, it has been possible to identify two conceptions that underlie the Oslo process. One is that this will enable Israel to reduce the cost of the occupation, using a Palestinian patronage regime, with Arafat as the senior cop responsible for the security of Israel. The other is that the process should lead to the collapse of Arafat and the PLO. The humiliation of Arafat, and the amplification of his surrender, will gradually lead to loss of popular support. Consequently, the PLO will collapse, or enter power conflicts. Thus, the Palestinian society will lose its secular leadership and institutions. In the power-driven mind of those eager to maintain the Israeli occupation, the collapse of the secular leadership is interpreted as an achievement, because it would take a long while for the Palestinian people to get organized again, and, in any case, it is easier to justify even the worst acts of oppression, when the enemy is a fanatic Muslim organization. Most likely, the conflict between the two competing conceptions is not settled yet, but at the moment, the second seems more dominant: In order to carry out the first, Arafat's status should have been strengthened, with at least some achievements that could generate support of the Palestinians, rather than Israel's policy of constant humiliation and breach of promises.[17]

Nevertheless, the scenario of the collapse of the PA did not materialize. Palestinian society resorted once more to their marvelous strategy of "sumud"—sticking to the land and sustaining the pressure. Right from the start, the Hamas political leadership, and others, were warning that Israel is trying to push the Palestinians into a civil war, in which the nation slaughters itself. All fragments of the society cooperated to prevent this danger and calm conflicts as soon as they were deteriorating to arms. They also managed, despite the tyranny of Arafat's rule, to build an impressive amount of institutions and infrastructure. The PA does not consist only of the corrupt rulers and the various security forces. The elected Palestinian council, which operates under endless restrictions, is still a representative political framework, some basis for democratic institutions in the future. For those whose goal is the destruction of the Palestinian identity and the eventual redemption of their land, Oslo was a failure.

In 1999, the army got back to power, through the "political generals"—first Barak, and then Sharon. (They collaborated in the last elections to guarantee that no other, civil candidate would be allowed to run.) The road opened to correct what they view as the grave mistake of Oslo. In order to get there, it was first necessary to convince the spoiled Israeli society that the Palestinians are not willing to live in peace and are threatening its mere existence. Sharon alone could not have possibly achieved that, but Barak did succeed, with his "generous offer" fraud. After a year of horrible terror attacks, combined with massive propaganda and lies, Sharon and the army feel that nothing can stop them from turning to full execution.

Why is it so urgent for them to topple Arafat? Shabtai Shavit, former head of the Security Service (Mossad), who is not bound by restraints posed on official sources, explains this openly:

> In the thirty-something years that he [Arafat] leads, he managed to reach real achievements in the political and international sphere.... He got the Nobel peace prize, and in a single phone call, he can obtain a meeting with every leader in the world. There is nobody in the Palestinian gallery that can enter his shoes in this context of international status. If they [the Palestinians] will lose this gain, for us, this is a huge achievement. The Palestinian issue will get off the international agenda.[18]

Their immediate goal is to get the Palestinians off the international agenda, so slaughter, starvation, forced evacuation, and "migration" can continue undisturbed, leading, possibly, to the final realization of Sharon's long-standing vision, embodied in the military plans.

The immediate goal of anybody concerned with the future of the world, should be to halt this process of evil unleashed. As Alain Joxe concluded his December 17 article in *Le Monde*:

> It is time for the Western public opinion to take over and to compel the governments to take a moral and political stand facing the foreseen disaster, namely a situation of permanent war against the Arab and Muslim people and states—the realization of the double fantasy of bin Laden and Sharon.

---

1   *Ha'aretz*, October 18, 2000.

2 *Yediot Aharonot*, March 9, 2001.

3 Details of the document were published in *Ma'ariv*, July 6, 2001.

4 Amir Oren, *Ha'aretz*, November 23, 2001.

5 For the details of this operative plan, see Anthony Cordesman, "Peace and war: Israel versus the Palestinians: A second Intifada?" Center for Strategic and International Studies, December 2000, and Shraga Eilam, "Peace with violence or transfer," *Between the Lines*, December 2000.

6 The document can be found online at www.gamla.org.il/english/feature/intro.htm.

7 From section 2 of the "White Paper."

8 *Miami Herald*, April 5, 1997.

9 *Yediot Aharonot*, November 25, 2001.

10 Barnea and Schiffer, *Yediot Aharonot*, December 7, 2001.

11 Clause 1, translated from the Hebrew text that appeared in *Ha'aretz*, December 12, 1997.

12 For a survey on some of the PA's assassinations of Hamas terrorists, see my article, "The A-Sherif affair," *Yediot Aharonot*, April 14, 1998, an expanded version of which is available online at www.tau.ac.il/~reinhart/political/A_Sharif.html.

13 *Ha'aretz*, April 6, 1998.

14 David Hirst, "Arafat's last stand?" *Guardian*, December 14, 2001.

15 *Ha'aretz*, January 8, 1999.

16 *Yediot Aharonot*, April 27 1997.

17 The article (in Hebrew only) can be found online at www.tau.ac.il/~reinhart/political/politicalE.html.

18 Interview, *Yediot Aharonot*, weekend supplement, December 7, 2001.

DAVID BARSAMIAN

Interview with Edward Said

DAVID BARSAMIAN writes:

Edward W. Said was born in Jerusalem, Palestine, in 1935, and attended schools there and in Cairo. He received his B.A. from Princeton and his M.A. and Ph.D. from Harvard. Said, University Professor at Columbia University, is a prolific writer. His latest books include Reflections on Exile and Other Essays *and* The End of the Peace Process: Oslo and After. *He also writes a regular column for the Arabic newspaper* Al-Hayat *in London. For many years, Said has been the main spokesperson for Palestinian rights in the United States and has paid a price for his high-profile activism. His office at Columbia was set on fire, and both he and his family have "received innumerable death threats," he writes.*

For more than a decade, Said was a member of the Palestine National Council. Since resigning from the council in the early 1990s, Said has become one of the most public critics of Yasser Arafat and the so-called peace process. His was a rare voice of resistance amid all the euphoria when the Oslo accords were signed on the South Lawn of the White House in September 1993. He understood instantly what Oslo meant and called it "a Palestinian Versailles."

My first collection of interviews with Said resulted in The Pen and the Sword, *published by Common Courage Press. A new col-*

This interview ran in two issues of the International Socialist Review *(ISR 18, June–July 2001, and ISR 19, August–September 2001). The subtitles in this version reflect the titles of the two installments in the ISR.*

lection is planned. Said, even while battling leukemia, maintains a rigorous speaking and writing schedule. I interviewed him in Santa Fe, New Mexico, in early May 2001.

"What they want is my silence"

SINCE THE Al-Aqsa Intifada began in late September, 2000, a number of events have occurred, including the election of Ariel Sharon as prime minister of Israel. What's your assessment of the current situation on the ground in Palestine?

IT'S STALEMATED. I don't think there's any clear direction, except on both sides there's a return to earlier, almost primordial positions—for the Palestinians to stay on the land and to resist to the best of their ability and for the Israelis to get them off the land. That's Sharon's policy. The policy is to use what they call "restraint" but what, in fact, is disproportionate force, including helicopter gunships, missiles, and tanks against a basically unarmed and defenseless civilian population, and to do it out of a position of tremendous asymmetry, which is often obscured by the media. This isn't a battle between two states. It's a battle between a state with basically a colonial army attacking a colonized population, using all forms of collective punishment.

Politically, there really isn't any way forward. What the Israelis want is the status quo without Palestinian resistance and what the Palestinians want is, officially at least, the resumption of negotiations to the point that was reached in the last days of the Clinton administration. But for the people, what they want is the end of Israeli occupation.

HAVE THE Palestinians done a better job in telling their story, getting their narrative out?

I DON'T think so, simply because the weight of Israeli power is so great that the Palestinians don't have a chance. There is no organization. There are a few Web sites that, if you want, you can go to and get up-to-date Palestinian information on what's happening. But in the sense that there's a narrative—that there are easily available maps that show that what is at stake is military occupation versus liberation—none of that is easily available.

What the leading papers show is what they constantly refer to as "Palestinian violence" that seems to be gratuitous and directed at Jews. You have a massive propaganda effort on the part of Israel, which has employed two, some say three, public relations firms in the United States; has the entire U.S. Senate at its beck and call; and has an enormous amount of financial, political, and other resources blocking any effort at the United Nations to protect Palestinian civilians against Israeli military onslaught.

The net result is that there is a very skewed situation, in which Palestinians are dying. There are now more than 400 dead and upwards of 14,000 seriously injured, without any political benefit. It's a tragic and, to me, absolutely unacceptable situation.

THE AL-AQSA Intifada now has been largely relegated to the back pages of the newspapers. For example, today, the Albuquerque Journal *has a small item on page 4.* The New York Times *has a piece on page 9. And the local Santa Fe paper,* The New Mexican, *has nothing at all. Unless there is some major atrocity or conflagration, it's largely low-level background noise now.

MY IMPRESSION is that this is very much the popular Israeli feeling, that the Arabs are a nuisance and their presence is a fly in the ointment. Daily life for most Israelis in places like Tel Aviv, Haifa, and Hertzlia goes on. They're completely insulated from what is taking place. Even the settlers on the West Bank and Gaza don't have to see or deal with Palestinians. They're protected from them, just as whites were protected from Blacks during apartheid [in South Africa] because of the homeland system and because the roads went around in such a way as to avoid the vision of them.

Meanwhile, constant encroachment and economic suffocation are taking place. No one is recording that. It can't be recorded by conventional means. Then the Israelis are trying to project an image of beleaguered victimhood, that this is a continuation of what Hitler did to the Jews. It's the most unscrupulous kind of propaganda, basically blaming the victims.

IN TODAY'S **New York Times,** *there is a full-page ad from the American Jewish Committee rehearsing some of the shibboleths surrounding the conflict. How can the Palestinians make their case heard in the face of such enormous outreach?*

THE ADS are terrible. They're basically lies—not just lies, but they remove the context entirely. They quote passages from the Egyptian and Syrian press, something that a mufti may have said, without supplying the context, which is that Palestinians are under attack by a Jewish state that is doing what it does in the name of the Jewish people, and therefore there's a causal relationship between the resentment and hatred that people feel in the Arab and Islamic world toward Jews—not because of classic European anti-Semitism, but because of what Israel is doing, which is barbaric. There's no other word for it.

Second, what the ad doesn't show is the vast amount of outpouring of racist sentiment on the part of Jews. A few days ago, the main rabbi of the Shas Party, Ovadia Yosef, said that the Palestinians should be exterminated. They're snakes. They should be killed. If you were to cull the press of Israel, you'd find far worse sentiments expressed about Arabs, Muslims, and Palestinians than in this silly collection of random sayings, most of them probably manufactured by the American Jewish Committee for the American consumer, who doesn't know better.

Americans have no idea what their money is financing. All of this is paid for by the United States. All of the oppression of the Palestinians is taken out of the $5 billion that American taxpayers are giving Israel without any strings attached, along with the power to use arms that are meant for defensive purposes for offensive purposes.

In the meantime, Palestinians unfortunately haven't yet come to the awareness that what we need is an organized campaign, which I think can be done. There's a large Palestinian diaspora community that hasn't been mobilized. There are many resources in Palestine, in the Arab world, which haven't been mobilized. We're still at a very primitive level of fighting for turf—who's going to lead what.

We're still under the thumb of a tyrannical and, in my opinion, at this point, useless Palestinian Authority that wants to try to control information so as to keep itself in power and to go back to negotiations, which nobody wants. Certainly most Palestinians don't want to return to interim negotiations for an interim settlement that gives the Israelis the right to do what they're doing and continue the settlement, which has been ongoing never more than under the last prime minister, Ehud Barak. Most people think that Barak was a generous, nice man who was defeated because he was too soft on the Palestinians. The fact is that he was as brutal as Sharon. The rate of settlement under his regime was never greater under the four or five previous prime ministers.

So this is a continuation of a policy that has been unremittingly active in oppressing and subduing Palestinians in methods that far outstrip anything that was done in South Africa under apartheid. This needs to be pointed out, and it hasn't been, because the Palestinian leadership and many of the elite still believe that the way to move forward is to get Bush's attention, to try to get the attention of the American administration, which is heedless.

If you look at what Colin Powell said when he asked that the Israelis withdraw from Gaza, after they made that famous incursion around the middle of April [2001], he basically blamed the Palestinians for provoking them. Then he said Israel should withdraw because it's disproportionately violent. But basically the administration, like all American administrations, is hostile to Palestinian aspirations. Therefore, we should concentrate on constituencies in the United States that are friendly to us—the universities, the churches, the African American community, the Latino community, the women's community. We've simply neglected them.

WHAT'S AT the root of that neglect? Why hasn't there been more outreach?

PROBABLY THE root is the sense of terrible desperation and encirclement. There's no way of overestimating the pressure under which all Palestinians live. Here we are, being slaughtered, basically, by a ruthless enemy, and all we have in our defense are young men throwing stones at tanks, missiles, and helicopter gunships. That is the basic reality.

The Palestinian Authority (PA) is unable to lead. For one, its movements are severely restricted by the Israelis. Arafat has been stuck in Ramallah for months. Second, Israel has a policy of extra-judicial assassination, so everybody who occupies a leadership position in the Palestinian community is threatened directly with murder by Israel.

Most people are having a terrible time economically to put food on the table for their children. Most people are unable to work. There's 60 or even 70 percent unemployment. There's a sense in which we are alone. We are surrounded by enemies, and the world is paying us no attention, after 100 years of struggle against this determined enemy. That's the main reason.

The other reason is ignorance. The Palestinian elites—the intellectuals and others—still think that there's a shortcut to influencing America, which is the main actor in this besides Israel. Without America, nothing of this could be done. There's an ignorance of how the United States is constructed and what the source of pressure, the points of pressure might be.

Wherever they've been used, for example, tactics of civil disobedience have worked. In 2000, there was a successful effort to stop Ben & Jerry's ice cream from using water taken from an Israeli settlement on the Golan Heights. So Ben & Jerry's became the focus of pressure and boycott, and in the end they stopped. There was a Burger King franchise sold to an Israeli settlement, Efrat, just south of Bethlehem. There was a concentrated boycott highlighting this, and it was also stopped. The franchise was rescinded. These tactics in fact work.

But what you need is a new leadership, an alternative leadership of intellectuals who make that a principal focus and don't become diverted by things like worrying about the Arab League or whether the British or the Germans are going to do something. What we need is a disciplined focus on the main actors. One is Israel and the Israeli people, who have to be addressed. We've never done that. The second is America and the American people, those sectors of this gigantic country that might join us in a battle against this unending war of ethnic cleansing.

It's important to learn the lessons in the wider society of the U.S. and liberation movements around the world. We haven't taken advantage of that. There's a lot of good will and a lot of people willing to help us.

DO YOU think that the fear that's present in your generation is somewhat less in the younger generation?

THERE'S NO question about it. Not only us, but there's a lot of understandable contempt for what this generation has wrought. All you have to do is look at the panorama in the Arab world. The problem is—and I've found this with working with young people in some of the new Arab organizations—they haven't been able to draw from my generation the experiences and the accumulation of knowledge and achievement that we've made. These new organizations are reinventing the wheel, starting from scratch. They're going back and doing things that have already been done and don't need to be done again and can be built on rather than ignored and contemptuously swept aside.

There's a problem of generational continuity which has to be worked out. I think it is being worked out. There is a tremendous reservoir of competence and achievement among young people that I see every time I go to universities around the country—young Arab Americans allied with African Americans, women, Native Americans, who are very sophisticated. What we need now is an apparatus, a rethinking of how all of them can work together.

YOU JUST gave a talk in Bellingham at Western Washington University. What was the reception like there? I ask that because it's not Berkeley, Madison, or Boulder.

I GAVE a large lecture on humanism which didn't deal with Palestine. But, earlier in the day, I talked to a group of about 50 or 60 students from anthropology, literature, and political science. I found a startling, I wouldn't say unanimity, but openness, and not only openness, but acceptance of the Palestinian position. There were no Arab Americans. They were all from Washington, basically from the Northwest. They had a very good understanding of the Palestinian situation, of the political situation in the Middle East, and the work of the Zionist lobby in this country.

Even more ironically, one of their professors, one of the leading professors at that university, happens to be an American Jew who is not a Zionist. It's in his class and thanks to his teaching and the reading that he does of my books, Noam Chomsky's, and those of others that has brought these kids around. That's a perfect example.

A few weeks earlier I was at Princeton. I've been giving a lot of lectures at universities. The minority is seen as right-wing extremist Zionists. The rest are very open and compassionate. I was in London last week. I gave a talk. There must have been 2,000 or 2,500 people there, a lot of them Arab, but a lot of them English. I also spoke at the School of Oriental and African Studies. Hundreds of students turned up from all over the Third World.

There, too, what startles me is the amazing openness and willingness to listen to the Palestinian position. We've never tapped that in any systematic way. That's what strikes me as so stupid on the part of the conventional Arafatist leadership. So I try my best to draw some of that off to focus it on healthy Palestinians.

Now it's a question of survival. But I think we have to go beyond survival to the battle of culture and information. And there are people in Israel who are also very anxious to hear what we have to say. We have to provide them with a message that Zionism has never done anything for them. More Israelis are beginning to understand that Israel, despite its enormous military strength and economic and political power, is more insecure than it ever was. There's a reason for that. Since the leadership is unable to provide them with an understanding of it, we have to do it. So we have a lot of tasks on hand, but they are doable, and they don't involve suicide and a kind of brave, but in the end futile, throwing of stones and exposing yourself to the depredations of the Israeli military.

YOU'RE A lightning rod for criticism, from the National Post in Canada to the Wall Street Journal to Commentary to the New Republic. That ties up a lot of your time in responding, doesn't it?

I DON'T respond. It's a total waste of time. These are propagandists who have a racist hatred of Palestinians, Arabs, and Muslims that seems to be irremediable. And besides, it's not the readers of the *New Republic* or the *National Post*. It's their owners.

I suppose it flatters me that they think I'm important enough to keep attacking me. What it does do, in fact, is to interest more people in my work and my writing. That's the way I respond to them, by producing more. I think what they want is my silence. Unless I die, it's not going to happen.

They call all resistance "terrorism"

ROBERT FISK, the Middle East correspondent for the **Independent**, *comments that "ignorance of the Middle East is now so firmly adhered to in the U.S. that only a few tiny newspapers report anything other than Israel's point of view."*[1]

I DID a homemade survey of the major papers in the metropolitan centers—Los Angeles, New York, Chicago, Atlanta, and Boston. They are uniformly reporting from Israel, that is to say, using reporters who are stationed in Jerusalem, which is Israel because it's been annexed, or Tel Aviv. They have very few reporters in the Arab world reporting the Palestinian point of view. Second, they report things that are sent back to their editorial offices in their home bases, and the stories are changed to reflect the same bias, the same line.

The mantra is Palestinian violence and Israeli insecurity. That is the theme of all the reporting in which hundreds of Palestinians have been killed, thousands maimed and wounded—ignoring the reports of Amnesty International, Human Rights Watch, United Nations committees, the UN High Commissioner for Refugees' report. I could give you a dozen citations about what is taking place that are easily verifiable.

None of this gets reflected in the major newspapers, and certainly not on TV. Even the so-called virtuous programs, like the *NewsHour* on PBS and National Public Radio, hew to the same line, largely—and they told me this when I inquired—because of letter-writing or e-mail campaigns that flood them with complaints, orchestrated obviously by public relations outfits, designed to keep the news focused on Israel and Israel's plight.

There are a few intrepid people writing critical pieces in the *Orlando Sentinel,* the *Seattle Post-Intelligencer,* Z magazine, the *Des Moines Register,* and the *Hartford Courant.* You find them here and there. But they are few and far between and do not reach the major newspaper-reading public.

TERRORISM IS an ongoing focus for the U.S. media. The State Department has just issued its annual report. With the litany of terrorist states—Afghanistan, Pakistan, Iran, Iraq, Libya, Sudan, and Syria—all of them are Muslim-majority countries. "Terrorism is a persistent disease," Colin Powell said as he released the report.[2] What geopolitical function does the focus on terrorism serve?

FIRST OF all, this relentless pursuit of terrorism is, in my opinion, almost criminal. It allows the United States to do what it wishes anywhere in the world. Take, for example, the 1998 bombing of Sudan. That was done because Bill Clinton was having trouble with Monica Lewinsky. There was a paper-thin excuse that they were bombing a terrorist factory, which turned out to be a pharmaceutical factory, producing half the pharmaceutical supply for the country, which a few weeks later was in the grip of a plague. Hundreds of people died as a result of the plague because there were no pharmaceuticals to treat them because of the willful bombing by the United States.

Terrorism has become a sort of screen created since the end of the Cold War by policymakers in Washington, as well as a whole group of people, like Samuel Huntington and Steven Emerson, who have their meal ticket in that pursuit. It is fabricated to keep the population afraid and insecure, and to justify what the United States wishes to do globally.

Any threat to its interests, whether it's oil in the Middle East or geostrategic interests elsewhere, is labeled as "terrorism," which is exactly what the Israelis have been doing since the mid-1970s in response to Palestinian resistance to their policies.

It's very interesting that the whole history of terrorism has a pedigree in the policies of imperialists. The French used the word "terrorism" for everything that the Algerians did to resist their occupation, which began in 1830 and didn't end until 1962. The British used it in Burma and in Malaysia. "Terrorism" is anything that stands in the face of what we want to do. Since the United States is the global superpower and has or pretends to have interests everywhere—from China to Europe to southern Africa to Latin America and all of the Americas—"terrorism" becomes a handy instrument to perpetuate this practice.

Terrorism is also now viewed as a resistance to globalization. That connection has to be made. I notice, by the way, Arundhati Roy made that connection, as well, that people's movements of resistance against deprivation, against unemployment, against the loss of natural resources—all of that is termed "terrorism."

Into this vicious cycle feed a few groups like bin Laden's and the people he commands, whether they are in Saudi Arabia or Yemen or anywhere else. They're magnified and blown up to insensate proportions that have nothing to do with their real power and the real threat they represent. This focus obscures the enormous damage done by the United States, whether militarily, environmentally, or economically, on a world scale, which far dwarfs anything that terrorism might do.

Lastly, very little is said about homegrown terrorism, the militias and armed groups in this country, or Timothy McVeigh. I remember very clearly after the blowing up of the federal building in Oklahoma City, my office was deluged with phone calls because I think Steven Emerson, who was instantly called an "expert on terrorism," said this has all the marks of Middle Eastern terrorism.

That cycle of connections is deeply damaging to individuals of Arab and Muslim origin in this country. During the 2000 election campaign, anything having to do with Islam or Muslims was used as a way of discrediting your opponent. Hillary Clinton returned a $50,000 contribution from the Muslim Alliance, which is a very conventional, quite politically neutral group, because they smacked of terrorism, she said. Those kinds of labels can be like racial profiling that involves not only African Americans and Latin Americans, but also Arab Americans.

Interestingly, the State Department report you cited shows conclusively that the Islamic world is number 10 on the list.[3] The greatest source of terrorism is the U.S. itself, and some of the Latin American countries, not at all the Muslim ones. But they're used, partly manipulated by the Israeli lobby, partly by Defense and State Department interests, to keep America in its policies and to intimidate people.

THE U.S.- and U.K.-led sanctions against Iraq are clearly crumbling. What accounts for that?

THEY'VE FAILED. In the first place, the point of the sanctions was to bring down Saddam Hussein, but he got stronger. Second, the Iraqi civilian population has suffered enormous harm, genocidal harm, thanks to the United Kingdom and the United States. Sixty thousand children are dying every year since the sanctions were imposed. And countless unnumbered others have been affected through cancer and other diseases. It's led to the impoverishment of the entire population. Two UN commissioners of the oil-for-food program resigned because of the inhumanity of the sanctions.

Also, Iraq does not exist, contrary to U.S. policymakers' fantasies, in a vacuum. It is, along with Egypt, one of the central Arab countries. Its economy has always historically been tied to that of its neighbors, especially Jordan. What has happened is that the Jordanians have now been supplied by Iraq with oil at 50 percent of its cost, and Jordan trades with Iraq. There are other kinds of organic connections between Iraq and its neighbors, including some of the Gulf countries. So the sanctions can't possibly continue in the form that they were envisioned.

As a result, we have Colin Powell traveling throughout the Middle East in February [2001], advocating something called "smart sanctions." That struck me as a complete misnomer and again a fantasy—to suggest that the U.S. can in fact cause people to go against their own interests. That won't happen. The whole thing has been a total, futile, disastrous policy.

This is the irony of it. The power and wealth of the United States is such that most people have no awareness of the damage that has been caused in their name—or the hatred that has been built up against the U.S. throughout the Middle East and the Islamic world—for no purpose other than to guarantee the continued dominance of policymakers and a few people whose interests are tied to this ridiculous and inhuman policy.

ONE OF the countries that has broken the sanctions and actually sent flights into Baghdad is Turkey. It is in the

*situation of being the site of the major U.S. air base that
bombs Iraq and also a country that has invaded northern Iraq
a number of times in pursuit of Kurdish resistance fighters.*

AND WHICH is supplied by the U.S. in pursuit of its war against
the Kurds, to the extent that it makes what happened to the Alba-
nians in Kosovo look like a Sunday school picnic. Turkey, one
mustn't forget, is in very close alliance with Israel. They have joint
military maneuvers. There's a military alliance with the United
States and with Israel, and yet, because commercial and regional
interests override those, Turkey is now trading with and getting
oil from Iraq, the second-largest oil supplier in the region.

*DO YOU think the Israeli military and economic alliance with
Turkey is part of a grand strategy to encircle the Arabs?*

NO, BECAUSE Egypt is involved. It's not to encircle the Arabs. It's
to encircle what are considered to be intransigent states, like Syria,
Iraq, and Iran. It's not directed against the Arabs, but rather against
those states that have seemed to be too anti-Israeli or too sympa-
thetic to the Palestinians. But it's a mindless, irrational strategy. In
the final analysis, these are deeply unpopular policies and can't possibly last. It's like Syngman Rhee in South Korea, or Ky and Thieu
in Vietnam. U.S. policymakers never learn. They repeat the same
mistakes, with the same human and economic and political costs.
They will persist in doing it, because their education and their perspective is the same, handed down from generation to generation.

*NOBEL PRIZE winner and current Israeli Foreign Minister
Shimon Peres recently gave an interview to the Turkish press
denying the Armenian genocide.[4]*

THERE, TOO, Turkish policy and Israeli policy are very similar.
They both have an interest in suppressing knowledge and acknowledgment of what the Turkish government did to the Armenians early in the 20th century because they want to reserve the
right to function in the same way. I'll give you an example. In
1983, there was an Israeli government radio program that was
about trying to understand what happened to the Armenians. It
was forbidden to go out on the air simply because they used the
words "holocaust" and "genocide," which in Israel are reserved

only for what happened to the Jews. This kind of policy is perpetuated by what Shimon Peres did, stupidly, instead of trying to widen the circle of acknowledgment and understanding of what might happen to people, whether in Rwanda or to the Armenians or the Bosnians or elsewhere in the world where these horrible things have occurred, and where all human beings have an interest in making sure that they don't happen again. They want to organize memory in such a way that it's focused exclusively on certain groups and not on other groups that suffered these historical calamities.

YOU'VE SPOKEN out on many occasions on the right of return. Are you making any headway on getting recognition of a right of return?

I THINK we are, especially in people's awareness that there is a right of return. I don't mean only necessarily to Palestine. People cannot be driven from their homes or even choose to leave their homes and not have the right to return. That's the larger principle. That right was left out of the Oslo peace process, invidiously, though Palestinians now constitute the largest number of disenfranchised refugees since World War II still in existence and still to be found in refugee camps.

The right of return can also serve to draw attention to the plight of Palestinians in Arab countries, Syria and others, where they haven't been patriated and been given rights of residence, work, or travel. So it's not just in Israel—although Israel is the main cause of this—but elsewhere in the Arab world in general where Palestinians are treated harshly.

I would like to think that this is part of a bigger movement, drawing attention to the rights of immigrants to enter countries if they've been driven from their own. If they're not able for political and physical reasons to return, they should be given rights of residence wherever they are. It's a worldwide phenomenon that deeply interests me.

We live in a period of migration, of forced travel and forced residence, that has literally engulfed the globe. This has resulted in a series of very reactionary immigration laws, not only in Israel, that are motivated by some myth of purity that citizens of these countries, like Italy, Sweden, Britain, and the U.S., have a right to ward off these lesser people, these inferior people—from Africa and Asia mostly—who seek refuge or to return to their homes.

The principle is the same, whether people are not allowed to return to their homes in Palestine or are not allowed to find new homes in countries like Lebanon, the U.S., or Sweden because they're considered to be strangers and alien. The whole concept of who is a stranger, who is an alien, and who is a native has to be rethought to include the fate of people whose ancestors were exterminated and people who came in and forcibly became settler colonists in countries like Israel and the United States. It's a vast phenomenon and urgently in need of rethinking in ways that I hope the Palestinian right of return movement can dramatize.

---

1   Robert Fisk, "I am being vilified for telling the truth about Palestinians," *Independent*, December 13, 2000.

2   Secretary of State Colin L. Powell, "Statement upon release of patterns of global terrorism 2000," April 30, 2001, Washington, D.C., available online at www.state.gov.

3   U.S. Department of State, *Patterns of Global Terrorism—2000*, available online at www.state.gov.

4   "Peres: Armenian allegations are meaningless," *Turkish Daily News*, April 10, 2001.

TIKVA HONIG-PARNASS
AND TOUFIC HADDAD

September 11 and beyond: A view from Palestine

THE SEPTEMBER 11, 2001, attacks in New York and Washington, D.C., led the U.S. to declare a "war on terrorism." This war started in Afghanistan, but the Bush administration has made clear that it plans to expand the war elsewhere.

Meanwhile, Israel has used the "war on terrorism" to step up its military repression of the Palestinians. This repression increased greatly following the October 17, 2001, assassination of Rehavam Ze'evi, a far-right member of Prime Minister Ariel Sharon's government who had resigned only two days before. The Popular Front for the Liberation of Palestine (PFLP) claimed responsibility for the assassination, declaring that it was in retaliation for Israel's assassination of the PFLP's general secretary, Abu Ali Mustafa, in August 2001.

To get a perspective on how the events of September 11 and subsequent developments have affected the struggle for Palestine, International Socialist Review *editors Anthony Arnove and Lance Selfa interviewed Tikva Honig-Parnass and Toufic Haddad, co-editors of the journal* Between the Lines. *During the 1948 war that established the Israeli state by expelling 800,000 Palestinians, Tikva fought in the Palmach—a kibbutz-based strike force of the Zionist militia Haganah. Today, she is an outspoken critic of*

Zionism and a firm advocate of Palestinian rights. Toufic is a Palestinian American activist based in the West Bank.

WHAT HAS been the impact of September 11 and the "war against terrorism" on Israel's war against the Palestinians?

TOUFIC: The impact was felt almost immediately. Within 24 hours of the attacks in New York and Washington, Israel took advantage of the international media's preoccupation with the events in the U.S. to escalate its policies in suppressing the current Palestinian uprising (Intifada). This was seen during brutal incursions into the West Bank city of Jenin (in Area A,[1] supposedly under full sovereignty of the Palestinian Authority) and in the Gaza Strip.

The destruction reaped 21 Palestinian dead within three days, enormous material damage, and a clear elevation in tactics used for suppressing the Intifada. This included the drawn-out and extended reoccupation of Area A (two weeks in the case of Jenin, which was occupied by 60 tanks) and the hunting down and assassinating of Palestinian activists taking refuge in Area A. These tactics were subsequently repeated, and even further escalated, when Israel reoccupied six Palestinian cities in the West Bank on September 17. The destruction in this case was even more grave, resulting in 55 Palestinians killed within 10 days.

All these measures have been explicitly conducted beneath a new campaign the Israeli government has waged in light of the bipolar new world order, with Part II being constructed as, and popularly (mis)titled, the "war against terror." Israel is intent upon framing itself as the victim of "terrorist aggression," and Sharon has even gone so far as to say that the Taliban are the Palestinian Authority (PA) and [PA President Yasser] Arafat is Israel's bin Laden. Israel seeks to capitalize upon the false comparison by exploiting the absence of a "third way" in the "with us or against us" war against terror.

Any attempts to elucidate the nuances of gray—let alone speak of the lucid reality of a people under occupation that have a right to resist it—are being swept away in what has fast become an international barrage against the most elementary human values, freedoms, and rights. In the absence of international support, both governmental and grassroots, for the Palestinian struggle to achieve their national rights to self-determination, an end to the Israeli military occupation, and the return of the Palestinian refugees to their homeland, from which they were expelled 53 years prior—all of which, I might add, is codified in a litany of United Nations (UN) resolutions and the Fourth Geneva convention—Israel can and has gotten away with its new policies.

TIKVA: After the short shock at the human catastrophe of the September 11 attacks, Israel went back to its traditional, self-centered, morally insensitive approach to foreign disasters and focused mainly on examining the implications of the attacks on its own war against the Palestinian people. Both Israeli "left" and "right" have long ago accepted fully the hegemonic establishment of the U.S. as the dominant global empire. Therefore, the majority of the Israeli population could easily adopt the presentation of the antiterror war as the war for "democracy and enlightenment."

Moreover, there was no need here to manufacture national unity and feelings of the urgency of security issues, as has been the case in the United States. Israeli society has been united since the founding of the Jewish Zionist state (and in decades before) around the Zionist culture of statism, which has cultivated the supremacy of "security" over individual human rights and has demonized any opposition to Zionist colonialism in the name of "national security." This political culture has granted full legitimacy to the legal basis for implementing the violation of human rights whenever the state needed, in the form of the "antiterror" laws which were legislated under the "emergency situation" declared by the British Mandate and which is valid to this day.

The Israeli public discourse also very easily adopted the argument that the Arabs are the cause of terrorism which now threatens the security of the entire world as it has been threatening Israel since its foundation. And the analogy which was made between the Taliban and the Palestinian Authority (Arafat is "our bin Laden") of course led to the conclusion that the war against the Palestinian resistance should be intensified with the help of the "enlightened" world, as well as the war against Iraq and other

Arab states which have not yet accepted the role which the U.S. had assigned to the Jewish Zionist state in the "new Middle East."

Five weeks after the September 11 attacks, Minister of Tourism Rehavam Ze'evi, the most blatantly racist Israeli leader, was assassinated by members of the military wing of the Popular Front for the Liberation of Palestine (PFLP) in a retaliation attack for the assassination six weeks prior of Abu Ali Mustafa, the PFLP general secretary and a member of the historic leadership of the Palestinian national movement. Both the "antiterror war" and the killing of Ze'evi served now as excuses for Israel to unleash a murderous reoccupation of Palestinian towns and villages in Area A (putatively under full Palestinian control), to intensify the assassination policy against Palestinian activists and leaders, and to strengthen the sieges and curfews imposed all over the 1967 Occupied Territories.

These brutal atrocities have been in accord with the strategic aim accepted by the majority of the Israeli government and backed by the U.S. administration—namely, to defeat the Intifada and ultimately to force the Palestinians to surrender to the U.S. and Israel's dictates and relinquish their national aspirations.

WHEN THE U.S. built its coalition for war, it made noises about supporting a Palestinian state. In the aftermath of the December 1, 2001, Hamas bombings, the U.S. has given a green light to the most brutal repression Israel can administer in the Occupied Territories. Why?

TIKVA: It is true that in the first period following September 11, Sharon's attempt to use the war against terror in order to advance his own terror was perceived by the U.S. as a threat which could undermine the coalition for the war in Afghanistan. Bush thus felt the need to issue a statement in support of the establishment of a "Palestinian state"—an old, empty slogan which has been already accepted in the past by even Sharon himself, who repeated it again close after the declaration of Bush.

The Palestinian state, as is well known by now, is not meant to be more than a number of fragmented, autonomous enclaves, separated by Israeli settlements, which were designed to ensure Israel's control of those enclaves with the help of the Palestinian rulers in suppressing any resistance inside these enclaves. The declaration for a Palestinian state was accompanied with the misleading message about a "new" U.S. plan.

By the first week of December, it became apparent that Sharon's consistently provocative policy had succeeded in bringing about his long-aspired goal of receiving a U.S. green light to drown the Intifada in rivers of blood, even if this requires bringing about the collapse of Arafat's regime. In the last few months, the operational plans "Field of Thorns" for the West Bank and "Field of Living" for the Gaza Strip, both published five years ago, have been replaced by more updated versions, which are ready for realization upon short notice after the relevant order is given.

The morning after Sharon declared the PA "an entity which supports terror," with Bush's blessing, the path for the most brutal military operations and inhuman atrocities was opened. This is the right time to remind our readers of some of the recent provocations systematically committed by Sharon's government, which were intended to lead to this frightening stage—namely, strengthening the oppression and collective punishment on civilians and the assassination of political and military activists, with the aim of escalating the military confrontation, thus creating the justification for crushing the Intifada and burying the Oslo process.

All of Israel's provocations have been accompanied with the hope that Arafat will finally disappear from the scene, provided that Israel is not held responsible for that. However, after the recent series of Hamas military operations at the beginning of December—in which 26 Israelis were killed and more than 200 wounded—this condition is no longer applicable.

Bush's statement, following his meeting with Sharon on December 2, that "Israel has the right to defend itself," indicates that the U.S. has lifted the "limitations" it had placed upon Israeli military operations since the outbreak of the Intifada and has granted Israel the legitimacy to launch its own "war against terror," including doing away with the rule of Arafat unless he proves very soon that he is able and willing to suppress the Intifada.

During the weekend prior to [U.S. special envoy Retired General Anthony] Zinni's arrival on November 26, the Israeli army committed brutal attacks against Palestinians. The Israeli attacks aimed to elicit retaliatory operations, which were believed to pave the way to Sharon's meeting with Bush, who would hopefully confirm U.S. approval for the "big hit" for which Sharon has been waiting so long. Twenty Palestinians were killed in the West Bank and Gaza Strip, among them five children from the Astal family in Khan Younis refugee camp.

However, the biggest provocative operation was the assassination of Mahmoud Abu Hannoud, a senior leader of Hamas's military wing and highly respected among the Palestinian public. As *Ha'aretz* correspondent Dani Rubinstein reported, "[Hannoud's] assassination was performed with the explicit intention to provoke Hamas and to bring about retaliatory terror operations by the Islamic organizations." Moreover, Abu Hannoud's assassination was committed after two and a half months in which, following the September 11 attacks, Hamas agreed to a partial cessation to their military operations, especially suicide bomb attacks inside Israel, in order to help the PA be part of the "international coalition which fights terror." And, indeed, in this period, a significant decrease in Hamas military operations took place.

However, precisely due to this, the relative quiet had to be stopped. Indeed, soon came the Hamas retaliation operations in Haifa and Jerusalem in which 26 Israelis were killed and dozens wounded. The harvest yielded was enough to satisfy Sharon for a while. Although Bush insisted on not killing Arafat yet, the lifting of many limitations on Israel's military operations is doomed to further escalate the bloody confrontation, thus leading Sharon to the "promised land."

HOW HAVE Palestinians in the Occupied Territories responded to this new wave of repression?

TOUFIC: With the assassination of Rehavam Ze'evi on October 17, 2001, Sharon gained an opportunity to "turn the dial up a notch," targeting the greatest enemy to Israel's apartheid solution for Palestine: Palestinian popular support for the Intifada. With the pretext secured after Ze'evi's assassination, Israel thus sought to inflict increasingly deeper costs on the civilian population and their sense of determination and stability, while ruthlessly targeting the activists themselves who embody these popular aspirations.

In addition (and consistent with Israeli responses throughout the Intifada), it also targeted PA legitimacy internationally ("Arafat is a terrorist"; "the PA are the Taliban") and locally by undermining PA sovereignty with deep and lengthy incursions into Area A and bombing of PA facilities.

As though this weren't enough, Israel also sought to weaken the Intifada by navigating a strategy that flushed out those elements within Palestinian society and the PA that have interests (be they economic, political, or military) in a post-Arafat era and are capable of influencing political decision making today in the direction of direct PA intervention in (and possible cessation of) the Intifada.

The trail of devastation left in the wake of Sharon's post–Ze'evi assassination campaign was unprecedented in its scope and scale. Within 24 hours of the assassination, Israel had invaded and partially reoccupied six of the eight West Bank Palestinian cities. By the time of the final withdrawal from Jenin on November 27, 182 Palestinians were killed. Eighty-eight Palestinians alone were killed in the month of October; 54 in November. The drawn-out incursions showed classic Zionist fingerprints of sowing terror among the civilian population. Bethlehem witnessed 24 of its residents (including four children and two women) killed throughout the course of 10 days, and $17 million in damage, especially to the Aida and Azzeh refugee camps.

It was precisely the unrepentant Israeli campaign against both Palestinian civilians and Intifada activists that regalvanized what had to be described as popular fatigue with the Intifada, given the heavy toll Palestinian society has paid throughout the past 15 months. This sentiment was compounded by a popular intuition that the internal Palestinian position regarding the Intifada needed to be seriously addressed and defined, especially in the wake of the PA killing of three demonstrators in Gaza (protesting the U.S. bombardment of Afghanistan), and the "flirtatious" insinuations that the PA might be willing to return to the days of political arrests.

This popular fear emerged in the wake of Ze'evi's assassination, when approximately 60 activists, primarily from the PFLP, as well as from the Islamic Jihad, were arrested by [PA West Bank security head] Jibril Rajoub's Preventive Security apparatus. The same apparatus also arrested prominent Islamic Jihad activist Mohammed Tawalbeh from the Jenin refugee camp on November 14, promptly whisking him away to Nablus. The event aroused a 3,000-strong popular demonstration in front of the governor's headquarters in Jenin, where the Preventive Security Service has its offices, resulting in several PA cars being burned, rocks thrown, and even rumors of a tossed grenade.

Similar dissatisfaction with political arrests was also seen in the Gaza Strip. Head of [Gaza] Preventive Security, Mohammed Dahlan, had 80 Preventive Security Force officers in southern Gaza openly disobey arrest orders, and 15 senior commanders threatened to resign if a policy of political arrest was pursued. There were even rumors that Dahlan himself presented his resignation to Arafat over the affair but later rescinded it after it was ignored. Overall, the message was clear: A return to political arrest would not be accepted by the Palestinian street (and possibly wide sectors within the PA security establishment) and threatened to spark violent internal dissent.

Despite these internal uncertainties, it was the killing of five children in Khan Younis and 13-year-old Kifah Ubeid from the Deheishe refugee camp in Bethlehem on November 25, 2001, that forced Palestinians to consider a basic fact concerning their bleak reality: After 15 months of Intifada, their children are still being killed doing the simplest of things, such as walking to school. This reality caused Palestinian society to make the grim decision to push forward with the Intifada, and that, despite all its contradictions, inefficiency, disorganization, and multi-headedness, the Intifada is preferable to a future where their children's children will be subject to living under occupation.

The stick and carrot ultimatum of "arrest and be saved" no longer holds any weight—certainly not among the Palestinian street and political parties, and increasingly so in wide sectors of the PA security personnel (at least among the lower cadre). This creates the situation whereby, even if Arafat or high-ranking PA personnel were intent upon conducting a serious campaign of political arrests, the popular opposition is so unanimous that the move would be akin to political suicide. Though this may indeed be Israel's intention, it is unlikely Arafat would ever give Israel the pleasure of a Palestinian civil war.

While these are moments of great anxiety, frustration, and gritting teeth within Palestinian society, one is also tempted to wonder if this is the opening stage in the birth of genuine reevaluation of the national trajectory—one that does away with any of the Oslo process presumptions which call for the amputation of Palestinian rights through the creation of a Palestinian "partner for peace," willing to collaborate with Israeli dictates for its apartheid solution for Palestine.

While it will be steeped in the blood of hundreds of Palestinians—a thought so incomprehensible, so disturbingly blunt, unmasked, and drenched in the silence of the international community and the Arab regimes—it will also prove to be a moment of truth which impels Palestinians, in due time, to give birth to a movement that unflinchingly engages and unrepentantly reflects the popular Palestinian national aspirations both within the homeland and in the diaspora.

ARAFAT AND other PA leaders still talk about restarting the peace process with greater U.S. involvement. Will anything come from this?

TOUFIC: The Palestinian people do not have any illusions about the fact that a "return to the negotiations"—which has the air of sounding so benign, but in reality is completely destructive to Palestinian rights—will bring about more despair, confiscated land, and settlements. In fact, the current Intifada has much to do with Palestinian rejection of the negotiated process, which throughout the course of the 10-year "peace process," beginning in Madrid after the 1991 Gulf War, gave Israel the opportunity and time to deepen and consolidate its control over the 1967 occupied Palestinian territories of the West Bank and Gaza Strip. The negotiated process was nothing less than a guise behind which Israel doubled its settlements, built military installations and bypass roads throughout the 1967 Occupied Territories, cantonized Palestinians in Area A, and effectively made the emergence of a viable independent state on these lands impossible.

It is also important to note here that there exists a class of Palestinians within the PA that definitively seeks a return to the negotiations, thus providing the U.S.-Israeli pantomime its Palestinian interlocutors. This class, well seasoned throughout the peace process and showered with benefits—monopolies, privileges of movement, trade, and VIP status—is serious in its calls for a return to negotiations because they seek to return to the days before the outbreak of the Intifada, which has been destabilizing to their interests. In this sense, they consistently try to find ways to push forward their agenda, emphasizing the futility of resisting Israeli measures, obsequiously courting the intervention of the Americans, and trying to titillate the U.S. and Israel [with pledges] that they are willing to arrest Palestinian activists and suppress the Intifada if negotiations are to restart. Unfortunately, it is primarily these people that foreign and Western journalists address, thus making it appear as though Palestinians are willing to accept a "negotiated process"—which they fear means a repeat of the might-makes-right previous 10-year peace process.

TIKVA: All these months, Sharon has determinedly adhered to the mantra of "seven days of cease-fire" on the Palestinian side as a condition to the implementation of the Tenet and Mitchell reports.[2] Namely, "seven days of cease-fire" will be followed by six weeks of "cooling down," which will lead to the "steps of building trust," the core of which is the freezing of settlement construction (which supposedly is to lead to negotiations based on the principles of the Oslo agreement). However, only on the surface can Sharon's demands be considered irrational, due to the lack of any chance that Arafat can implement a cease-fire without being able to point to some form of political horizon. Is it not precisely because of the lack of such a horizon, implied by [former Israeli Prime Minister Ehud] Barak's suggestions in Camp David, that the Intifada began? Rather, from Sharon's perspective, the seven-day cease-fire is indeed a very rational condition: It has helped him postpone, and even annul, the chance to reach the moment in which he will be forced to freeze settlement construction and thus reveal his commitment to continue Israeli control over most of the Occupied Territories.

The joint positions of Bush and Sharon regarding the need to crush Palestinian resistance by military force also found expression in the nature and aims of the new U.S. delegation to the area, headed by Zinni, and part of [Secretary of State Colin] Powell's political initiative to "bring both sides to the negotiating table." However, the feeling among senior leaders within the Israeli army (making no mistake that their "feelings" are based on reliable information) is that Zinni was sent as a diversionary tactic in order to save time while the U.S. goes to "war against terror."

To make sure that Zinni's mission is confined to attempts to contain the fire and not to allow it to "deteriorate" to political affairs, Sharon rejected the demand of [Israeli Foreign Minister Shimon] Peres to head the Israeli delegation. Instead, he nominated Retired Major General Meir Dagan, thus emphasizing the sheer "technical-military" mandate of Zinni.

The nomination of Dagan indicates not only the specific aims of Sharon regarding Zinni's mission; Dagan's appalling personal history in initiating and implementing the murderous policies of the infamous Israeli undercover units is evidence of the extent to which the killers who executed these policies are today part of the Israeli mainstream and are considered honorable members of the diplomatic corps. The general acceptance of this nomination indicates a change in Israeli society, the great majority of which has come to support Sharon's policies.

WHAT WILL happen in the Middle East and Palestine if the U.S. expands its "war on terrorism" to Iraq or elsewhere?

TOUFIC: Each case is different, though certain things remain basic. A U.S.-led strike against Iraq or any other Arab country would strike far closer to the heart of Arab sympathies than what has been taking place so far in Afghanistan. The Taliban regime is non-Arab and considered extreme by the standards of the Arab masses, though this fact does not mean they support the U.S.-led assault. Rather, the Arab masses oppose it, sympathizing with the plight of the Afghan people and critically viewing it as another imperial attempt to set up a puppet regime in Afghanistan and get a military foothold in Central Asia.

They furthermore support bin Laden's denunciation of Israeli and American interests in the region, which support the corrupt dictators of the Arab world that provide cheap oil for the U.S. But they stop short of [bin Laden's] means (implementation of Islamic law) as the solution for the problems that plague the Middle East. What we see, then, is an ambiguity wide enough to be exploited by the U.S., which permits their campaign in Afghanistan (with the support of the pro-U.S. Arab regimes), particularly in the absence of organized popular opposition throughout the Arab world.

In the case of a U.S.-led strike against an Arab country, this ambiguity would be removed or greatly reduced. One should not overlook the remnants within the Arab masses of what can be termed a latent Nasserite-like Pan-Arabism, which emphasizes the unity of the Arab peoples and is threatening to imperial interests in the region. This involves a call for freedom from direct or indirect foreign imperial control and the setting of an independent Arab agenda, including for the crucial oil reserves beneath the Arab world's soil. This was demonstrated with the outbreak of the current Intifada, which witnessed large popular demonstrations throughout the Arab world.

In the case of Iraq, there is wide consensus among the Arab peoples of the brutality of the U.S.-led sanctions and great sympathy with the Iraqi people for the suffering they have endured. A U.S.-led campaign against Iraq would ignite a wave of sympathy that would stoke latent sympathies that the Iraqi people are already the victims of a cruel, unjust, imperial-led campaign. The issue does not only end with the Iraqi people and their suffering, but taps into a wider Arab sentiment that the U.S. is consistently attempting to bash the head of any Arab regime that is defiant of U.S. imperialist interests in the region—from opposing Israel's role as the local bulldog or opposing the American military presence in the Gulf. An attack against Iraq would thus set a course that would flesh out the contradictions within the pro-American Arab regimes and their populaces.

In the case of strikes against other Arab regimes—Lebanon, Syria, Libya, Sudan, perhaps Algeria—the reaction would be similar. Much, of course, will depend upon the nature of the justification/propaganda campaign the U.S. initiates. Here, however, it is important to emphasize a crucial point. One must not forget that the U.S. already commands an advantageous position within the region. It is thus not to U.S. advantage to threaten this position unless the "threat" genuinely merits it.

In my opinion, genuine organized threats do not really exist, though in U.S. thinking, one can never be too cautious. What we see then in Afghanistan is a tremendous display of power that seeks to emphasize American "seriousness" in any efforts at organized resistance to U.S. hegemony. This was seen in the U.S.-led campaign in Kosovo and previously in the 1991 Gulf War.

In U.S. thinking, perhaps the time has come for America's opponents (be they Arab governments or Arab peoples) to "re-remember" this lesson, especially in light of significant but somewhat small retreats for American interests in the region with the outbreak of the current Intifada and the victory of the Lebanese resistance in liberating southern Lebanon from 18 years of Israeli occupation. In this sense, the "war against terror" in some cases in the Middle East may be a paper tiger which has the same effect of keeping the Arabs in line through sheer fear—which is superior, if possible, to sheer force.

With this said, however, one can never be too sure what a pro-nonrenewable fuel government as the Bush administration may become involved in, be it through the influence of pro-industrial, defense, and Zionist lobbyists, and which so far has been able to comfortably sell war to its people beneath the ever-malleable "war on terror."

IN YOUR view, what is the solution to the crisis? Is there hope for peace in the Middle East?

TOUFIC: There has always been a hope for peace in the Middle East if the basic UN resolutions and international humanitarian conventions are observed. Sadly this has not been the case, primarily out of consistent Israeli rejection of implementation of these resolutions and conventions, particularly the rejection of the right to return of what are today 5 million Palestinian refugees who were forced out and exiled from their homes in historic Palestine in what was nothing less than a Zionist ethnic cleansing campaign in 1948.

The problem, though complicated, relates to the fact that the Zionist movement has always sought the creation of an exclusive Jewish homeland in Palestine—a land that was inhabited by the Arab-Palestinian people. The Zionist desire to establish an exclusive Jewish state, together with imperial collusion in this matter, has meant a consistent history of Palestinian dispossession from their homeland, beginning in 1948 and continuing to this very day. The issue thus has to do with the nature of the Zionist movement and state, which a priori institutionalizes the primacy of Jewish rights over non-Jewish rights, be they individual or collective—especially in the latter case when they relate to national collective rights and, most importantly, to land. As long as Israel remains a Zionist state, it is impossible to think of scenarios that could bring about hope, because Zionism itself preserves fundamental inequalities between people.

True hope can only be seen in the establishment of a system that justly addresses the historical roots of the conflict, involves implementation of UN resolutions and the abandoning of the primacy of Jewish rights over non-Jewish rights—in essence, de-Zionizing Israel. Once this is done, fertile ground exists for a system that respects the equality and rights of all people, traditions, and religions who hold Palestine dear. This, however, is not possible without a process that concretely aims at amending the historical injustices and plight of the Palestinian people. Only then can the possibility of a secular, democratic Palestine come about that creatively addresses the needs of its citizens.

TIKVA: The U.S. is the power which now initiates the stirring of the region through the war against terrorism, which the possibilities of its disastrous developments are yet unknown. The aim of this war is to establish U.S. hegemony in the Middle East and thus pave the way for harnessing the region to the capitalist globalization processes that the Oslo agreements were designed to ensure. These agreements were believed to solve the Palestinian "problem," which threatens to "destabilize" the region, within a bantustan state[3] and to sustain an apartheid regime throughout entire

Palestine, under the rule of the Jewish Zionist state that is still an important strategic asset for the United States.

U.S. policy in the Middle East, which supports the oppressive Arab regimes and Israel's military occupation and which, together with Israel, has prevented any diplomatic settlement in accord with UN decisions, denies any hope for a genuine peace between Palestinians and Israelis, as well as in the Middle East at large.

The Oslo framework granted the Israeli Ashkenazi[4] bourgeoisie a significant role in the economic division of labor of the "new Middle East." Despite its following the neoliberal policies dictated by international banks, it enjoys in Israel a secure position incomparable to any of the European countries that have also demolished their welfare systems and replaced them with a "free economy."

All Jewish political parties have been representing the interests of capital. Not only is there no difference between the neoliberal ideology of right and left, but it is precisely the Labour Party, which has led the support for Oslo, that serves as the political home for the Ashkenazi capitalists. They use the Zionist ideology, with the notion of the Jewish state at its center, to depoliticize and unite the Jewish population, including the working class, behind the Zionist colonialist project.

The [working class] is split along national and ethnic lines, with the Palestinian citizens of Israel and the Jewish Misrahim[5] comprising the majority of the lower layers of the proletariat, lacking any independent organization, even in terms of trade unions fighting for minimal workers' rights. The past powerful Histadrut,[6] which traditionally served the needs of Zionism in cooperation with Jewish capital, has been dismantled from all its economic assets, which in the past made it the second-biggest employer to the state itself, and is now serving the sheer interests of the "Big Committees," which comprise mainly the Ashkenazi elite of the organized working class.

The only genuine democratic forces in the Israeli political scene that challenge the Jewish Zionist state and undermine it in their daily politics are emerging among the Palestinian national minority inside Israel. The National Democratic Assembly Party, headed by MK[7] Azmi Bishara, has been playing a central role in this process by taking a step forward from the traditional demand for "equality of citizen rights" to that of "collective rights as a national minority." This demand negates the very foundations of the Jewish state, as has been emphasized again and again by Barak: "We, as a Jewish state, can agree to equality of individual rights of Arabs which does not harm the democratic Jewish-Zionist state. But the Jewish state cannot accept the aspiration to define another national collective identity within it, with the long run vision of 'a state of all its citizens' held by extremists."

The strengthening of the national identity of the 1948 Palestinians and their growing solidarity and cooperation with their brothers in the 1967 Occupied Territories was indicated in their joint declaration and participation in the Durban [South Africa] UN Conference Against Racism [in September 2001]. There, they protested against their oppression within the same apartheid framework of the Zionist state. Indeed, the Palestinians inside Israel may grow to become a threat to the "stability" within "the only democracy in the Middle East," and, through that, to the entire region as well. The question of Palestine has been for decades defined only in terms of the 1967 Occupied Territories, which it is said can be solved in an independent state "alongside Israel."

The Jewish nature of the state of Israel, which is the cornerstone of U.S. policy towards the Middle East, and which implies the rejection of the right of return of Palestinian refugees, has never been really challenged by the international community. The assumption, however, that underlined the 1947 UN decision to partition Palestine—namely, that the atomization and marginalization of the Palestinian people can easily be achieved—has been refuted during the last year. After more than 50 years since the establishment of the state of Israel, we have been witness to the return of the old concern of imperialism and Zionism that an uncontrolled uprising of a united Palestinian people will stir the oppressed masses in the Arab countries and in the entire Middle East.

That is the reason for the war that has been opened recently by the Israeli establishment against the Palestinian MKs and the Palestinian minority of Israel at large. Focusing largely on MK Azmi Bishara, his parliamentary immunity was stripped [in November 2001] in order to put him on trial for "supporting terror and inciting terror" as was expressed in a speech in which he supported the Hezbollah struggle against the Israeli occupation in southern Lebanon. This is the first time that an MK has been stripped of his immunity because of his political ideas. This is definitely a new front that has been opened against the Zionist implementation of an apartheid regime all over Mandatory Palestine,[8] which may prove to be as important as the struggle of the Palestinians in the 1967 Occupied Territories.

The continued military attack on the Intifada, which is not resisted fiercely by the Palestinian Authority, may indeed result in the collapse of Arafat's rule. The challenge from the Palestinian people to Arafat is growing daily. However, it well may be that the forces which can build a popular liberation struggle are indeed absent from the current political scene.

On the one hand, there is a comprador bourgeoisie,[9] which is dependent on Israel and thus has no interest in leading a liberation struggle. On the other hand, there is the lack of real left forces which oppose the PA policy of integration into the imperialist reordering of the world and that can do more than propose an "improved" Palestinian bantustan state, which is the PFLP's strategy today. This situation may push the masses deeper into the bosom of the Islamic movement and strengthen the trends that took the present Intifada away from the mass popular form it had in the first two months—that is to say, the adoption of the strategy of military operations waged by small groups while the masses are merely passive observers, even though they will morally support the fighters.

Some of the heads of the Israeli army insist that the military victory which they think is possible can be maintained by nominating the more "cooperative" heads of the units of [PA] Preventive Security to rule the different autonomous enclaves. No doubt, they are already working towards [that solution] with some of them.

Whatever alternative will emerge after Arafat, the first stages of that era will probably be characterized by chaos and not by a wide mass organization for a systematic struggle against Zionism and imperialism. No doubt, many in the Israeli establishment are hoping for that to happen, and their policy, supported by the U.S., may inevitably lead to it.

The hope for peace in the Middle East is conditioned on the successful defeat of the very U.S. and Israeli "peace" initiatives aimed at gaining "stability" at the expense of the Palestinian and Arab people in the region. This requires a mass, democratic movement against U.S. imperialism and despotic Arab regimes that hinder economic and social development. Only such a transformation of Palestinian and Arab societies may change the current relation of forces that will lead to a powerful uprising against the Jewish Zionist state and U.S. interests in the region.

In Palestine, a joint mass struggle of Palestinians in the 1967 territories and inside Israel ("the 1948 Palestinians") should be directed against the emergent apartheid regime, whose war against both is doomed to escalate. The right of return should be raised consistently—both because it is the refugees' right and because it implies the struggle for transforming the nature of the Jewish state, paving the way to a secular, democratic state in all of Palestine.

The anti-imperialist dimension of the Palestinian national struggle must be strengthened to join the progressive forces in the Arab world in a systematic struggle against capitalist globalization of the Middle East. As we may predict, in the long run, a determined democratic struggle against imperialism and Zionist colonialism will inevitably result, with a growing consciousness that socialism is the only alternative to the barbaric oppression of the Palestinian people and the Arab masses. That is the only hope for a lasting peace.

---

1 Under the Oslo accords, Area A is the part of the Occupied Territories that was supposed to come under full Palestinian control.

2 U.S.-sponsored plans to end the Intifada. Former senator George Mitchell and CIA Director George Tenet led the teams, which issued reports in 2001.

3 Bantustans were created by the apartheid South African state as "homelands" for Africans. They were economically reliant on the white apartheid government, which appointed Black collaborators to run them. Bantustans were overthrown and/or abolished with the end of apartheid in 1994.

4 Jews with family origins in Europe or North America.

5 Poor and working-class Jews whose families came from Middle Eastern countries.

6 The General Organization of Hebrew Workers in the Land of Israel, founded in 1920, is often described as a trade union, but it was not independent of the Zionist state or the labor Zionist parties. In pre-state days, it organized Jewish workers to displace Arab workers. It later built up huge holdings in factories, banks, and other capitalist enterprises.

7 "MK" is the abbreviation for "Member of the Knesset," the Israeli parliament.

8 "Mandatory Palestine" refers to the territory originally mandated to the British in 1922 and encompasses all of modern Israel.

9 "Comprador bourgeoisie" is a term first used by Mao and the Chinese Communist Party in the 1930s to describe elements in the capitalist class of a colonized country that collaborate with the colonial oppressor.

PALESTINIAN DEMOCRATIC FRONT
AND ISRAELI SOCIALIST ORGANIZATION

A joint Arab-Israeli statement, 1967

THE FOLLOWING statement appeared for the first time in Eng-lish in the London Bulletin of the Bertrand Russell Peace Founda-tion in August 1967. It represented an effort by Israeli and Palestinian revolutionaries to present a common analysis of the 1967 war, in which Israel seized the West Bank, Gaza, the Sinai Peninsula, and the Golan Heights. As in its earlier statement in op-position to Israel's war, this statement puts forward a common po-litical response to the crisis. Its opposition to a "Zionist Bantustan" remains relevant today.

The Israeli Socialist Organization (ISO), founded in 1962, orga-nized Jews and Arabs in an anti-Zionist, revolutionary Marxist or-ganization. The ISO became known as "Matzpen" ("compass") in reference to its newspaper. The ISO functioned as an organization until the mid-1970s, when it experienced a damaging split. Today, many of its former members remain active in solidarity work with Palestinians or in organizing immigrant workers in Israel.

The Palestinian Democratic Front was a clandestine group of Palestinian socialists operating in Jordan prior to Israel's seizure of the West Bank. It worked with ISO members for several years before the outbreak of the 1967 war.

Activists from both organizations continued to develop their ideas—applying revolutionary Marxism to Israeli, Palestinian, and Middle Eastern politics—in the journal Khamsin, published *in the 1970s and 1980s.*

*We reprint this statement as an example of the political tradi-
tion in which the* International Socialist Review *stands.*

WE, THE Palestinian Democratic Front and the Israeli Socialist
Organization, published our first joint statement on the recent crisis in the Middle East on June 3, prior to the Israeli attack. We
stated there our principled, internationalist position with regard to
the history, the pre-war situation, and the imminent war. We now
reaffirm our first statement and follow up with a second one, stat-
ing our position with regard to the situation created by this war.

The predominant political phenomenon of our times is the
struggle of the people in the unindustrialized continents—Asia,
Africa, and Latin America—to free themselves from the political
and economic domination of the industrialized imperialist powers.
Every other political phenomenon is judged, first of all, according
to its relation to this worldwide conflict. In this context, there is
little doubt that the recent war in the Middle East, and its outcome, have served the interests of imperialism in this area and
throughout the world. Can the consequences of the Israeli attack
be isolated from the crushing of the anti-imperialist struggle in Indonesia or the U.S. intervention in Vietnam? It is evident, for example, from a recent statement of de Gaulle that even the
imperialists think that it cannot.

In the last months before the war, the anti-imperialist policies
of the Syrian government came increasingly into conflict with the
oil monopolies in the Middle East. This political background enabled Israel to launch an air attack on Syria on April 7, and
threaten Syria with a military invasion. Nasser, who opportunisti-
cally steers the anti-imperialist interests and sentiments of the
Arab masses in nationalist channels, found himself, under the
pressure of circumstances, forced to support the Syrian regime
against this threat. Moreover, American oil monopolies in Saudi
Arabia, worried lest the anti-imperialists in Yemen and Aden win
their struggle and endanger their interests, did their best to play
Egypt and Israel against each other so as to weaken Nasser's sup-

port to the anti-imperialists in South Arabia. Nasser, being a nationalist and an opportunist, did not hesitate in the circumstances to sign a pact with Hussein, the well-known puppet of imperialism, ignoring the contradictions between the regimes and their objectives. Even worse, he resorted to racialist propaganda against the Israeli population.

We, as internationalists, fully support the struggle of the Arab masses for political, economic, and social liberation against the recent and all other aggressions; this does not mean that we support the nationalist leaders who purport to carry out this struggle. We would like to remind those who lend uncritical support to such nationalist leaders of the examples of Chiang Kai-chek, Attaturk, Sukarno. The struggle for genuine political and social liberation can be won only under a principled, internationalist leadership.

After WWI, Sherrif Hussein and his sons Faisal and Abdalian (Hussein's grandfather and predecessor on the throne) promised the Arab masses that they would achieve independence by serving British imperialism. Between the two world wars, Haj Emin el-Husseini, Fawzi el-Kaukii, and others (and during WWII, Rashid Ali el-Katlani, General Aziz el-Masri, and others) sought to do so by serving the interests of Nazism and Italian fascism (some nationalist leaders even named Mussolini "Saif ul Islam"). Now we are asked to believe that the nationalists—the Nasserites, the Baathists, and the nationalist left which trails behind them—will carry this struggle to its end and even bring about a socialist revolution. The recent "all Arab" alliance of the "progressive" El-Attassi, the anti-imperialist Nasser, the pro-imperialist Hussein, and the racialist Shukairy fits into this pattern of failure all too clearly.

As for the Zionist leadership of Israel, we have already pointed out in our first statement that the alliance between political Zionism and first Ottoman, then British, and nowadays U.S. imperialism was not an accident. Political Zionism, because of its colonialist history and because of its principled segregationist policies towards the Arabs of Palestine, has a vital interest in preserving imperialist influence in the Middle East and has acted as an integral part of the imperialist power system. Political Zionism was always lined up against the struggle of the indigenous population of Palestine to liberate itself from foreign domination. Weizmann's pact with Faisal (1921), Ben-Gurion's secret pact with Abdallah (1949), his participation in the Suez aggression, and the recent attack are merely highlights of one and the same policy, which—in the recent case—because of the racialist propaganda of radio Cairo, Damascus, Amman was disguised as a defensive policy. While this propaganda led the Israeli population to believe it was fighting for its survival, the Zionist leaders of Israel took their chance to realize a lifelong dream of territorial aggrandizement. The policies of annexing new territory, especially Old Jerusalem, are not new. They were always latent in the Zionist aims, and could be expected to show themselves when the opportunity arose. This opportunity was presented to them by Arab nationalism.

This round in the anti-imperialist struggle can be summed up by saying that while the Israeli people were lined up behind the wrong leadership on the wrong side of the barricade, the Arab people were lined up behind the wrong leadership on the right side of the barricade.

Internationalists inside Israel must tirelessly explain that as long as the state is lined up with the imperialist system there can be no peace or normalization of relations with the Arab world. The Arab masses will, eventually, sweep away every ruler and policy—Arab or otherwise—supporting imperialism. Moreover, as long as Israel maintains its Zionist segregationist policies against the Arabs, any talk of "peace" is hypocrisy or, at best, self-illusion. There can be no normalization of relations with segregationist and pro-imperialist policies. A dictated "peace" or a "Pax Americana" with Hussein is no remedy to this conflict. The temporary setback to the anti-imperialist struggle brought about by this war will soon pass, and the struggle will be resumed with new vigor and under a better leadership. There can be no coexistence between imperialism and the anti-imperialist movement; it is doubtful whether there can even be a respite. The Zionist and pro-imperialist policies of the Israeli leadership antagonize not just this or that Arab leader, but the entire population of the Arab world. This fundamental antagonism cannot be overcome by military victories.

Internationalists inside the Arab world must tirelessly explain that the nationalist leadership cannot be relied upon to fight resolutely against imperialism, that it is always tempted to seek compromise or resort to opportunist policies, as the Nasser-Hussein pact has shown; that by resorting to racialist propaganda, this leadership commits a crime against the anti-imperialist struggle; that by borrowing imperialist ideology and morals to further its own aims, it defeats these aims and defiles them. Shukairy's calls to kill all Jews, women and children included, from radio Cairo are not some "minor defect" which may now be forgotten. Even Syria, considered by some to be the "most progressive" Arab state, spoke of destroying Israel, "neglecting" to mention what would happen to the Jewish population. Under no circumstances do we forgive such crimes or, for tactical reasons, abstain from denouncing them. Those who do so cause grave damage to the anti-imperialist struggle. As for Israel, every attempt of Arab nationalists to destroy the state by force only consolidates the entire Israeli population behind the Zionist leadership. Israel will be changed from the inside by its own anti-Zionist internationalists who will, in due time, join ranks with the internationalists in the Arab world in a joint struggle against imperialism and for establishing a genuine socialist republic throughout the Middle East.

Faced with the state of affairs created by the Israeli attack we say:

- We oppose all territorial annexations brought about by this war, but we find it necessary to point out that the root of the trouble in the Middle East is not a territorial issue; the roots of the problem lie in the existence of a segregationist and pro-imperialist power structure in Israel which dispossessed an entire people of their human and political rights; and in the inability of Arab nationalist policies to deal with it.

- A dictated Israeli peace, a "Pax Americana," between Israel and Hussein, whether public or secret, and similar Western arrangements will not solve the conflict between Israel and the Arab states; they will only defer it.

- The creation of a Zionist Bantustan for the Palestinian Arabs while maintaining the segregationist policies towards them will not solve the "Palestine problem" any more than a South African Bantustan can solve the problems resulting from the existence of a racialist state in South Africa.

The only viable solution is:

- To abolish completely all segregationist measures of the Zionists against the Palestinians (this includes the implementation of their right to repatriation) and turning Israel into a normal state of its own population.

- Active participation of the non-Zionist Israel in the anti-imperialist struggle of the Arab people.

- Enabling the Palestinians to decide themselves about their political fate.

Knowing that the present rulers, on both sides, have no intention of implementing these solutions, we have little doubt that the conflict will continue as long as these regimes remain in power. To all those indulging in self-illusions we say: There is no salvation to the political problems of people through policies which, tacitly or overtly, implement measures of economic, social, racial, or national supremacy of one group of people over another.

MOSTAFA OMAR

The Palestinian national liberation movement: A socialist analysis

SINCE THE Oslo accords were signed in 1993, endless rounds of negotiations between the Palestine Liberation Organization (PLO) and Israel have failed to secure an end to the Israeli occupation of the West Bank and Gaza, a Palestinian state, or the right of return for 5 million Palestinian refugees. Moreover, living conditions for the Palestinians in the Occupied Territories have actually deteriorated. Poverty and unemployment have skyrocketed. And Israel has expanded its settlements.[1] In the wake of the September 11, 2001, attacks in the U.S., Israel seized the initiative to implement plans that may lead to the elimination of the "peace process" altogether.

This failure has led a large number of Palestinians to question the PLO's strategy. Many no longer trust that negotiating "partial withdrawals" or "redeployment of troops" will actually lead to a just solution. Many have lost faith in the PLO and its leader, Yasser Arafat. As Palestinian professor and Arafat critic Edward Said put it:

> In the Palestinian case, the tragedy of a dispossessed and militarily occupied people is compounded by a leadership that made a "peace" deal with its more powerful enemy, a deal that serves Israel's strategic purposes by keeping Palestinians, whose land has been practically lost to Zionist conquest, in a state of depression and servitude.... The fact is that by his behavior Mr. Arafat no

longer represents the majority of Palestinians, and now survives without dignity by virtue of U.S., Israeli, and Arab support.[2]

In September 2000, as a result of deteriorating living conditions since Oslo and increasing frustration with the PLO's political impotence, the Palestinians began their second mass uprising in 15 years, the Al-Aqsa Intifada.[3] Since then, hundreds of thousands of Palestinians have taken to the streets of the West Bank and Gaza to confront the Israeli army and settlers directly. Despite brutal repression by Israel and repeated attempts by Arafat to rein in Palestinian anger, the Palestinians have shown, once again, tremendous courage and willingness to make huge sacrifices to win their freedom.[4]

Unfortunately, the heroic struggles of the Al-Aqsa Intifada are insufficient to stop Israel. The Palestinians simultaneously face a number of difficult obstacles: Israel's brutal repression, unconditional U.S. political and military support for Israel, betrayals and repression by the PLO itself, and maneuvers by pro-U.S. Arab regimes to end the Intifada before other Arab workers begin to emulate it.

Although formidable, these obstacles are not insurmountable. But in order for the Palestinians to overcome them, a mass movement needs to be built across the Arab world to challenge both U.S. imperialism and the Arab regimes backed by it. Such a movement could provide the necessary political and economic support for the Palestinians to challenge Israel.

The success of any mass movement in challenging the U.S. and the Arab regimes and supporting the Palestinians against Israel is linked to the question of building a socialist alternative in the Arab world. The case for this alternative starts from the realization that Arab workers, who produce all the oil and wealth in the area, have to fight for real, democratic control over society in order to rid themselves of the miserable conditions imposed by the ruling Arab regimes and the United States.

But a socialist alternative in the Arab world would have to learn from the mistakes of an older generation of radicals that looked to Stalinist Russia and certain "progressive" Arab regimes, such as Syria and Iraq, as models for social change.[5] This means rejecting the compromises with Zionism of the PLO; looking to the struggles of ordinary people in Palestine against Israel; recog-

nizing that solidarity with the Arab working classes, not negotiations, is the way to stop Israel; and fighting for a secular and
democratic Palestine based on equality between Arabs and Jews.

Building a socialist alternative in the Arab world, especially in
Palestine, requires clarity on a number of key political questions.
Why did the PLO surrender to Israel and Washington? Whose class
interests does the PLO represent? Why did many Palestinians turn
to Hamas? What happened to the Palestinian left, the Popular and
the Democratic Fronts for the Liberation of Palestine? Why does
the left tail Arafat's policy? Is it really necessary (or realistic) to
look to the struggles of Arab workers as the way to liberate Palestine?

These questions cannot be properly answered without a reexamination of the history of the Palestinian national liberation
movement, especially of the rise and fall of the PLO and the Palestinian left. Such a reexamination is necessary to achieve theoretical clarity for those of us who want to continue to resist both
Israel and U.S. imperialism. This essay hopes to make a small contribution toward that goal.

The pre-1948 nationalist movement

In the three decades that preceded the 1948 al-Nakbah ("catastrophe"), the Palestinians carried out a brave struggle to resist the
Zionist project of building a Jewish state that would serve as an
outpost for Western imperialism in the Middle East. Throughout
the 1920s and 1930s, the Palestinians challenged Britain's colonial
mandate over Palestine and its policy of facilitating Jewish immigration and settlement. In 1929, Palestinians organized demonstrations and protests against Jewish settlements and businesses, in
what became known as the Al-Baraq Rebellion. The British army
viciously suppressed these protests.[6]

The intensification of Jewish immigration, triggered by the rise
of fascism in Europe during the first half of the 1930s, placed
more pressure on Palestinians. The Palestinians resumed the fight
against British colonialism and Zionism, turning to armed struggle as a means of resistance. Led by the Muslim Brotherhood's
Sheikh Izz al-Din al-Qassam, a network of militias drawn primar-

ily from peasants and urban intellectuals attacked British and Zionist interests all over Palestine.[7] Mandate police killed al-Qassam in a gun battle in 1935, but the armed struggle continued.

In 1936, a mass social struggle joined with the armed struggle. In April, following weeks of clashes between Palestinian protesters and Jewish settlers, Arab dockworkers at the port of Jaffa struck to protest British support for Jewish immigration. Under mass pressure, the Palestinian elite, under the leadership of Jerusalem's Mufti, Hajj Amin Al-Husseini, was forced to call a general strike. Within days, the strike spread to other major Palestinian ports, cities, and villages. All sections of Palestinian Arab society, including workers, peasants, small businesses, and even sections of large business, joined the strike. The strike demanded an end to Jewish immigration, a ban on the sale of land to settlers, and the replacement of the British mandate by a government drawn from the majority population. Palestinians organized a mass civil disobedience campaign and stopped paying taxes to British authorities. Meanwhile, al-Qassam militias attacked British and Zionist interests all over the country.[8]

The general strike lasted for six months, before the British managed to end it with brutal repression. Armed struggle continued for two more years. Eventually, the British army and Zionist militias managed to crush the armed struggle. In total, this mass rebellion (which became known as the 1936 Revolt) lasted for three years.

Despite the Palestinians' heroic struggles and sacrifices, the 1936 Revolt failed. This was attributable to two main factors. First, the poorly armed Palestinian militias were no match for the overwhelming military superiority of the combined British and Zionist forces. Moreover, Zionist displacement of Palestinian workers in strategic workplaces throughout Palestine helped the British to "block Arab nationalist efforts to spread the general strike and fully paralyze the country's economy."[9] Second, fearing a total loss of control over the Palestinian masses, the Palestinian elite, backed by reactionary Arab regimes close to Britain, weakened the rebellion through its compromises with Britain and its constant maneuvers to end the revolt.

Indeed, the conservative role the Palestinian elite played during

the 1920s and 1930s presented many obstacles to the development of a successful struggle against Zionism. This elite, composed of big landowners and merchants, generally opposed British
colonialism and the establishment of a Jewish state. However, two
factors mitigated this elite's opposition to colonialism. On one
hand, different wealthy Palestinian families competed for support
from British authorities to edge out their rivals. On the other
hand, economic ties between the Palestinian elite as a whole and
the other pro-British Arab ruling classes, such as those in Egypt
and Jordan, prompted the Palestinian elite to avoid confrontation
with Britain. This explains, for example, why some members of
the elite called for an end to attacks on Zionist interests during the
Al-Baraq rebellion in 1929, or argued for a disastrous policy of
strengthening relations with Britain to win the latter away from
supporting Zionism. Some Palestinian notables even went so far
as to argue that Britain should maintain its mandate over Palestine
as a last line of defense against Zionism![10]

Indeed, some wealthy families, such as al-Nashashibis and al-
Husseinis, organized different nationalist parties. However, these
families aimed to use the nationalist struggle as a way to advance
their own narrow commercial and political interests. Their ani-
mosity toward each other and their fear of the masses of Palestinian peasants and workers always outweighed their opposition to
British colonialism and Zionism.[11] In other words, the Palestinian
elite was more interested in maintaining its wealth and its ties with
Arab regimes than it was in leading a fight against British colonialism and Zionism.

In contrast, throughout the same period, Palestinian workers
and peasants made enormous sacrifices in the nationalist struggle.
In the cities, workers organized numerous strikes and street
protests. In the countryside, peasants fought bravely despite years
of British terror.

The heroism of these workers and peasants was insufficient to
overcome the conservative influence of the Palestinian elite in the
nationalist struggle. In pre-1948 Palestine, the working class was
still a tiny minority of the population, without much union or political organization. The peasants, on the other hand, lacked the

social cohesion necessary to play an effective political role. These weaknesses meant that the Palestinian masses were ill prepared to take on the giant task of successfully challenging the British army and a well-funded and well-armed Zionist settler movement.

The Palestine Communist Party: A false start

Divided between rival factions in the Palestinian elite, the nationalist movement remained fragmented and weak. Under these circumstances, there was a clear need for a progressive left alternative. Unfortunately, the Palestine Communist Party (PCP), the only socialist organization in Palestine prior to 1948, suffered from serious political weaknesses that prevented it from challenging the leadership and control of the conservative Palestinian elite.

Founded in 1924 with help from the Communist International (Comintern), the PCP aimed to unite Arab and Jewish workers in a struggle to build a socialist Palestine.[12] However, the PCP, like other Communist Parties around the world, ceased to be a revolutionary organization by the early 1930s, following Stalin's ascendancy to power in Russia. Thus, the PCP formulated its policies based on the needs of Russian foreign policy in the Middle East, not on those of workers' struggles against colonialism. This meant that the PCP followed orders from Moscow—even those that led to its isolation from the Arab masses.

Throughout the 1920s and 1930s, party membership remained almost wholly Jewish, owing to its origin in a split from the left-Zionist Socialist Workers Party. The PCP did not produce its first Arabic publication until 1929. The Al-Baraq Rebellion that year caught the party unprepared. Party publications and spokespeople simultaneously characterized the rebellion as an anti-imperialist uprising and an anti-Jewish pogrom. The Comintern, then in its ultra-left Third Period phase, saw the 1929 events as the beginning of a revolutionary upsurge in Palestine. It ordered the PCP to "Arabize" itself from top to bottom and to call for a "workers' and peasants'" government in Palestine. The party then denounced Arab nationalist leaders as collaborators with imperialism.

When the Comintern junked the Third Period in 1935, it adopted a policy of "revolution in stages," calling for its members in oppressed countries to unite with the "progressive bourgeoisie" in an anti-imperialist "people's front." In Palestine, this policy translated into an uncritical tailing of the traditional Arab leadership. Whether in its ultra-left phase or its Popular Front phase, the PCP abandoned a principled attempt to build a multinational organization to win Jewish workers away from Zionism and Arab workers away from allegiance to reactionary Arab notables.

In 1943, the PCP split on national lines. Jewish members, accusing the party leadership of "ultranationalist" politics, reorganized the PCP as a party accepting the Zionist idea that the *yishuv*, the Jewish community of Palestine, constituted a national group entitled to self-determination. The PCP's decision to abandon the goal of fighting for a united, socialist Palestine drove most of the Arab cadre to quit the party. Later that year, some of these cadres, such as Bulus Farah, regrouped in the National Liberation League (NLL).

The NLL attempted to correct some of the mistakes of the PCP. First, the NLL rejected the PCP's accommodation to Zionism. Instead it looked to the Arab nationalist struggle as the way to fight against Britain and Zionism. It believed that Arab workers and peasants, not the Palestinian elite, would be the leading force in that struggle. Therefore, the NLL tried to establish connections with existing Arab trade unions and to organize new ones.[13] But, similar to the PCP, the NLL suffered from a major political weakness. Whereas the PCP practically tailed Zionism by denouncing the whole Arab nationalist movement, the NLL more or less tailed the reactionary Arab leaders. So the predominant socialist opposition in Palestine remained hopelessly split on national lines. Tony Cliff spells out the tragedy of both groups:

> On VE Day the PCP marched under the blue-white Zionist flag, their slogans being "Free Immigration," "Extension of colonization," "Development of the Jewish National Home," and "Down with the [British government's 1939] white paper" (restricting Jewish immigration). The National [Liberation] League participated in the Arabic National Front, which included feudal and bourgeois parties, and called for a fight "Against Zionist immigration," "Against the transfer of land to Zionists," and "For the white paper."[14]

This meant that the NLL ultimately failed, even on a small scale, to build a socialist alternative to the Palestinian elite. The small Trotskyist organization to which Cliff belonged criticized the PCP's misleadership. Despite heroic efforts and police repression, the Trotskyists never organized more than a few dozen Palestinians and Jews.

A final blow to genuine socialist politics in Palestine came when the USSR decided to back the United Nations (UN) partition plan for Palestine in 1947. Until then, the PCP had opposed partition, despite its softness on Zionism. When the Soviet Union announced its support for the formation of Israel, a state it hoped to turn into a Russian ally in the region against the U.S. and Britain, the PCP followed suit. Jewish PCP members joined the Haganah to fight Arab resistance to the formation of the state of Israel in 1948. Meanwhile, the Soviet Union's support for partition threw the NLL into disarray, with some leaders supporting partition and others opposing it.

During the war, large numbers of NLL cadres attempted to organize military resistance to Zionist forces. But NLL supporters of partition distributed leaflets to Arab troops calling on them to return to their own countries to overthrow their corrupt rulers—ending military resistance to a partitioned Palestine.

In the end, the NLL was too small and politically confused to play any significant role in preventing the catastrophic destruction of Palestinian Arab society that ensued. After the war, the NLL ceased to exist as an organization. Its members were either killed on the front lines or arrested and imprisoned by Egypt or Jordan, which respectively took over the Gaza Strip and the West Bank.[15]

Rebirth of a national liberation movement

The 1948 al-Nakbah set back the Palestinian nationalist movement for years. In the immediate aftermath of the war, the destruction of Palestinian Arab society and the transformation of 70 percent of the population into refugees living under authoritarian Arab regimes made it very difficult to organize resistance.

But by the mid-1950s, as Palestinians became embittered with the unwillingness of the Arab regimes to solve the refugee problem or to challenge Israel, the Palestinian nationalist movement started to revive. A group of Palestinian intellectuals and professionals who lived and studied in Arab countries—among them Yasser Arafat—formed the Palestinian Liberation Movement (Fatah) in 1958. Drawing on the experience of the Algerian war of independence against France, Fatah advocated "armed struggle" (guerrilla warfare) to liberate Palestine. Fatah grew in size and popularity.

In the aftermath of Israel's victory over Egypt, under President Gamal Abdel Nasser, and other Arab regimes in the June 1967 war, Fatah's armed struggle gave millions of people across the Arab world hope in the possibility of fighting back. Fatah's 1968 "Battle of Karameh," where under-equipped Palestinian guerrillas held off the Israel Defense Forces near the Jordanian town of Karameh, inspired thousands of Palestinians and others from all over the world to join its ranks.

In 1969, Fatah succeeded in taking over the PLO, an organization that Arab governments had founded in 1964. As originally conceived, the PLO allowed the Arab governments—most notably, Nasser's Egypt—to pay lip service to the Palestinian struggle, while keeping control over its activities. Its chair, Ahmed Shuqayri, a Palestinian lawyer, made headlines with inflammatory rhetoric (famously threatening to "drive the Jews into the sea"). But Shuqayri's bluster covered for a weak and undynamic organization. By 1969, Fatah's prestige put it in a position to take the PLO's reins as Nasser pushed Shuqayri aside. Fatah turned the PLO into a mass organization that included all the newly formed left-wing and revolutionary organizations.[16]

The Palestine National Charter, revised in 1968, showed the influence of the guerrillas on the Palestinian movement. The PLO continued to identify Palestine as the "indivisible territorial unit" within the borders of the pre-Israel British mandate. Moreover, it asserted, "armed struggle is the only way to liberate Palestine. Thus it is the overall strategy, not merely a tactical phase…. Commando action constitutes the nucleus of the Palestinian popular liberation war." In addition, the charter stated that Palestinians "reject all solutions which are substitutes for the total liberation of Palestine."[17] The radical language reflected the heady days of early guerrilla success.

Fatah's "Palestine first" ideology appealed to Palestinians who wanted action, not diplomatic wrangling with Arab regime sponsors. But Fatah didn't want to answer the question: "Whose Palestine?" Fatah regarded itself as a representative of all social classes in Palestinian society. It argued that any class differences among Palestinians must be put aside in order to wage a successful struggle. Fatah's nationalist ideology ignored the irreconcilability of class antagonisms among Palestinians.

The 1948 catastrophe affected wealthy and poor Palestinians in different ways. While a large number of wealthy Palestinians were able to transfer their assets to neighboring Arab countries in the months leading up to the catastrophe, the vast majority of Palestinian peasants and workers ended up in UN refugee camps. So, while wealthy Palestinians were able to regroup and eventually play a central economic role in Arab countries, the majority of refugees lacked any social, economic, or political rights.

Fatah's nationalist ideology suited the interests of the Palestinian bourgeoisie. This group, on one hand, needed a movement such as Fatah to achieve the goal of building its own state. But, on the other hand, the Palestinian bourgeoisie needed to ensure that poor refugees would not rebel against its oppressive Arab allies. Fatah promised to fulfill both of those needs: mobilizing the Palestinian refugees to fight Israel while avoiding confrontation with Arab governments.

Fatah adopted a "principle of nonintervention" in the internal affairs of Arab countries. The PLO under Fatah received billions in aid from Arab regimes, including the medieval Gulf monarchies. In exchange, the PLO refused to take stands on political and social questions affecting the Palestinians and other populations of its Arab sponsors. In the oil-rich Gulf monarchies, Palestinian workers toiled for 50 years to build the economies of these states while they were denied basic economic and human rights. Still Fatah failed to support the struggles of Palestinian oil workers in the 1950s against the giant American oil company, ARAMCO.[18] It also failed to challenge the policies of the Arab regimes, such as Egypt and Jordan, that jailed and tortured Palestinian activists, not to mention thousands of other Arab trade unionists and radicals. The nonintervention principle meant that Fatah compromised, time and again, with regimes that oppressed Palestinian refugees and lacked any interest in challenging either Israel or Western influence in the area.

Despite its initial successes, the PLO paid for the "principle of nonintervention" with a number of serious political and military setbacks. The organization's crushing defeat in Jordan during the events of September 1970 was the most prominent of these. In the late 1960s, the PLO had established itself as the main political and military force in Jordan, virtually eclipsing the hated regime of King Hussein. It had the political support of Palestinian refugees, who made up 70 percent of Jordan's population. Time and again, however, Arafat turned down appeals from Palestinian activists, and even some Jordanian army officers, to depose the king and replace his regime with a democratic one. A democratic Jordan, many radicals believed, would provide a model for other Arab people to emulate. It could also unleash the potential of mass struggle that would be needed to fight a strong military regime such as Israel.

But the PLO's hesitations proved costly. In September 1970, King Hussein used the crisis precipitated by Palestinian leftists' airline hijackings as a pretext to launch an all-out military attack on the PLO. Arafat once again refused to enter into an all-out confrontation with the king's regime. A confrontation with the king, from Arafat's point of view, would have caused massive political instability in the region. It could have also endangered the PLO's support among other Arab dictators. The PLO's passive resistance allowed the king's army to massacre hundreds of Palestinian activists while subjecting the refugee population to a reign of terror. Finally, Arafat agreed to transfer PLO institutions and militias from Jordan to Lebanon.[19]

The PLO was never able to recover from its defeat in Jordan. If the Arab defeat in the 1967 war showed the impotence of the Arab regimes against Israel, "Black September" convinced the PLO leader Salah Khalaf that

> [i]t was only too evident that the Palestinian revolution could not count on any Arab state to provide a secure sanctuary or an operational base against Israel. In order to forge ahead toward the democratic, inter-sectarian society that was our ideal, we had to have our own state, even on a square inch of Palestine.[20]

Khalaf's statement put a radical-sounding gloss on an emerging shift in the PLO's goals. In the immediate aftermath of the 1973 Arab-Israeli war, the U.S. launched the "peace process" of negotiations between Arab states and Israel. The U.S. aimed to win Arab recognition of Israel in exchange for Israel's return of Arab land it occupied in 1967 and 1973. Arab regimes, yearning to establish closer relations with the U.S., pressured the PLO to abandon its radical goals. And PLO leaders increasingly looked to international diplomacy to win the "mini-state" they desired. Phil Marshall spells out the political impact of Fatah's decision:

> Fatah accepted, dropping its principal aim—the liberation of the whole of Palestine—in favor of the prospect of the mini-state, which was to be pressed on Israel by the U.S. Although the Fatah leadership had long debated the character of the Palestinian "entity" for which it struggled—the extent of its territory, whether it should coexist with Israel, and whether it should give citizenship to Israeli Jews—it had never publicly conceded the Zionist movement's right to control any area of Palestine.[21]

Indeed, in 1974, Arafat officially called for a two-state solution and accepted UN resolutions that partitioned Palestine. In a famous speech to the UN General Assembly, Arafat offered Israel a "historic compromise," while waving a gun with one hand and an olive branch with the other. This compromise effectively amounted to recognition of the state of Israel and, in some ways, became a prelude to Oslo.

The PLO's Charter, revised in 1974, reflected the shift away from armed struggle to the mini-state solution:

> The PLO will struggle by every means, the foremost of which is armed struggle, to liberate Palestinian land and to establish the people's national, independent and fighting sovereignty on every part of Palestinian land to be liberated. This requires the creation of further changes in the balance of power in favor of our people and their struggle.

The PLO completed its evolution to "peaceful coexistence" with Israel at its 19th Palestine National Council (PNC) meeting in 1988, where Arafat issued a Palestinian "Declaration of Independence." Meeting as the grassroots-led Intifada was tying down thousands of Israeli troops in the Occupied Territories, the PNC took the initiative to advance its diplomatic agenda for the mini-state. In unambiguous language, Arafat and the PNC laid out a number of historic concessions to Israel.

The PNC recognized Israel. It endorsed the 1947 UN resolution that partitioned Palestine. It proposed that the independent Palestinian state be located in the West Bank and Gaza—only 23 percent of pre-1947 Palestine. It renounced "terrorism" (i.e., the armed struggle) and endorsed diplomacy as the means to achieve the mini-state. These 1988 Palestinian concessions paved the road to Oslo.[22]

The Palestinian left: An alternative to Fatah?

In the late 1960s and early 1970s, a new Palestinian left could have challenged Fatah's leadership of the PLO. Two main organizations, the Popular Front for the Liberation of Palestine (PFLP) and the Democratic Front for the Liberation of Palestine (DFLP), criticized Fatah's "principle of nonintervention" and attempted, briefly, to build a left-wing current in the national liberation movement.

Radical Arab nationalist intellectuals, led by George Habbash, founded the PFLP immediately after the June 1967 war. The inability of self-proclaimed "socialist" Arab regimes, such as Nasser's Egypt, to live up to their promises of fighting Israel and U.S. imperialism, pushed these activists to search for more radical means to liberate Palestine. Inspired by the successes of the Cuban revolution and other anti-imperialist struggles in Algeria and Vietnam, and influenced by a combination of Maoist and Stalinist ideas, the PFLP declared itself to be a "Marxist-Leninist" organization. It viewed the Palestinian cause as one part of a worldwide struggle against imperialism. It believed that the plight of the Palestinians was closely connected to the oppression of the Arab masses by Arab dictatorships and imperialism. Therefore, it argued that the liberation of the Palestinian people was tied into the struggle for a socialist society in the entire Middle East.[23]

The PFLP rejected the notion that any of the nationalist Arab regimes was actually "socialist." These "petit bourgeois" regimes, the PFLP argued, were unable and unwilling to challenge Israel or U.S. imperialism because of their dependence on the international capitalist economy. A deep class antagonism between workers and peasants, on one hand, and the Arab bourgeoisie, on the other, characterized the Arab regimes. Thus, the PFLP argued, the Arab regimes could survive only through support from imperialist powers and suppression of the Arab masses.

Furthermore, the PFLP rejected Fatah's "principle of nonintervention" in the affairs of Arab regimes. In contrast to Fatah's dependence on the Arab regimes, the PFLP believed that the victory of the Palestinian struggle was contingent on the success of the Arab masses in defeating those regimes. That's why it coined the famous slogan: "The road to Jerusalem begins in Cairo, Damascus and Amman." This slogan reflected its own commitment to a broader vision of the needs of the struggle.

Hence, the PFLP made some attempt to orient itself on the struggles of Palestinian and other Arab workers and peasants. In Jordan, at the height of PLO influence in the late 1960s, the PFLP attempted to organize both Palestinian and Jordanian agricultural workers and intervened in various industrial struggles. It also organized its own popular militias, attracting many Palestinian, Jordanian, and other Arab activists. During the events of Black September in 1970, these militias fought bravely, yet unsuccessfully, to stop King Hussein's assault on the PLO.

In 1970, the PFLP was forced, along with the other PLO factions, to leave Jordan for Lebanon. During the 1970s and 1980s, it tried to maintain its commitment to the liberation of Palestine. During the Lebanese civil war, for example, the PFLP fought on the side of other Lebanese leftist and Islamic militias against the Israel-backed, pro-fascist Maronite militias. Its members helped to defend Palestinians and the PLO against the Israeli onslaught in the 1982 Lebanon war. And its cadres, along with other forces, played on-the-ground leadership roles in the early stages of the 1987–93 Intifada in the Occupied Territories.[24]

The PFLP led a "Rejection Front" of Palestinian organizations against the PLO's adoption of the "mini-state" formula in 1974. Despite its radical critique of PLO strategy, the PFLP suffered from a series of major contradictions and weaknesses. These problems prevented it from building a revolutionary alternative to Fatah.

First, while it rejected, correctly, the notion that some Arab regimes were socialist, the PFLP made a false distinction between reactionary regimes that accommodated to imperialism and progressive nationalist ones that were forced to fight against it. Thus, based on this distinction, the PFLP allied itself with a number of repressive Arab governments, such as the Ba'athist regime in Iraq and the Assad regime in Syria. Ultimately, these alliances cost the PFLP its political independence and reduced it to a tool in the hands of some Arab rulers.

Second, the PFLP, similar to the rest of the Stalinist left in the Arab world, allied itself with what it considered to be "real" socialist societies, the Soviet Union and the Eastern Bloc. This meant that, throughout the 1970s and 1980s, the PFLP was regularly manipulated by the Soviet Union and forced to adapt to the Cold War needs of Russian foreign policy in the area. Its vision of Marxism-Leninism was expressed in the Cuban Revolution, where a small group of guerrillas defeated a U.S.-backed dictator and, a few years later, declared Cuba a socialist society. Cuban workers and peasants did not take part in making the revolution.

Finally, the PFLP's chief tactical contribution to the growing Palestinian movement in 1968–72 was its use of airline hijackings to publicize the Palestinian cause.[25] As a result, it substituted the actions of its small, committed membership for the mass struggle of the Arab workers and peasants it aimed to relate to. As the Palestinians faced one of the world's chief military powers in the Israeli state, it became apparent that guerrilla tactics alone could not win. And although millions of people across the Arab world supported the Palestinians' armed struggle, the nature of that struggle prevented them from taking part. Therefore, the reliance on this tactic left the PFLP (and PLO) militias relatively small in size and unable to pose a serious military threat to Israel. Also, more critically, it isolated the PFLP from the mass struggles that took place against the Arab regimes and U.S. imperialism in the late 1960s and early 1970s—especially the workers' and students' movement in Egypt (1968–72).[26]

Unfortunately, the PFLP's political weaknesses left it ill equipped to respond to changing circumstances in the Middle

East. Egypt's decision to recognize Israel brought a reunification
of all Palestinian factions in 1978–79 against further Arab state
concessions to Israel. In 1978, the PFLP shut down the Rejection
Front, and returned to its role as internal critic of Fatah in the
PLO. By the mid-1980s, as the PFLP failed to have much impact
on Fatah's search for the mini-state solution, it joined Fatah and
other PLO factions in support of the 1983 Arab summit proposal
for a mini-state in Gaza and the West Bank. Effectively, the PFLP
adopted Fatah's two-state solution.[27]

The DFLP began in 1969 as a left-wing split from the PFLP.
While it shared the PFLP's politics overall, the DFLP rejected the
distinction between reactionary and nationalist Arab regimes. This
distinction, the DFLP argued, simply allowed the PFLP to rely on
petit-bourgeois regimes that were inconsistent in their fight against
imperialism. Instead, the DFLP argued correctly that the Arab
working classes are the only social force capable of defeating Israel
and U.S. imperialism. Also, the DFLP was the first of the Palestinian
resistance groups to work with allies in the Israeli left. It pioneered
the idea that Palestinians should fight for a "secular, democratic
state" in Palestine, where Arabs and Jews would have equal rights.

However, following the defeat of the PLO in Black September,
the DFLP shifted sharply to the right. Using the mechanical, Stalinist theory of stages, in which "democratic" demands (e.g., national liberation) were to be prioritized and achieved before the
struggle for socialism could begin, the DFLP abandoned its previous radical positions. The DFLP now argued that the revolutionary left should put the goal of socialism or the total liberation of
Palestine on hold. Instead, the left must strive, in the short term, to
build a Palestinian state "in any liberated piece of land Israel
could be forced to give up."

In 1974, DFLP leader Naïf Hawatma called for the formation
of a Palestinian "national authority" in Gaza and the West Bank.
Believing that the Palestinian mini-state could be achieved through
the peace process, the DFLP did not join the Rejection Front. It reversed its key positions. The Palestinian bourgeoisie, it started to
argue, and not the working class, would play the leading role in
such a campaign. As a result, workers would have to subordinate

their interests to the common national goal. This meant that four long years before Arafat himself dared to utter it, the Palestinian left was actually ready to recognize the state of Israel and accept the two-state solution. This political collapse of the DFLP and its retreat from a stress on the importance of class struggle brought it much closer to Fatah positions. Since the early 1970s, the DFLP has, even more than the PFLP, simply tailed Fatah's compromises and zigzags.[28]

Even when an upturn in activity provided an opening to shift the Palestinian struggle to terms more favorable to the DFLP's original positions, it missed the opportunity. In 1987, the DFLP published the first manifesto of the United Leadership of the first Intifada. Rather than taking advantage of its position at the base of the mass uprising to win the Palestinian movement away from Fatah, it stressed unity with Fatah. This missed opportunity contributed to a situation in which Fatah was able to bring the United Leadership under its control and political leadership.[29]

The Islamic opposition

The failure of the PLO and its left wing over the past 30 years to provide a clear, effective leadership in the national struggle or to win any of the rights that millions of Palestinians desperately await has hurt the credibility of secular organizations. Moreover, the antidemocratic and corrupt practices of the Palestinian Authority (PA) have turned many more ordinary Palestinians against it. These conditions explain why, in recent years, a large section of Palestinian society has looked to the Islamic Resistance Movement (Hamas) and, to a lesser degree, the Islamic Jihad, to resist Israel.

Hamas's formal opposition to the Oslo accords and Palestinian negotiators' endless concessions resonates with people who recognize the futility of negotiations. Its insistence on the liberation of the whole of Palestine connects with the aspirations of Palestinian refugees to return to their country.

From 1967 until the outbreak of the first Intifada in 1987, the Muslim Brotherhood dominated the Islamic movement in Palestine. The Brotherhood attracted a considerable number of people who were alienated by the miserable conditions under Israeli occupation. However, the Brotherhood refused to play any active role in resisting Israel. Instead, it focused on missionary work, such as the construction of mosques, and providing various social and health services to needy Palestinians. The organization's nonpolitical position increasingly frustrated many of its younger cadres. As a result, in the late 1970s, some of these cadres began to look to the more radical Egyptian Islamic Jihad. This younger generation admired the political activism of the Egyptian organization, known predominantly for its role in the assassination of (the pro-Israel) President Sadat in 1981. Eventually, these disgruntled elements broke with the Muslim Brotherhood to form Palestinian Jihad.

Jihad rejected the nonpolitical stance of the Brotherhood, as well as the PLO's two-state solution compromise. It maintained, as the PLO and its left did at one point, that an armed struggle (this time by an "Islamic vanguard") was still necessary to liberate the whole of Palestine. Therefore, throughout the 1980s, Jihad carried out military attacks on Israeli targets, though Israel's overwhelming military superiority kept Jihad's influence relatively limited.[30]

The outbreak of the first Palestinian Intifada in 1987 fundamentally changed the fortunes of the Islamic opposition. Under the pressure of the first Intifada, the Muslim Brotherhood realized that it either had to drop its nonpolitical approach or risk losing all credibility among Palestinians. Therefore, in 1988, the Brotherhood formed a political wing, Hamas, to organize resistance to Israel.

Hamas's own charter reflected the Palestinians' disappointment with the failure of the PLO's diplomatic efforts and maneuvers to secure any of their lost rights. Sections of Hamas's charter express this sentiment:

> There is no solution to the Palestinian problem except by Jihad (Holy Struggle). The initiatives, proposals and International Conferences are but a waste of time, an exercise in futility. The Palestinian people are too noble to have their future, their right and their destiny submitted to a vain game.[31]

Hamas advocated the creation of an Islamic state in Palestine. It rejected Arafat's decision to recognize the state of Israel at the 1988 session of the Palestine National Congress in Algeria. And, while the PLO was busy preparing to use the Intifada as a bargaining chip to force Israel to the negotiating table, Hamas began to gain more popular support by playing a leading role in street protests and confrontations with the Israeli army.

In 1992, Hamas founded its own military wing, the Al-Qassam Militias, named after the martyred leader of the 1930s armed struggle. Since then, these militias have launched numerous military attacks on Israeli targets. In 1993, Hamas refused to recognize the Oslo accords. Using the tactic of suicide bombings, Hamas has continued its attacks on Israeli targets. Under pressure from Israel to crack down on Oslo opponents, the PA imprisoned and tortured hundreds of Hamas activists.

As millions of Palestinians grew impatient with the continued arrogance of Israel and Arafat's endless compromises, Hamas gained more popular support. The willingness of its members to sacrifice themselves in military attacks on Israeli targets earned them the respect of people who face Israeli bombardment on a daily basis.[32] By early 2002, Palestinian opinion polls showed support for Islamist groups drawing even with, or even exceeding, support for Arafat's secular Fatah movement.

The increased support for Islamist currents does not mean that the Islamists offer any solution for Palestinians. In fact, for the Palestinian movement, which has been historically secular and left oriented, increased support for Islamist politics marks a big step backward.

Formally, Hamas rejects the ideas of what it calls "Eastern communism" and "Western crusaders" in favor of an "Islamic society." In reality, like other Islamist groups, Hamas believes in the sanctity of private property and supports a market-based economy. This belief leads it to have a contradictory position toward U.S. imperialism. On one hand, it finds itself pitted against the U.S. due to U.S. support for Israel. On the other, Hamas tends to adopt the market ideas pushed by the U.S.—and its financial arms in the area, the International Monetary Fund (IMF) and World Bank— that are responsible for the misery of millions of Arab workers and peasants. Furthermore, due to its conservative ideology, Hamas is unable to challenge the different Arab regimes that ally themselves with the U.S., especially the right-wing Islamic monarchies in the

Gulf, such as Saudi Arabia. In this way, Hamas agrees with Fatah's principle of non-interference in the affairs of Arab countries.

Hamas's backward social positions, especially regarding women, Jews, and Christians, constantly undermine the struggle against Israel. Hamas's own characterization of the struggle against Israel as a continuation of an age-old struggle between Muslims and Jews mirrors Israel's own propaganda. Moreover, this characterization alienates Palestinian Christians (and Arab Christians in general), who have always been a key part of the struggle against imperialism. Hamas's anti-Jewish propaganda, while a reaction to Israel's crimes against the Palestinian people, diverts attention away from Israel's real role as a watchdog for U.S. imperialism in the area. Finally, Hamas's belief that women should focus on their duties as mothers and wives relegates women to a secondary position in the nationalist struggle. While seemingly a response to high unemployment among Palestinians, this position essentially reinforces the oppression of women and weakens the struggle.[33]

Hamas's leadership is drawn primarily from middle-class elements. Therefore, it tends to sympathize with the goals of the Palestinian bourgeoisie. Like Fatah, Hamas also believes in the necessity of an alliance between all classes in Palestinian society. In practice, this means that the interests of Palestinian refugees and workers must be subordinated to those of Arafat and the bourgeoisie. On more than one occasion, Hamas leadership has indicated its readiness to accept Oslo and live with the state of Israel. As early as 1993, Sheikh Ahmed Yassin, the political leader of Hamas, indicated that the movement could accept a two-state solution: "It is perceivable to declare a cease-fire with Israel for 10, perhaps 20 years if a Palestinian state is established."[34]

Despite Hamas's critique of the PLO's insistence on a strategy of compromise, it continues to defer to the PLO (and Arafat) as the legitimate leader of the Palestinian nationalist movement. Hamas regards itself simply as one component of that movement:

> The PLO is among the closest to the Hamas, for it constitutes a father, a brother, a relative, a friend. Can a Muslim turn away from his father, his brother, his relative or his friend? Our homeland is

one, our calamity is one, our destiny is one and our enemy is common to both of us.[35]

While the PA imprisoned and tortured its members, Hamas insisted on the need "to maintain open dialogue with Arafat and cooperation with the PA in all areas of self-autonomy." This conciliatory approach towards the PA has angered many rank-and-file cadres of the organization.

The ambiguity of Hamas's relationship with the PA was revealed in the organization's indecisiveness regarding the 1996 Palestinian Legislative Council elections. Hamas leaders in Amman, Jordan, called for a boycott of the elections. Hamas leaders based in Gaza argued for participation in the elections, and three Gazan "moderates" announced their intentions to run as candidates. These three pulled out of the race at the last minute, but clearly identified Hamas sympathizers won seven of the 88 open seats. Hamas supporters voted at just under the average of supporters of other Palestinian political tendencies.[36] Wendy Kristiansen summarizes the political dilemma Hamas faces:

> Arafat has indicated that any continued political role for Hamas may be conditioned on its behavior: if it desists from outright opposition (political as well as military) to the PA's agenda, it may be allowed to continue its social and welfare activities. Yet it is Hamas opposition—championing Palestinian resistance to Oslo—that has been the basis of the support it has built up over the years.[37]

These tensions within Hamas continued to boil under the surface. But, every now and then, they explode in the open. In September 1995, under pressure by the PA, Hamas's leadership declared a cease-fire with Israel. However, shortly after, Israel assassinated one of Hamas's top military commanders, Yehia Ayash. In retaliation, Hamas militants broke the cease-fire to carry out a number of suicide bombings in Israel. The PA, under Israeli pressure, arrested hundreds of Hamas militants. But, in a number of leaflets, Hamas militants issued a serious warning to the Palestinian police force to stop arresting their comrades. This was as much a threat directed at Hamas's leadership as it was against Arafat's police.[38]

Like the PFLP and DFLP, Hamas does not look to the actions of the masses of Palestinians as the key to defeating Israel. Instead, it substitutes the actions of a tiny minority of militants for the struggle of the majority. Its reliance on individual military attacks against Israel, although popular, fails to involve the majority of ordinary Palestinians in the struggle against Israel.

Oslo and the crisis of perspectives

Three decades ago, millions around the world regarded the PLO as one of the main national liberation movements in the world, on par with the Vietnamese National Liberation Front and the African National Congress of South Africa. Tragically, today the PLO is a shadow of its former self. It has all but given up on its initial goals of liberating Palestine and replacing Israel with a secular, democratic state.

The Oslo "peace process" trapped the main forces of the Palestinian national liberation movement in a cul-de-sac. The PLO, reconstituted as the Palestinian Authority in the West Bank and Gaza after the 1993 Oslo accords, unashamedly cooperates with both Israel's internal security service (Shinbet) and the CIA to curb Palestinian militants. It claims that such cooperation is needed to persuade Washington to support a Palestinian state. It uses its massive security forces (more than 50,000 strong) to jail, torture, and even murder those Palestinians who oppose Oslo.[39] The PLO has ceased to be a force in the struggle against imperialism.

Incredibly, in the aftermath of the terrorist attacks on the U.S. in September 2001, the PLO declared itself a "partner of the U.S. in its war against terrorism." Not only did the PLO support the bombing of Afghanistan, one of the poorest countries on earth, but its security forces shot and killed Palestinians who protested against the war.

Large numbers of Palestinians view Arafat as safeguarding Israel's security—not conducting a struggle for liberation. Many are angry, since years of negotiations have failed to end the occupation, stop the expansion of Israeli settlements, or secure the refugees' right of return. They are also angry because poverty and unemployment levels for ordinary people have worsened, while Arafat and his cronies have made fortunes through corruption and monopolies.

Many people view the PLO's surrender to Israel and the U.S., as well as its internal brutality, as a case of "selling out." This view, however, overlooks the real reason behind the PLO's capitulation to the U.S. and Israel: the class interests that have always informed the organization's policies. The PLO claimed that it represented the interests of all Palestinians. In reality, it has always served the interests of the Palestinian bourgeoisie—especially this class's desire to form its own mini-state through negotiations and compromise with the U.S. and Israel. It has never wanted to rely on popular struggles of Palestinian or Arab masses, which could endanger the stability of both it and its Arab allies.

This fear of mass rebellion from below, which is characteristic of all ruling classes, explains why the PLO has always had a contradictory attitude toward mass struggles. The PLO needs some form of struggle to pressure Israel into making concessions, but it constantly has to try (sometimes unsuccessfully) to keep any such struggles, especially the Intifadas, under its own control. It also explains why the PLO always supports its Arab allies when they are faced with a threat from their own working classes. In 1970, for example, the PLO chose to leave Jordan rather than challenge and destabilize the authoritarian regime of King Hussein. In 1988 and 1989, it chose to support the Algerian and Jordanian governments against two popular uprisings that the first Intifada inspired.[40]

In response to the Oslo accords in 1993, the established Palestinian left harshly criticized Arafat for signing a treaty that only benefited Israel and failed to guarantee any of the Palestinians' fundamental rights. The two organizations joined with eight other radical Palestinian organizations to boycott the PA. In 1996, the PFLP formally withdrew from the PLO. But after 1994, the PA increasingly shaped Palestinian politics. PFLP and DFLP leaders opposed participation in the 1996 legislative council elections. This provoked an organizational split in the DFLP, spawning another party (FIDA) that ran candidates and took a position in the PA. Supporters of the PFLP in the electorate largely ignored the leadership's calls for boycotts, and many party members ran as independents without official PFLP backing.[41]

As Arafat prepared to enter into "final status" negotiations with Israel when the Oslo accords' transition period ran out in 1999, the

DFLP and PFLP entered into negotiations with Arafat to prepare a united national stance. Most Palestinian political observers interpreted these moves as these groups' admission that they had failed to develop a coherent opposition to the Oslo process. At the time, the late PFLP leader Abu Ali Mustafa admitted that the opposition "has failed to transform its political discourse into practical, material action."[42] In 1999, both groups endorsed Arafat's plan to reach a "final status" agreement with Israel.

The failure of the secular left to build a left opposition to Fatah and the Palestinian Authority stems from their failure to apply their initial insights on the reactionary nature of the Arab ruling classes to the Palestinian bourgeoisie itself. As the Jerusalem-based socialist magazine *Challenge* explained:

> At first, when the Oslo Accords were signed, the leftist parties began a campaign against them, calling on the Palestinians to boycott the Palestine Authority (PA) which had joined the colonialist system. The aim was to bring the bourgeoisie back into the national camp. When this failed, the organized Left decided to acknowledge Oslo as a fait accompli; it began calling for national unity, this time on the basis of simply "overlooking" Oslo. Instead of doing its utmost to isolate the bourgeoisie from the masses, the Palestinian Left put all its efforts into finding a national common denominator with the bourgeoisie. The latter, of course, never committed itself to this common denominator. The bourgeois simply used the concept to cover up their surrender so as to keep their grip on the masses. The illusion of national unity among all classes served bourgeois interests and prevented the Left from fulfilling its strategic task: to create a political alternative.[43]

Both the PFLP and DFLP have simply become a left, loyal opposition to Arafat.[44] In fact, their influence has fallen so far that journalist Graham Usher, a longtime observer of Palestinian politics, declared them politically impotent:

> The future alliance of the national movement is between mainstream nationalists, Fatah, and the Islamicists. The leftists, the Communists, the Democratic Front (DF), and the Popular Front (PF) are nowhere. They are history. They have no road. They follow Fatah and Hamas. The Popular Front resumed armed actions in the last two months [in summer 2001—*ed.*] purely and simply because they are copying Fatah, Hamas, and Islamic Jihad. Same with the Democratic Front.

> So the secular left...no longer makes the decisions. It's Hamas
> and Fatah. Arafat has had to share power with [Hamas].[45]

Perhaps for this reason, Arafat felt emboldened to arrest the PFLP general secretary, Ahmad Saadat, in February, 2002—fulfilling Israel's demand to arrest PFLP leaders who claimed responsibility for the October 2001 assassination of Israel's far-right tourism minister, Rehavam Ze'evi.[46]

Since Oslo, the PLO has felt itself under pressure from above and below. From above, it is under pressure from the U.S. and Israel to continue with concessions and crackdowns on militants. From below, mass anger at endless and fruitless concessions, which exploded in the form of the Al-Aqsa Intifada, limits Arafat's ability to make certain concessions. Arafat was not totally off the mark when he reportedly told President Bill Clinton that he feared he would be assassinated if he were to make any more concessions to Israel during the 2000 Camp David negotiations.

The socialist alternative

Both the first Intifada and the Al-Aqsa Intifada have shown that, despite its massive military might and U.S. support, Israel cannot silence the Palestinian question. However, they have also shown that the struggle of the Palestinians alone cannot defeat Israel. Today, the situation in Palestine is difficult. Barbaric bombings by the government of Ariel Sharon, as well as Arafat's collaboration with Israel in cracking down on opposition forces, has weakened the Intifada.

In its initial stages, the Al-Aqsa Intifada combined mobilization of the Palestinian population with military attacks on Israeli soldiers and settlers. Because the Arafat regime saw the Intifada as a bargaining chip to restart negotiations with Israel, it wound up the popular aspects of the uprising and increasingly turned the conflict into sporadic military confrontations. Following the September 11, 2001, terrorist attacks in the U.S., the Sharon government stepped up its military assault on the Palestinians. Sharon declared his intention to use the "war on terrorism" to crush all resistance and to impose an apartheid system on Palestinians. This raised the stakes in the liberation struggle. Only a strategy that involves the mass of Palestinians—not one that vacillates between isolated guerrilla actions and negotiations that simply reinforce Israeli domination over Palestine—can defend the liberation movement.

In the near term, a strategy of a mass Intifada—combining military tactics with mass actions of Palestinian "civil society" (such as trade unions and popular committees)—can move the struggle in a direction more favorable to the Palestinians. This kind of strategy has the potential to raise the costs of the occupation and to break Israeli morale. It can give confidence to those on the other side of the Green Line—military resisters, Israeli supporters of Palestinian rights, and Palestinians living in Israel—to demonstrate their solidarity. This kind of strategy would also shift the balance in Palestinian society toward ordinary Palestinians and democracy and away from the Arafat cronies and corrupt PA officials who sought to rule an Oslo-imposed Bantustan in collaboration with Israel.

Even if the Palestinians drove Israel out of the territories occupied in 1967, this achievement would not amount to the liberation of Palestine. The Zionist state would still exist, and Palestinians would not have won their right to return to their historic homeland. Palestinian oppression is firmly built into the U.S.-supported state system in the Middle East. Therefore, Palestinian liberation depends on ending that state system and forming a democratic, secular state in all of historic Palestine where Jews and Arabs can live as equals. The only force capable of achieving that task is the working class of the region. This point in no way diminishes the centrality of Palestinian struggle and sacrifice. It only stresses that for Palestinians to finally liberate themselves, Arab workers have to shake off their chains, too.

Millions of ordinary Arab people live in poverty under oppressive governments that the U.S. supports. In addition, they see how U.S. power enforces genocidal sanctions on Iraq that have killed hundreds of thousands of Iraqis and left its economy in a shambles. And they see how U.S. power backs up Israel's denial of basic human rights to millions of Palestinians. This combination of growing class inequality in the region and the miserable conditions of both the Iraqi and Palestinian peoples is pushing many over the edge.

The Egyptian working class, the largest of the Arab working classes, has endured 30 years of government attacks on its standard of living through cuts in social services, privatization of the once-massive public sector (accompanied by layoffs of millions of workers), and lack of union or political rights. These attacks have led workers and peasants to attempt to fight back. During the second half of the 1990s, thousands of poor peasants protested the government's reversal of land reform. And a number of key strikes in steel, printing, and textiles challenged privatization schemes.

Deepening class anger and growing support for Iraqis and Palestinians underpinned the outbreak of mass demonstrations across Egypt immediately after the Al-Aqsa Intifada began and during Israel's spring 2002 onslaught on the Occupied Territories. Tens of thousands of workers, lawyers, and students (from the college to the elementary level) took to the streets of major cities (and even villages) to show their solidarity with the Intifada. The demonstrations demanded that the Mubarak government cut diplomatic relations with Israel. These solidarity demonstrations quickly turned into protests against the Mubarak government itself. The demonstrators very quickly raised slogans and chants denouncing widespread corruption, lack of political freedoms, and austerity measures imposed by the government and the IMF. The neoliberal reforms are fueling a rising militancy among workers that has made the Egyptian government very nervous.[47]

In Jordan, for many years, Palestinian refugees and the majority of ordinary Jordanians have suffered due to harsh economic conditions caused by the sanctions against Jordan's main trade partner, Iraq, as well as vicious austerity programs imposed by a corrupt monarchy. As in Egypt, during the 2002 Israeli invasion, thousands of people took to the streets to support it. Since then, the Jordanian government, on more than one occasion, had to call the army to control pro-Palestinian demonstrators.

Demonstrations have also taken place in Morocco, Syria, and even in the Gulf countries of Saudi Arabia and Kuwait, where protests were previously unknown. The evolution of solidarity

protests with the Intifada into antigovernment protests highlighted, once again, the close connection between the plight of the
Palestinians and struggle of the Arab working classes for democracy. It showed the radicalizing impact that the Palestinian struggle has always had on Arab workers. Time and again, the
Palestinian national liberation struggle has inspired both Arab
workers and students to resist their own repressive governments,
as well as U.S. domination in the Middle East.

Millions of Arabs who were demoralized by Israel's 1967 victory over the Arab regimes drew hope from the armed resistance
of the PLO. The PLO's resistance proved that it was still possible
to fight both Israel and U.S. imperialism. The PLO's initial military successes against Israel (1968–70), in turn, gave confidence to
ordinary Arabs to resist their own bankrupt and humiliated
regimes. Mass movements of workers and students in Egypt
(1968–72) and Jordan (1970) challenged these regimes. Recipro-
cally, thousands of youths and revolutionaries from around the
Middle East flocked to join the PLO's militias.

Spontaneous struggles of Arab workers or students will not be
enough to defeat Israel and U.S. imperialism. A socialist alternative
rooted in the day-to-day struggles of Arab workers against the oppression and the corruption of their own regimes must be built. It
must reject the PLO's (and the Arab regimes') collaboration with
Israel and the United States. And, it must fight for an Arab world
run democratically by the workers who create all its oil wealth.
The nationalist tradition, embodied most in the mainstream PLO,
ran into the cul-de-sac of Oslo. This offered an opening to the Islamists, whose militancy covers for a reactionary social agenda.

Real hope for the future in Palestine lies in the building of a
genuine socialist alternative to these politics. Building such an alternative will not be an easy task in Palestine or in the rest of the
Arab world, given the level of repression by the PA and other Arab
governments. Moreover, a new generation of socialists has to overcome the legacy of Stalinism and its harmful impact on the left.
This will require the rediscovery of the real Marxist tradition,
which has always looked to struggles of the working class—and
not to Stalinist Russia or some authoritarian Arab regime that calls

itself "socialist" or "progressive"—as the way to change society. It will be critical for us to learn from the mistakes of the old Stalinist organizations and connect these lessons to the struggles of today.

Building a socialist alternative in the Arab world might not be an easy task. Yet, the liberation of Palestine and the future of democracy in the Arab world depend on it.

---

1 For a brief description of the living conditions for Palestinians since Oslo, see Rania Masri, "The Al-Aqsa Intifada: A natural consequence of the military occupation, the Oslo accords, and the 'peace process,'" in this volume.

2 Edward Said, *The End of the Peace Process: Oslo and After* (New York: Pantheon Books, 2000), p. 188.

3 The first Intifada lasted from 1987–93. For a brief overview of its causes and impact on Israel and the Arab world, see Phil Marshall, *Intifada: Zionism, Imperialism, and Palestinian Resistance* (London: Bookmarks, 1989), pp. 149–76.

4 For a detailed discussion of the conditions that led to the outbreak of the Al-Aqsa Intifada and the hardships endured by the Palestinians in the West Bank and Gaza, see the Middle East Research and Information Report (MERIP), "MERIP primer on the uprising in Palestine," available online at www.merip.org.

5 Marshall, pp. 191–208.

6 Center for Socialist Studies (CSS), *The Palestinian Question: A Revolutionary Perspective* (Cairo, Egypt: The Center For Socialist Studies, 2001), pp. 28–29.

7 The Muslim Brotherhood is an Islamic organization that was first formed in Egypt in the late 1920s, then spread to other Arab and Muslim countries. It holds a conservative and contradictory ideology. During the 1920s and 1930s, the Brotherhood's ideology combined certain elements of anticolonialism with an apologetic approach toward the Arab and Muslim monarchies that cooperated with it. For more background on the different Islamic organizations in the Arab world, their history, and their political positions, see Chris Harman, *The Prophet and the Proletariat* (London: Bookmarks, 2000).

8 Marshall, pp. 40–41.

9 Marshall, pp. 40–43

10 CSS, pp. 32–36; Zachary Lockman, *Comrades and Enemies: Arab and Jewish Workers in Palestine, 1906–1948* (Berkeley: University of California Press, 1996), p. 241.

11 Marshall, pp. 59–61.

12 The Russian Bolshevik Party formed the Comintern in 1919 to organize mass communist parties around the world. A number of Arab socialists, especially from Egypt and Palestine, were fascinated by the example of the Russian Revolution and its recognition of the right of self-determination for oppressed

nationalities in the tsarist Russian empire. This led to the formation of small communist parties in a number of Arab countries, including Palestine.

13 Joel Beinin, *Was the Red Flag Flying There? : Marxist Politics and the Arab-Israeli Conflict in Egypt and Israel, 1948–1965* (Berkeley: University of California Press, 1996), pp. 42–43.

14 Tony Cliff, *A World to Win: Life of A Revolutionary* (London: Bookmarks, 2000), pp. 24–25.

15 Beinin, p. 43.

16 Marshall, pp.115–20; CSS, pp. 43–47.

17 See "The Palestine National Charter as revised by the Fourth PNC meeting, July 1968" (extracts), in Helena Cobban, *The Palestinian Liberation Organization: People, Power, and Politics* (Cambridge: Cambridge University Press, 1984), pp. 267–68.

18 Marshall, pp. 99–101. In the mid 1950s, Palestinian oil workers led a series of militant strikes against oil companies in Saudi Arabia and the other Gulf states. In 1956, Palestinian workers organized protests against the invasion of Suez. This prompted the Gulf countries to ban strikes in the oil fields as well as the entry of Palestinian blue-collar workers.

19 Marshall, pp.123–27; CSS, pp. 47–51.

20 Quoted in Cobban, pp. 60–61. Israel assassinated Khalaf in 1990.

21 Marshall, p. 132.

22 For a summary of the PLO's shift to the "mini-state" strategy and an analysis of the 1988 decisions, see Muhammad Muslih, "Towards coexistence: An analysis of the resolutions of the Palestine National Council," *Journal of Palestine Studies*, Spring 1990, pp. 3–29.

23 CSS, pp. 95–96.

24 CSS, pp. 95–104; Marshall, pp. 115–27.

25 The PFLP abandoned—and then repudiated—hijackings in the early 1970s.

26 Marshall, pp. 177–96.

27 Samih K. Farsoun with Christina E. Zacharia, *Palestine and the Palestinians* (Boulder, Colo.: Westview Press, 1997), p. 193.

28 CSS, pp. 95–104; Marshall, pp. 97–100.

29 See "Debate with the Palestinian left: The Palestinian bourgeoisie and the National Program," *Challenge*, May–June 2001, available online at www.hanitzotz.com/challenge/67/mis.html.

30 CSS, pp. 104–05.

31 The full text of the Hamas Charter is available on the Palestine Center Web site at www.palestinecenter.org/framecpap.html.

32 CSS, pp. 105–09.

33 See full text of the Hamas Charter, and CSS, pp. 104–14.

34 CSS, pp. 112–13.

35 Hamas Charter.

36 See Wendy Kristiansen, "Challenge and counterchallenge: Hamas's response to Oslo," *Journal of Palestine Studies*, Spring 1999, pp. 19–36.

37 Kristiansen, p. 33.

38 CSS, pp. 104–14.

39 Said, pp. 35–36, 84–85, 106.

40 Marshall, pp. 188–89.

41 On the Palestinian elections, see Ali Jarbawi, "Palestinian politics at a cross-roads," *Journal of Palestine Studies,* Summer 1996, pp. 37–38, and Khalil Shikaki, "The Palestinian elections: An assessment," *Journal of Palestine Studies,* Spring 1996, p. 18.

42 Abu Ali Mustafa, "The Palestinian secular opposition at a crossroads," *Journal of Palestine Studies,* interview, Winter 2000, p. 84. In August 2001, Israel assassinated Mustafa.

43 "Debate with the Palestinian left," *Challenge.*

44 An October 1, 2000, PFLP statement, issued days after the Al-Aqsa Intifada began, called for a "return to the decisions of the international legitimacy as postulated in the related United Nations and security council resolutions, as the terms of reference for further peace talks and as an alternative to the Israeli force and the American-biased position" ("Popular Front for the Liberation of Palestine," press releases, available on the Netherlands-based Anti-Imperialist League Web site at www.lai-aib.org.

45 Graham Usher, unpublished interview with Anthony Arnove, Ahmed Shawki, and Nigel Harris, Jerusalem, July 2001. A theoretical slide has accompanied the DFLP and PFLP loss of political initiative. Once considering themselves a vanguard in the region against U.S. imperialism, the DFLP's former general secretary, Naïf Hawatma, recently wrote, "The Palestinian national liberation movement must set itself the goal of communication and reaching a common understanding with the U.S. This could help convince the U.S. to pressure Israel to respect all previous UN resolutions and international law." And PFLP founder George Habbash recently declared, "It is no longer necessary to fight against U.S. imperialism or defeat it in order to defeat Israel" (CSS, pp. 101–04).

46 The PFLP assassinated Ze'evi in response to Israel's assassination of its general secretary, Abu Ali Mustafa, in August 2001.

47 See Emad Mekay, "Egyptian labor reforms fuel militancy" *Asia Times,* February 13, 2002.

About the authors

ANTHONY ARNOVE edited *Iraq Under Siege* (South End Press, 2000) and Howard Zinn's *Terrorism and War* (Open Media Pamphlet, 2002). He is a member of the International Socialist Organization and the National Writers Union.

NASEER ARURI is Chancellor Professor of Political Science at the University of Massachusetts at Dartmouth. He is the author of *The Obstruction of Peace: The U.S., Israel, and the Palestinians* and editor of the forthcoming *Palestinian Refugees: The Right of Return*. He formerly served as a member of the Palestine National Council and the Palestine Liberation Organization Central Committee.

DAVID BARSAMIAN is the director of Alternative Radio in Boulder, Colorado, and author of *The Decline and Fall of Public Broadcasting* (South End Press, 2001).

PAUL D'AMATO is an associate editor of the *International Socialist Review.*

PHIL GASPER, a member of the International Socialist Organization, teaches philosophy at Notre Dame College.

TOUFIC HADDAD and **TIKVA HONIG-PARNASS** are co-editors of the Jerusalem-based *Between the Lines.*

RANIA MASRI, Ph.D., is a member of Al-Awda, the Palestine Right to Return Coalition, and a national board member of Peace Action and the Education for Peace in Iraq Center.

MOSTAFA OMAR is a longtime activist for Palestinian solidarity and a member of the International Socialist Organization.

TANYA REINHART, professor of linguistics and cultural studies at Tel Aviv University, has been one of the most outspoken critics of the Israeli government's treatment of the Palestinians. Her articles regularly appear on ZNet, Indymedia Israel, and in the Israeli press.

EDWARD SAID was born in Jerusalem, Palestine, in 1935, and attended schools there and in Cairo, Egypt. A well-known spokesperson for Palestinian rights, he is University Professor at Columbia University. His latest books include *Reflections on Exile and Other Essays* and *The End of the Peace Process: Oslo and After.* He writes a regular column for the Arabic newspaper *Al-Hayat* in London.

LANCE SELFA, a columnist for *Socialist Worker* newspaper, frequently contributes to the *International Socialist Review.*

AHMED SHAWKI is the editor of the *International Socialist Review.*

HADAS THIER is a member of the International Socialist Organization in New York.

Additional resources

SELECTED BIBLIOGRAPHY

Aburish, Saïd K. *Arafat: From Defender to Dictator.* New York and London: Bloomsbury Publishing, 1998.

———. *A Brutal Friendship: The West and the Arab Elite.* New York: St. Martin's Press, 1998.

Ahmad, Eqbal. *Eqbal Ahmad, Confronting Empire: Interviews with David Barsamian.* Edited by David Barsamian. Cambridge: South End Press, 2000.

———. *Terrorism: Theirs and Ours.* Open Media Pamphlet Series. New York: Seven Stories Press, 2002.

Aruri, Naseer. *The Obstruction of Peace: The U.S., Israel, and the Palestinians.* Monroe, Maine: Common Courage Press, 1995.

Beinin, Joel. *Was the Red Flag Flying There? Marxist Politics and the Arab-Israeli Conflict in Egypt and Israel, 1948–1965.* Berkeley: University of California Press, 1990.

Beit-Hallahmi, Benjamin. *The Israeli Connection: Who Israel Arms and Why.* New York: Pantheon, 1987.

Bennis, Phyllis. *From Stones to Statehood: The Palestinian Uprising.* Foreword by Ibrahim A. Abu-Lughod. Photographs by Neal Cassidy. Brooklyn: Olive Branch Press, 1990.

Berberoglu, Berch. *Turmoil in the Middle East: Imperialism, War, and Political Instability.* Albany: State University of New York Press, 1999.

Blaming the Victims: Spurious Scholarship and the Palestinian Question. Edited by Edward W. Said and Christopher Hitchens. New York and London: Verso, 1988.

Brenner, Lenni. *Zionism in the Age of the Dictators.* Westport, Connecticut: Lawrence Hill, 1983.

The Case against Torture in Israel: A Compilation of Petitions, Briefs, and Other Documents Submitted to the Israeli High Court of Justice. Edited and translated by Allegra Pacheco. Jerusalem: The Public Committee Against Torture in Israel, 1999.

Chomsky, Noam. *Fateful Triangle: The United States, Israel, and the Palestinians.* Updated edition. Cambridge: South End Press Classics, 1999.

———. *Powers and Prospects: Reflections on Human Nature and the Social Order.* Boston: South End Press, 1996.

———. *Rogue States: The Rule of Force in World Affairs.* Cambridge: South End Press, 2000.

———. *World Orders, Old and New.* Updated edition. New York: Columbia University Press, 1996.

Cliff, Tony. "Middle East at the crossroads." In *Neither Washington nor Moscow: Essays on Revolutionary Socialism.* London: Bookmarks, 1982.

Cliff, Tony. "Politics in the Middle East." In *International Struggle and the Marxist Tradition: Selected Writings,* vol. 1. London: Bookmarks, 2001.

Cohen, Avner. *Israel and the Bomb.* New York: Columbia University Press, 1998.

Davis, Uri. *Israel, An Apartheid State.* London and Atlantic Highlands, New Jersey: Zed Books, 1987.

Farsoun, Samih K., with Christina E. Zacharia. *Palestine and the Palestinians.* Boulder, Colorado: Westview Press, 1997.

Finkelstein, Norman G. *Image and Reality of the Israel-Palestine Conflict.* New York and London: Verso, 1995.

Fisk, Robert. *Pity the Nation: Lebanon at War.* Third edition. New York and London: Oxford University Press, 2001.

Flapan, Simha. *The Birth of Israel: Myths and Realities.* New York: Pantheon Books, 1987.

Forbidden Agendas: Intolerance and Defiance in the Middle East. A *Khamsin* anthology. Edited by Jon Rothschild. London: Al Saqi Books, 1984.

Hanegbi, Haim, Moshe Machover, and Akiva Orr, "The class nature of Israeli society," *New Left Review* (January–February 1971).

Harman, Chris. *The Prophet and the Proletariat: Islamic Fundamentalism, Class, and Revolution.* London: Bookmarks, 1999.

Hass, Amira. *Drinking the Sea at Gaza: Days and Nights in a Land under Siege.* Translated by Elana Wesley and Maxine Kaufman-Lacusta. New York: Henry Holt/Owl Books, 2000.

Hunter, Jane. *Israeli Foreign Policy: South Africa and Central America.* Boston: South End Press, 1987.

The June 1967 War after Three Decades. Afterword by Edward W. Said. Edited by William W. Haddad, Ghada H. Talhami, and Janice J. Terry. Washington, D.C.: Association of Arab-American University Graduates, 1999.

Lens, Sidney. *The Forging of the American Empire: From the Revolution to Vietnam: A History of U.S. Imperialism.* New York: Thomas Y. Crowell Co., 1971.

Leon, Abram. *The Jewish Question: A Marxist Interpretation.* Translated by Ernest Mandel. New York: Pathfinder Press, 1971.

Liebman, Arthur. *Jews and the Left.* New York: John Wiley and Sons, 1979.

Lockman, Zachary. *Comrades and Enemies: Arab and Jewish Workers in Palestine, 1906–1948.* Berkeley and London: University of California Press, 1996.

Marshall, Phil. *Intifada: Zionism, Imperialism, and Palestinian Resistance.* Chicago and London: Bookmarks, 1989.

Masalha, Nur. *A Land without a People: Israel, Transfer, and the Palestinians, 1949–1996.* London: Faber and Faber, 1997.

Morris, Benny. *The Birth of the Palestinian Refugee Problem, 1947–1949.* New York and Cambridge: Cambridge University Press, 1987.

———. *Righteous Victims: A History of the Zionist-Arab Conflict, 1881–1999.* New York: Alfred A. Knopf, 1999.

The New Intifada: Resisting Israel's Apartheid. Introduction by Noam Chomsky. Edited by Roane Carey. New York and London: Verso, 2001.

The Other Israel: The Radical Case against Zionism. Compiled by Arie Bober. Garden City, New Jersey: Anchor Books, 1972.

Owen, Roger. *State, Power, and Politics in the Making of the Modern Middle East.* Second edition. New York and London: Routledge, 2000.

Palestine: Profile of an Occupation. Khamsin series. London and Atlantic Highlands, New Jersey: Zed Books, 1989.

Pappé, Ilan. *The Making of the Arab-Israeli Conflict, 1947–1951.* New York: I.B. Tauris, 1994.

Reinhart, Tanya. *The Second Half of 1948: Israel and the Palestinian Uprising.* Open Media Pamphlet Series. New York: Seven Stories Press, 2002.

Rodinson, Maxime. *Israel: A Colonial-Settler State?* Translated by David Thorstad. New York: Monad Press, 1973.

———. *Israel and the Arabs.* Translated by Michael Perl. New York: Pantheon, 1968.

Rose, John. *Israel: The Hijack State.* Chicago and London: Bookmarks, 1986.

Roy, Sara M. *The Gaza Strip: The Political Economy of De-Development.* Second Edition. Washington, D.C.: Institute for Palestine Studies, 2001.

Sacco, Joe. *Palestine.* Introduction by Edward W. Said. Seattle: Fantagraphics Books, 2002.

Said, Edward W. *Covering Islam: How the Media and the Experts Determine How We See the Rest of the World.* Revised edition. New York: Vintage Books, 1997.

———. *The End of the Peace Process: Oslo and After.* Updated edition. New York: Vintage Books, 2001.

———. *Peace and Its Discontents: Essays on Palestine in the Middle East Peace Process.* New York and London: Vintage Books, 1995.

Said, Edward W. *The Pen and the Sword: Conversations with David Barsamian*. Introduction by Eqbal Ahmad. Monroe, Maine: Common Courage Press, 1994.

————. *The Question of Palestine*. Updated edition. New York: Vintage Books, 1992.

Schoenbaum, David. *The United States and the State of Israel*. New York and Oxford: Oxford University Press, 1993.

Schoenman, Ralph. *The Hidden History of Zionism*. Santa Barbara, California: Veritas Press, 1988.

Segev, Tom. *The Seventh Million: The Israelis and the Holocaust*. Translated by Haim Watzman. New York: Owl Books/Henry Holt, 2000.

Shahak, Israel. *Israel's Global Role: Weapons for Repression*. Introduction by Noam Chomsky. Belmont, Massachusetts: Association of Arab-American University Graduates, 1982.

————. *Open Secrets: Israeli Nuclear and Foreign Policies*. London and Sterling, Virginia: Pluto Press, 1997.

Shalom, Stephen R. *Imperial Alibis: Rationalizing U.S. Intervention after the Cold War*. Boston: South End Press, 1993.

Shepherd, Naomi. *Ploughing Sand: British Rule in Palestine, 1917–1948*. New Brunswick, New Jersey: Rutgers University Press, 2000.

Shlaim, Avi. *The Iron Wall: Israel and the Arab World*. New York and London: W.W. Norton, 2001.

Siegel, Paul N. *The Meek and the Militant: Religion and Power across the World*. London and Atlantic Highlands, New Jersey: Zed Books, 1986.

Tordai, J.C., and Graham Usher. *A People Called Palestine*. Stockport, England: Dewi Lewis Publishing, 2001.

The Transformation of Palestine: Essays on the Origin and Development of the Arab-Israeli Conflict. Edited by Ibrahim A. Abu-Lughod. Evanston, Illinois: Northwestern University Press, 1971.

Usher, Graham. *Dispatches from Palestine: The Rise and Fall of the Oslo Peace Process*. London and Sterling, Virginia: Pluto Press, 1999.

The War for Palestine: Rewriting the History of 1948. Afterword by Edward W. Said. Edited by Eugene L. Rogan and Avi Shlaim. Cambridge and New York: Cambridge University Press, 2001.

Weinstock, Nathan. *Zionism: False Messiah.* Introduction by Moshe Machover. Edited and translated by Alan Adler. London: Ink Links, 1979.

Whitelam, Keith W. *The Invention of Ancient Israel: The Silencing of Palestinian History.* New York and London: Routledge, 1997.

Younis, Mona N. *Liberation and Democratization: The South African and Palestinian National Movements.* Minneapolis and London: University of Minnesota Press, 2000.

ORGANIZATIONS AND PUBLICATIONS

Al-Awda: The Palestine Right to Return Coalition
P.O. Box 1172
Orange, CT 06477-7172
Fax: (717) 832-1123
E-mail: prrc@mail.com
Web: al-awda.org

Ali Abunimah's Bitter Pill
E-mail: abunimah01@yahoo.com
Web: www.abunimah.org

Alternative Information Center
P.O. Box 31417
Jerusalem 91313
Phone: 011-97-2-2-624-1159
Fax: 011-97-2-2-625-3151
E-mail: aic@alt-info.org
Web: www.alternativenews.org

Alternative Radio

David Barsamian, Director
P.O. Box 551
Boulder, CO 80306-0551
Phone: (800) 444-1977
Fax: (303) 546-0592
E-mail: ar@orci.com
Web: www.alternativeradio.org

BADIL Resource Center for Palestinian Residency and Refugee Rights

P.O. Box 728
Bethlehem, West Bank
Phone: 011-97-2-277-7086
Fax: 011-97-2-274-7346
E-mail: info@badil.org
Web: www.badil.org

Between the Lines

P.O. Box 681
Jerusalem
E-mail: btl@palnet.com
Phone: 011-97-2-2-563-0060
Web: www.between-lines.org

B'Tselem, The Israeli Information Center for Human Rights in the Occupied Territories

8 HaTa'asiya Street, 4th Floor
Jerusalem 93420
Phone: 011-97-2-2-673-5599
Fax: 011-97-2-2-674-9111
E-mail: mail@btselem.org
Web: www.btselem.org

Center for Economic and Social Rights

162 Montague Street, 2nd Floor
Brooklyn, NY 11201-3536
Phone: (718) 237-9145
Fax: (718) 237-9147
E-mail: rights@cesr.org
Web: www.cesr.org

Challenge

P.O. Box 41199
Jaffa 61411
Israel
E-mail: oda@netvision.net.il
Web: www.hanitzotz.com/challenge

Electronic Intifada

Fax: (775) 254-4323
E-mail: info@electronicIntifada.net
Web: www.electronicintifada.org

Ha'aretz (English edition)

21 Schocken Street
P.O. Box 233
Tel Aviv 61001
Israel
Phone: 97-2-3-512-1212
Fax: 97-2-3-681-0012
E-mail: feedback@haaretz.co.il
Web: www.haaretzdaily.com

Indymedia Israel

Rehov Cordovero 14
Tel Aviv
Phone: 011-97-3-518-3490
Fax: 011-97-3-518-5036
E-mail: indymedia@indymedia.org.il
Web: www.indymedia.org.il

Indymedia Palestine

E-mail: imc-palestine@lists.indymedia.org
Web: www.jerusalem.indymedia.org

International Socialist Review

P.O. Box 258082
Chicago, IL 60625-8082
Phone: (773) 583-7884
Fax: (773) 583-6144
E-mail: business@isreview.org
Web: www.isreview.org

In These Times
2040 North Milwaukee Avenue
Chicago, IL 60647-4002

Phone: (773) 772-0100
Fax: (773) 772-4180
E-mail: itt@inthesetimes.com
Web: www.inthesetimes.org

Jerusalem Center For Legal Aid and Human Rights
Irsal Street
Ramallah
West Bank

Phone: 011-97-2-2-298-7981
Fax: 011-97-2-2-298-7982
E-mail: jlac@palnet.com
Web: www.palnet.com/~rich

Journal of Palestine Studies
3501 M Street NW
Washington, DC 20007-2624

Phone: (202) 342-3990
Fax: (202) 342-3927
E-mail: ips@ipsjps.org
Web: www.ipsjps.org/jps

Kav La'Oved
17 Peretz Street
Tel Aviv 66853

Phone: 011-97-3-688-3766
E-mail: email@kavlaoved.org.il
Web: www.kavlaoved.org.il

Middle East Children's Alliance (MECA)
905 Parker Street
Berkeley, CA 94710-2525

Phone: (510) 548-0542
Fax: (510) 548-0543
E-mail: meca@mecaforpeace.org
Web: www.mecaforpeace.org

Middle East Report

Middle East Research and Information Project (MERIP)
1500 Massachusetts Avenue NW, Suite 119
Washington, DC 20005-1814

Phone: (202) 223-3677
Fax: (202) 223-3604
E-mail: ctoensing@merip.org.
Web: www.merip.org

The Palestinian Academic Society for the Study of International Affairs (PASSIA)

P.O. Box 19545
Jerusalem/Al-Quds
18, Hatem Al-Ta'i Street – Wadi Al-Joz

Phone: 97-2-2-626-4426 / 628-6566
Fax: 97-2-2-628-2819
E-mail: passia@palnet.org
Web: www.passia.org

The Progressive

409 East Main Street
Madison, WI 53703-2863

Phone: (608) 257-4626
Fax: (608) 257-3373
E-mail: circ@progressive.org
Web: www.progressive.org

Socialist Worker

P.O. Box 16085
Chicago, IL 60616

Phone: (773) 583-6725
Fax: (773) 583-6144
E-mail: letters@socialistworker.org
Web: www.socialistworker.org

Students for Justice in Palestine
2425 Channing Way
PMB #572
Berkeley, CA 94704-2260
   Phone: (510) 496-1269 x1948
   E-mail: justiceinpalestine@yahoo.com
   Web: www.justiceinpalestine.org

Trans-Arab Research Institute (TARI)
P.O. Box 495
Boston, MA 02112
   Phone: (781) 648-1245
   E-mail: tarisite@excite.com
   Web: www.tari.org

Washington Report on Middle East Affairs
American Educational Trust, Inc.
P.O. Box 53062
Washington, DC 20009
   Phone: (202) 939-6050
   Fax: (202) 265-4574
   E-mail: subscriptions@wrmea.com
   Web: www.wrmea.com

ZNet Mideast Watch
Z Magazine
18 Millfield Street
Woods Hole, MA 02543-1122
   Phone: (508) 548-9063
   Fax: (508) 457-0626
   E-mail: sysop@zmag.org
   Web: www.zmag.org/meastwatch/meastwat.htm

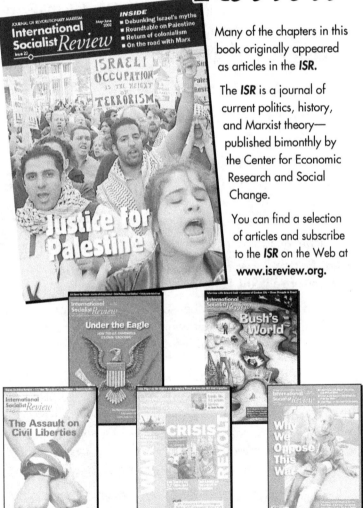

9 781931 859004